Personal Autonomy
Oppression

Personal Autonomy and Social Oppression addresses the impact of social conditions, especially subordinating conditions, on personal autonomy. The essays in this volume are concerned with the philosophical concept of autonomy or self-governance and with the impact on relational autonomy of the oppressive circumstances persons must navigate. They address on the one hand questions of the theoretical structure of personal autonomy given various kinds of social oppression and, on the other, how contexts of social oppression make autonomy difficult or impossible.

Marina A. L. Oshana is Professor of Philosophy at the University of California, Davis, U.S.

Routledge Studies in Contemporary Philosophy

For a full list of titles in this series, please visit www.routledge.com

Personal Autonomy and Social Oppression

Philosophical Perspectives

Edited by Marina A. L. Oshana

Routledge
Taylor & Francis Group

LONDON AND NEW YORK

First published 2015
by Routledge

2 Park Square, Milton Park, Abingdon, Oxon OX14 4RN
711 Third Avenue, New York, NY 10017, USA

*Routledge is an imprint of the Taylor & Francis Group,
an informa business*

First issued in paperback 2017

Library of Congress Cataloging-in-Publication Data
Personal autonomy and social oppression : philosophical perspectives /
    edited by Marina A.L. Oshana. — 1 [edition].
        pages cm. — (Routledge studies in contemporary philosophy ; 65)
    Includes bibliographical references and index.
    1. Autonomy (Philosophy)   2. Oppression (Psychology)   I. Oshana,
Marina, 1957– editor.
    B808.67.P47 2014
    128—dc23
    2014028108

ISBN: 978-0-415-84013-2 (hbk)
ISBN: 978-1-138-73152-3 (pbk)

Typeset in Sabon
by Apex CoVantage, LLC

Contents

viii   *Contents*

Preface

This idea for this book grew out of a two-day workshop on self-government and social transformation held at the University of California, Davis, in March 2012. The workshop took place on the heels of the "Arab Spring," which made it a good time to hold an event focused on research dealing with the transformative power of autonomous agency in oppressive contexts. In the last twenty years, there has been a great deal of work in philosophy on the social and relational dimensions of personal autonomy.[1] There has also been a substantial body of work offering different conceptions or theories of autonomy.[2] In addition, scholarship in philosophy, social psychology, political theory, and feminist theory has addressed the issue of social oppression.[3] But to date, no volume has focused on the possibility of relational autonomy and the conditions that support the relational dimensions of autonomy within socially and psychologically oppressive contexts. *Personal Autonomy and Social Oppression: Philosophical Perspectives* presents important new scholarship on this topic. Eleven previously unpublished papers address the impact of social conditions, especially subordinating conditions, on personal autonomy. The papers explore questions about the theoretical structure of personal autonomy given various kinds of social oppression as well as questions about the practical effect that contexts of social oppression have upon autonomous choice and action.

Part I of the book probes the interpretations of autonomy currently on offer for their plausibility given the presence of social and structural oppression. The first three chapters assess relational conceptions of autonomy. The fourth chapter in the section explores the impact of a kind of epistemic injustice on autonomy. The fifth chapter critically examines narrative conceptions of autonomy.

In Chapter 1, Marina A. L. Oshana examines the criteria that must be met to make autonomous agency possible under conditions of social injustice, especially injustice of a sort confronted by social reformers and civil rights activists of the 1960s. Taking the lives of social reformers such as Martin Luther King, Jr. and Shirin Ebadi as examples, Oshana argues that the constitutively relational conception of autonomous agency she advances is not, as some have charged, empirically untenable and unduly paternalistic. Rather, the account is broadly liberal in orientation and congruent with common sense despite the strong criteria it embodies. In Chapter 2, Jennifer Warriner tackles the controversial proposal that persons who live under oppressive social conditions may count as autonomous even if they have values that ostensibly are in conflict with autonomy, provided that such persons have proper regard for their authority as agents. This proposal has been made by some exponents of weakly substantivist accounts of autonomy, such as Paul Benson. Focusing on the lives of women in the Christian Patriarchy Movement who value gender hierarchy and female submission, Warriner argues that weakly substantivist accounts of autonomy cannot explain the autonomy of these women in a satisfactory way. In Chapter 3, Catriona Mackenzie discusses the objection to relational theories of autonomy according to which they fail to respond to what Serene Khader calls the "agency dilemma."[4] This is the challenge of recognizing the vulnerabilities of persons subject to social oppression or deprivation while also acknowledging and respecting their agency. In particular, feminist efforts to explain the impact of social oppression on autonomy must guard against seeming to support paternalistic and coercive forms of intervention in the lives of oppressed agents. Mackenzie contends that Khader's argument makes the mistake of confusing autonomy with choice and instrumental rationality. Mackenzie demonstrates how a nuanced relational theory can meet the challenge of the agency dilemma.

Beate Roessler's essay (Chapter 4) addresses social exclusion of the sort that transpires when persons belonging to certain groups are not taken seriously as trusted conversational partners and sources of knowledge. Roessler describes this form of exclusion as "epistemic injustice." She argues that a person's not being trusted as a source of knowledge can have distorting consequences for her self-knowledge and her autonomy. In making explicit the link between problems of epistemic injustice and ethical claims, Roessler's essay offers a new perspective on the various ways social oppression works in impeding a person's autonomy.

Part I concludes with Andrea Westlund's paper questioning narrative interpretations of autonomy. Westlund agrees that an autobiographical narrative may assist a person in providing a conditional framework against which to measure the significance of the person's decisions and actions, but she contends that the nature of such a narrative is not constitutive of a person's autonomy. To the contrary, an individual's autonomy, and also her responsibility for her actions, depends on her ability to reject problematic, stultifying narratives about her life. This ability is especially pressing when these narratives are fashioned under the influence of an oppressive social environment. Autonomy hinges on the agent's ability to selectively distance herself from provisional autobiographical narratives and on her ability to assume responsibility for the interpretive commitments that shape the narrative she endorses.

Part II of this volume focuses on the daily effects of social oppression and oppressive socialization upon an individual's capacity for autonomy. Two chapters focus on the impact of oppressive stereotyping on autonomy and three chapters focus on the impact of adaptive or deformed desires on autonomy.

In Chapters 6 and 7, respectively, Natalie Stoljar and Paul H. Benson explore the impact of oppressive stereotyping on a person's autonomy. Stoljar argues that the internalization of oppressive social scripts undermines the psychological freedom that is a necessary condition of autonomy. Even if agents reject the oppressive norms that are implied by oppressive stereotypes or scripts, their psychological freedom is impaired because they must adapt their behavior to the expectations of others that are implicit in the scripts, they must adopt an evaluative attitude to the norms of the scripts, and they must renounce the scripts if they are to regard themselves and be regarded as equal participants in everyday interactions with others. Benson's paper mines the empirical literature in social psychology for insight into the consequences stereotyping may have on autonomous agency by virtue of its effect upon a person's awareness of his social situation and his sense of social belonging. Evidence that points toward relational elements of autonomy is refined by examining related research on agents' uncertainty about their social belonging. Benson also considers how a familiar type of non-relational theory of personal autonomy would explain the apparent capability of stereotyping to degrade autonomous agency. His essay presents a more psychologically convincing treatment of some proposed features of relational autonomy than typically has been offered, as well as a treatment that largely avoids entering the fray over autonomy's evaluative content and its political implications for liberalism.

The topic of deformed desires and autonomy is the subject matter of Chapters 8, 9, and 10. In Chapter 8, Ann E. Cudd explores specific cases of adaptive preferences that arise out of oppressive circumstances and that lead persons to develop an affinity for oppressive social norms. Cudd argues that, despite arguments to the effect that such preferences can be "autonomous, authentic, or [have] positive normative weight personally and socially" (pg. 157, this volume), such preferences do not just injure the person who holds them but are much more widely injurious to the members of social groups oppressed by those norms. By putting such adaptive preferences into action, persons become complicit with the oppressive norms and with the circumstances that oppress them. As a result, adaptive preferences threaten morality and justice. Cudd concludes that we have a prima facie duty to counter such preferences by intervention.

In Chapter 9, Suzy Killmister explores precisely how oppression undermines personal autonomy and the steps persons might take to counter these effects. The core claim of the chapter is that oppression characteristically undermines personal autonomy through the imposition of double binds: oppressed agents are unable to fully realize all of their goals and values, and this reduces their scope for self-governance. This opens up the possibility that oppressed agents could increase their autonomy by altering their goals and values to fit the restrictions imposed by the oppressors. Killmister argues that while this possibility is conceptually feasible, it is not likely to result in increased autonomy, for whatever improvements would be had for one facet of autonomy would occur to the detriment of a different facet of autonomy.

In the tenth chapter, Anita M. Superson explores the ability of heterosexual women to identify themselves as autonomous sexual agents given the various external, internal, and social constraints that jeopardize their control over their sexual identity. Challenging the claim of some feminists that a prostitute offers the archetype of a woman who completely controls her sexual identity, Superson argues that prostitutes neither control their sexual identity nor are positioned to exercise their right to bodily autonomy. Under conditions of patriarchy, external, liberty-limiting constraints, internal constraints such as deformed desires, and social constraints such as sexist stereotypes combine to rob prostitutes of the freedom to determine what happens in and to their bodies.

In the last chapter of the book, Marilyn Friedman turns to the impact of internalized oppression on a person's self-conception. Friedman notes that because most people frame their self-conceptions in terms of socially ascribed categories, identifying oneself or being identified as belonging to a historically oppressed or persecuted group can generate internal conflict and impair local autonomy. The socialized self-conception is often degraded, group members may feel a special responsibility for confronting the oppressive circumstances that have produced the self-conception, and one's self-conception as a member of the group may be imprecise, making the determination of authenticity and autonomous acceptance with respect to that identity complicated. While group-based self-hatred can occur, Friedman argues that a member's criticisms of her own group do not necessarily exemplify group-based self-hatred, for there may exist legitimate grounds for moral criticism of the historically oppressed group.

As a collection, the eleven essays tackle live issues concerning the appropriate theoretical shape of the concept of autonomy and the practical capability of persons to live autonomously given a climate of social subjugation. The issues have special urgency for agents within liberal democratic states where the ideals of robust self-governance, equality, and state neutrality with respect to individual conceptions of the good are prized at the same time such ideals are often in tension with perfectionist interpretations of a self-managed life. The essays are equally timely in the face of nascent democracies, where aspirations to self-governance, responsible agency, self-understanding, and authentic self-identity remain liberatory ideals. We hope the essays will be of use to philosophers, social scientists, and political theorists, and to anyone with an interest in these matters.

Marina A. L. Oshana
University of California, Davis, U.S.
July 2014

NOTES

1. Much of the philosophical scholarship began with the publication of *Relational Autonomy: Feminist Perspectives on Agency, Autonomy, and the Social Self*, co-edited by Catriona Mackenzie and Natalie Stoljar (Oxford, 2000).
2. Monographs include Marilyn Friedman's *Autonomy, Gender, Politics* (Oxford University Press, 2002), Marina Oshana's *Personal Autonomy in Society* (Ashgate, 2006), and John Christman's *The Politics of Persons* (Cambridge University Press, 2010). Notable anthologies are John Christman and Joel Anderson, eds., *Autonomy and the Challenges to Liberalism* (Cambridge University Press, 2005) and James Stacey Taylor, ed., *Personal Autonomy: New essays* (Cambridge University Press, 2005).
3. Ann Cudd's *Analyzing Oppression* (Oxford University Press, 2006) is a noteworthy example.
4. Serene Khader, *Adaptive Preferences and Women's Empowerment* (Oxford University Press, 2011).

Acknowledgments

I would like to thank the authors of the papers for the dedication they have shown to this project and for their effort to adhere to the deadlines I set! Thanks are also due to the two anonymous reviewers for Routledge. Their comments surely improved the shape and the clarity of the book. I am also grateful to David Copp and Natalie Stoljar for editorial suggestions they provided in the early stages of the project.

Part I

Theoretical Problems

How Should We Conceptualize
Relational Autonomy?

1 Is Social-Relational Autonomy a Plausible Ideal?

Marina A. L. Oshana

1. CONSTITUTIVELY SOCIAL-RELATIONAL AUTONOMY

The position that the concept of autonomy is substantively socio-relational—that it is a concept that incorporates content-laden, normative specifications about the social situation of the autonomous person or about the values and commitments she embraces—has attracted a good deal of attention of late. Substantive accounts vary in the details, of course, and most treat the concept of autonomy as weakly substantive rather than strongly so.[1] The difference can be summarized as follows. Weakly substantive interpretations generally call upon autonomous agents to be in a certain self-referential psychological state. Autonomous persons are expected, for instance, to have good self-esteem or to regard themselves as worthy to answer for their conduct. A strongly substantive conception, by contrast, would typically charge that an autonomous person must include autonomy among the things she values or that her values must accord with an ideal of autonomy.

I have defended a social-relational account of autonomy that has been construed as belonging to the latter, strongly substantivist group. Certainly the social-relational account I defend is strongly substantivist in that it mandates the presence of content-specific states of affairs. Claims of a practical and a material nature are made upon the social environment. However, the account I have developed departs from the more traditional strongly substantive accounts in denying that autonomy is a matter of being committed to particular values or of valuing some ideal of autonomy or of feeling worthy to act. I concede that an autonomous person generally "cares about her own activity of reflecting on deeper, self-defining concerns without impediment and acting accordingly"[2] but deny that this interest is needed for autonomy and deny that this interest adequately marks a person as autonomous. Success in having one's lived experiences coalesce with one's deepest concerns does not suffice for autonomy. And while I grant that psychological self-rule is an important element of personal autonomy, my view is that personal autonomy is constitutively and intrinsically social and relational. Autonomy is a matter of having a stable social status of a particular type. It is not merely the case, to quote Paul Benson, that "persons' social relationships and attitudes influence their autonomy entirely as a matter of contingent circumstance."[3]

Of course, one might deny that autonomy calls for the integration of substantive constraints of either a weak or a strong variety, preferring instead a formal "content-neutral" or "proceduralist" conception of autonomy. Such conceptions typically limit the requirements for autonomous agency to certain minimal rational capacities or "competencies" and perhaps to constraints governing the measures a person follows in arriving at the defining interests that mold her behavior. On this approach, it is not necessary that the autonomous agent profess to value self-government, nor that she exhibit a particular level of self-esteem. A content-neutral approach might claim that an autonomous agent must exhibit a degree of competence sufficient to appreciate the nature of her motivations for choice, action, and attitudes, to appraise their desirability, and to stand up for them, if need be. Or the condition for autonomy might be the capacity to seek and attain one's own good on the basis of beliefs and desires that are rational. Rationality can be determined in various ways; recently, Andrea Westlund has suggested that the rational capacity central to the critical deliberation taken as decisive of autonomy is "the disposition to hold oneself answerable to external critical perspectives."[4] At this juncture, let me state I do not discount such capacities and procedures as significant in assessments of autonomy. But I do claim autonomy is more than simply an enhanced species of more minimalist, content-neutral incarnations of autonomy, or "autonomy with attitude."[5]

In what follows, I shall attempt to defend a social-relational account of autonomy against certain objections that have been levied against it and that have not been adequately answered by proponents of such accounts, myself included. I concede that I have left my interpretation of autonomy vulnerable to rather obvious criticisms; what follows is an attempt to diffuse the force of these criticisms. To specify, the discussion will be concerned with autonomy as a global property of a person. So understood, autonomy is first and foremost a matter of self-determination. While autonomy manifests as a characteristic persons exhibit in executing particular actions, it is a property of persons, a particular state of personhood, rather than a characteristic of choice or action of a particular variety. More precisely, autonomy is exercised over domains of a person's life that are significant for the person's agency and is assessed in light of a person's standing in these domains.[6] (Persons can be self-determining with respect to some areas of their lives while failing to be autonomous with respect to other areas of their lives, and a lack in some of these is arguably of no importance.) The global focus thus is not on autonomy simply as a quality of the temporally extended character of a person's life. The point of a global focus, rather, is that however many episodes of autonomous choice and action a person's life may include or however extended in time these episodes might appear, what decides autonomy is whether a person possesses influence and authority of a form and to an extent sufficient for a person to oversee undertakings in those domains that are of import to her agency. The account I defend holds that the existence of social relations that afford a person this influence and authority are mandatory if a person is to count as genuinely self-determining, whatever her choices are for and however laudably self-affirming they appear to be.

Although the social-relational account I advance does set an ideal for personal relations, I do not offer an account according to which the content of a person's preferences, values, and commitments must be congruent with this ideal or any other ideal of autonomy.[7] What a person prefers or values will be evident in the choices she makes and in her plans for actions. But it is possible that these preferences and plans can be opposed to autonomy at the same time the agent lives an autonomous life.[8] That is, while I deny that autonomy depends on a meshing of preferences and an independent ideal, I claim that it is to be explained in terms of the presence of relational circumstances in the world that make practical self-determination possible.

I characterize autonomy in this way because I am concerned with a specific set of issues having to do with self-determination under conditions of oppression and with social conditions of oppression (and injustice) in particular. What is at stake in these circumstances is the possibility and the value of agential life.[9] Agency of a distinctively human variety is exactly what an account of autonomy is supposed to capture. Intuitively, autonomous, self-governed, self-determined people are those in a position to oversee choices, actions, and personal relations of import to human agency, most notably when they live among others who may be able to derail their efforts. A plausible account of autonomy must be naturalistic—that is, it must be congruent with general empirical facts, such as the fact that people in societies occupy positions of social and relational interdependence. As I have contended elsewhere, psychological autonomy of a sort favored by content-neutral theorists is incapable of empowering a person in many areas of life that are crucial to successful agency where conditions of oppression are present or probable.[10] I have also claimed that neither a legal right of authority over one's affairs nor a moral right to make certain decisions for oneself and to control certain aspects of one's life without interference shall suffice for autonomy in these circumstances. Far too many persons who possess such rights are nonetheless deprived of autonomy just because they are prevented from wresting control over their lives. The question, then, is exactly what conditions must be met in order for the form of social-relational autonomy I advocate to be forthcoming. Why is it necessary, as I have claimed, that one is autonomous only when persons acting together are denied arbitrary power over one another? What happens when the external phenomena I claim are constitutive of autonomy are absent or fall below a certain threshold? Is it correct that people fail to be autonomous when it is a feature of the actual situation that they *would* lack the power to determine their affairs, governance over which is tantamount to governance over themselves, in the event that others *were* to attempt to deprive them of the authority to do so? Is every injustice a defeat of autonomy?

These are difficult questions. I have attempted to answer some of them and will not try to repeat the effort here.[11] Rather, the task of this chapter is to reply to three concerns that form part of a more general objection to my account. These are that the social-relational account denies the oppressed a voice in public deliberation; that the account denies social reformers status as autonomous; and that the account is empirically untenable. The general objection is that the account is too strong to be realized in this world. If my reply to the trio of complaints is modestly successful, I will have gone some distance to establishing that the characterization of autonomous agency I advocate is less unrealistic than critics make it out to be. Instead, the social-relational account is broadly liberal in orientation and (more importantly in my opinion) congruent with common sense.

2. CONSTITUTIVELY SOCIAL-RELATIONAL ACCOUNTS DENY THE OPPRESSED A VOICE

To begin, John Christman and Diana Meyers have charged (with variant emphases) that if autonomy is "the characteristic of persons who are can-didates for full participation in [. . .] collective decision-making processes," then constitutively social-relational accounts have the unpalatable conse-quence of denying beleaguered persons the standing that would empower them to act as public interlocutors on their own behalf and to openly chal-lenge those who subordinate them.[12] Accounts such as mine fail "to capture the sense of autonomy at the foundation of egalitarian democratic poli-tics."[13]

This objection merits serious attention. The worry concerns persons who lack the wherewithal to engage in the social and political sphere and whose interests as a result are overlooked in those arenas. We are told that what is at stake in a liberal account of the autonomy of political persons is the guarantee that person see themselves "as part of an individual and social narrative that they can authenticate from inside as part of a diachronic prac-tical identity of their own."[14] In most cases of hierarchical and oppressive social relations, the reason autonomy is lost is not the relations but the fact that persons cannot see themselves as "self-authenticating sources" (172), "of the biographical narrative[s]" that define them (180).

One response I can offer is that proceduralist accounts of the sort Christ-man and Meyers champion will not serve beleaguered and oppressed persons any better than do more demanding social-relational analyses of autonomy and that, in fact, the latter are far better positioned to explain exactly what is lacking in the lives of the dispossessed. Of course, persons who lack a voice *ought* to be entitled to autonomy. But first-person assur-ances that the subject is not causally, historically, psychically, or emotionally alienated from the ongoing social and political narrative will not amount to evidence of autonomy. If a person is not autonomous owing to a paucity of the required social-relational conditions, it does not follow that she ought to lack a full claim to autonomy and to the respectful, interlocutory treatment it promises. It does, however, mean that whatever claim to autonomy the person retains is without teeth. Any such claim cannot make contact with conditions on the ground, so to speak. People who enjoy autonomy of a proceduralist variety may be inclined to speak for themselves and may be competent to appreciate the nature of their circumstances, but they might be silenced and immobilized by these circumstances nonetheless.[15] By contrast, people who are socially and relationally self-determining are empowered to stand up for themselves as full agency requires; they are better positioned to demand their rights and actually overcome relations of oppression.

Matters are not so straightforward, of course. Among the oppressed we can count innumerable social reformers who resisted their oppression. I'll turn to these cases momentarily.

Other theorists of relational autonomy attempt a rejoinder by holding on to components of content-neutral accounts and weakly substantive accounts. Westlund, for example, argues for a "self-responsibility" account of autonomy that is constitutively relational in that it emphasizes the interpersonal and dialogical character of autonomy while retaining the pure formality of proceduralist accounts. Westlund's hope is that the self-responsibility account "will help us to make sense of strong intuitions about oppression and autonomy that have often seemed maddeningly at odds with one another."[16] Westlund's view is that the autonomous agent is one who is prepared to hold herself answerable to reflective critical moral commentary on the part of "herself and real or imagined others" regarding the desires, beliefs, and commitments that are her motivating reasons for action. This disposition reveals "a capacity that may be shared even by those enmeshed in problematic social relations that they themselves endorse."[17] So understood, autonomy places no constraints upon the content of the agent's belief, desires, and normative commitments, nor does it demand an idealized, egalitarian character of the agent's social circumstances. In this respect, Westlund's account shares conceptual space with the formalist orientation Christman and Meyers favor. What autonomy does demand is precisely what seems to be absent from the lives of the dispossessed, namely, a voice.

If Westlund's account survives scrutiny, it cannot be correct that people fail to be autonomous when their rights are subject to negotiation, as long as they are full partners in the negotiation process. It is the very practice of negotiation in which the person is involved that signals autonomy and that commands the attention of those who would challenge the person's standing. If this suffices for autonomy, then one needn't go so far as to charge that persons are autonomous only when they can defuse threats to their agency or that they must possess counterfactual control over mechanisms that would wrest control of their affairs, as I have claimed. It is enough for autonomy that persons are prepared to argue on their own behalf for the choices they make, the values and relationships they endorse, and the actions upon which they embark. If you have authority over your own voice, you have all the autonomy worth wanting. I am not persuaded by Westlund's account, and I will take up a worry about her approach in discussing the empirical plausibility of social-relational autonomy in section four. I would suggest that Westlund's conditions for dialogical competence include fairly robust substantive specifications about the social environment of the autonomous agent. Unless you are in fact an empowered member of the populace, you are less likely to be equipped for dialogical self-responsibility.[18] The fact of the matter is that most dispossessed persons are not so empowered. That observation aside, Westlund's assertion that interpersonal competence and a sense of oneself as authorized to speak on one's behalf suffice for autonomy signals the second objection to the social-relational account I want to address.

3. SOCIAL-RELATIONAL ACCOUNTS DENY AUTONOMY OF SOCIAL REFORMERS

The second objection posed by detractors of constitutively social-relational accounts is that such accounts cannot explain the dissimilarity between oppressed persons who submit to their oppression and persons who vigorously struggle against it. As Robert Noggle tells it,

> Martin Luther King, Rosa Parks, Harriet Tubman, and Nelson Mandela were clearly oppressed, and some even incarcerated, but they still chose to resist the systems that oppressed them. The social conditions in which they lived were, according to Oshana's theory, *ipso facto* incompatible with global autonomy. Yet there seems something odd about labeling people like King, Tubman, Parks, and Mandela as lacking in autonomy. What, if not autonomy, explains why these people did not acquiesce to their situation? [. . .] Oshana's theory . . . seems incompatible with what is the most natural thing to say about such cases, that despite the nearly overwhelming obstacles, these people managed to retain their autonomy, and used it in courageous forms of resistance to the social systems that tried to take it away. [. . .] Oshana is right to emphasize the threats posed to autonomy by oppressive social relationships. The question is whether we should define autonomy as consisting of non-oppressive relationships. Once we do this, we are forced to lump resisters and collaborators into the same category, and we become unable to recognize that persons can sometimes manage to live autonomous lives even in the midst of social forces designed to prevent this.[19]

Let me take a stab at this worry. It is undeniable that African Americans during the civil-rights era of the early and mid-1960s were dispossessed politically, economically, and educationally. African Americans lived in an environment in which self-determination was highly insecure. Perversely, the expressions of autonomy Noggle cites occurred because African Americans felt *compelled* to act by the conditions that subjugated them.[20] Even if these lions of social reform possessed immense faith in their authority to speak on their own behalf and offered evidence of competence and skill in this regard, impediments to self-determination were ever present factors of life. Indeed, this is precisely why persons such as Tubman, Mandela, and King were willing to risk so much: they were acutely aware of something lacking in their lives and in the lives of ordinary people on whose behalf they fought. The lives they led were not lives they wanted to lead; they did not seek to be social agitators simply for the thrill of it. The problem was less that African Americans lacked a voice and more that they lacked a legal right and genuine opportunity to make their voices heard. As I have argued elsewhere, "Conversation does not consist merely in presenting one's position. Rather, it requires all parties to the discussion have a standing that empowers them to be heard, to raise questions, and to persuade one another, and it involves recognition by those party to the discussion that each has this standing."[21] What the social reformers of the black civil rights movement lacked was an audience who listened and took them seriously. "Too long," King wrote, "has our beloved Southland been bogged down in a tragic effort to live in monologue rather than dialogue."[22]

Perhaps we can call King's actions and the actions of all these activists expressions of autonomy as *self-authorization* over important choices and major domains of life in defiance of subjugation. King regarded himself as normatively authorized to act. The question is whether he was autonomous as a result. I have claimed that one task of autonomy is to make sure that a person is not dominated by others, particularly when matters that are essential to agency are at issue. I have stated that in order to be autonomous, one must possess "influence and authority of a form and to an extent sufficient for a person to own her choices, actions, and goals, and to oversee undertakings of import to her agency." But must the autonomous agent wield practical control in the face of oppressive circumstances, as I claim? Perhaps it is harder to develop and to assert one's agency under threatening conditions, but that does not show autonomy cannot be possible under threatening conditions. Even less, must we analyze autonomy in ways that require the presence of nonoppressive states of affairs? To respond to the second objection, we need to determine whether, how, and to what extent persons who are burdened by circumstances of oppression and institutional injustice can be self-determining and self-governing. Having done so, we will be able to tell whether social-relational autonomy alone can explain how autonomous agency is possible in situations of social or psychological insecurity or (less grandly) whether it can do the best job of explaining self-determination and self-governance under these conditions.

One way of determining whether a person's situation in life undermines the practical control demanded of autonomy—and one way of distinguishing genuine threats to autonomy from more benign and commonplace lapses of practical control and authority—is by posing and seeking answers to three questions. One question asks, what circumstances does the person encounter? Are areas of significance to a person's life at risk? ("Significant" areas will encompass those in which a person has a fundamental interest. I will later suggest that many of these interests enjoy legal and moral protection.) A second question asks, what is required to counter the threats and the oppressive phenomena that may be features of these circumstances? How demanding is the type of exertion and level of exertion required in order to confront the conditions that may undermine a person's autonomy? The third question is, what does it cost a person to counter the oppression and insecurity? That is, what effect might the fact that prodigious toil, psychological exertion, and sheer doggedness are needed in order for a person to have practical control over choices, actions, and goals that are significant to her and that are foundational to agency have upon the person?

To the first question: Under Jim Crow, the circumstances were patently rife with risk and insecurity. Racial injustice encompassed:

> such things as carrying the stigma attached to "looking" and "acting" black; having one's life prospects diminished by institutionalized racism; suffering discrimination on the basis of presumed incompetence; enduring arbitrary exclusion from certain neighborhoods, schools, and social circles; being preemptively regarded as unsuitable for intimate social interaction; navigating the social world with knowledge that one is often the object of unjustified hatred, contempt, suspicion, or fear; seeking to avoid "confirming" an array of degrading racial stereotypes; serving as the perennial scapegoat for social problems and economic crises; and living with the knowledge that one is vulnerable, at almost any time, to an anti-black attitude, action, social practice, or institutional policy.[23]

As to the second question: The type of exertion and level of exertion demanded of a person in this state is unfathomable to me. In order for King and others to accomplish their goals, they had to not merely risk their lives and the lives of those they loved. They also had to depend on the kindness and bravery and social sanctuary of more powerful white Americans whose lives were far less at risk.[24] If King and many others did not fail miserably as self-determining and self-governing agents living autonomous lives, it was in large part because they had the good fortune of social support behind them. In King's case, it was due to the fact that, owing to his persistence and his charisma, he was able to capture the ear of some of the powerful. Still, as was true of every other American descendant of enslaved Africans, and as was true of all black South Africans under apartheid, King and Mandela fell well short of the conditions of social control, relevant options, and social-relational security had by their white counterparts. This is what they lacked and this is what they fought for. Like every other American descendant of enslaved Africans, King lacked many of the *de jure* rights of autonomy granted his white brethren. On a daily basis, he had to navigate a minefield of indiscriminate constraints and interferences that were calculated to prevent him from realizing his goals. (The "minefield" was at times literally explosive.) It consisted not simply of social hindrances but of systemic obstacles that were socioeconomically, politically, and legally reinforced. If we couple this with a risible paucity of options and the fact that King functioned in climate that was the very antithesis of secure and in which the probability of interference was high, then on the social-relational account I described earlier, King's having met the threshold for *de facto* autonomy is nothing short of extraordinary. It is remarkable that having confronted these extraordinary circumstances, the lions of social reform were able to triumph. But why should such outliers, such moral paragons, serve as the litmus test for autonomy?[25] King's success should rather serve as an example of an *exception* to the social-relational account rather than proof that the social-relational account is implausible. It seems misguided to say that *because* African-Americans developed remarkable wherewithal to insist that their voices be heard notwithstanding their grim circumstances and the exertion these cost, they were proof of the falsity of social-relational autonomy.

To the third question: What cost did combating Jim Crow have? I think it is significant that the struggle for civil rights began with learning to absorb the belief that each person was "somebody." To be somebody and to represent oneself as somebody who is visible is to be worth something. This can be a strain to keep in mind when institutionally fostered social subjugation and political marginalization threaten to define one's life.[26] Indeed, in his last, prophetic speech, King described the struggle as follows: "It is no longer a choice between violence and nonviolence in this world; it's nonviolence or nonexistence."[27]

It is an open question whether oppression squelches autonomy. Lives spent in devotion to a political cause may certainly be admirable and, more importantly, sources of great worth for the subject. But these can be nonetheless be lives in which autonomy is lacking. The three-pronged test is meant to assist us in closing the question.[28]

Nonetheless, even if I am correct that the variety of oppression, the degree of exertion called for to combat it, and the struggle it cost those who bore it are indicators of marginalized autonomy, I am reluctant to claim that persons who press for their political or moral rights against persons, institutions, or regimes that would impede them—that is, under circumstances that do poorly by the three-pronged test—fail to be autonomous. Indeed, many seem to be exemplars of autonomy—with little outside assistance, these persons have initiated and presided over actions expressly intended to foster conditions that permit human agency to flourish. Despite Jim Crow, African Americans established schools, social clubs, unions, newspapers, churches, and so on, the legacy of which continues to shape American culture today. For his efforts, *Time* magazine named King "Man of the Year" in 1963. In 1964, at the age of 35, he was awarded the Nobel Peace Prize, the youngest man, the second American, and the third black man to be recognized.[29] It would seem that neither these awards nor his numerous other accomplishments nor his legacy belong to a man whose life was fundamentally lacking autonomy. In fact, in his acceptance speech for the Nobel, King declared: "I refuse to accept the idea that man is mere flotsam and jetsam in the river of life unable to influence the unfolding of events which surround him." King wielded influence and authority to a high degree. He appears to have taken full ownership of his actions, despite the fact that he was compelled to do so by circumstance. As Gary Watson notes in speaking of Gandhi and King, "Nor does it seem plausible to suppose that they do not hold themselves or others morally responsible: they stand up for themselves and others against their oppressors; they confront their oppressors with the fact of their misconduct, urging and even demanding consideration for themselves and others."[30] In the aftermath of the demonstrations and strikes in Birmingham, Alabama, in May 1963, King was regarded as one as the more powerful men in America. Certainly he attained in the national imagination greater stature than that of Birmingham's chief of police Eugene "Bull" Connor.[31] Connor directed local police and fire departments to use force to halt the demonstrations, and the events that ensued—children being blasted by high-pressure fire hoses, clubbed by police officers, and attacked by police dogs—were broadcast to a horrified nation. This marked a turning point in the civil rights movement and cemented King's reputation.[32]

But I think this supports my point: King gained autonomy—understood as freedom from domination where matters of significance to the direction of one's life are concerned—only when national and international circumstances forced a seismic shift in attention to the movement he represented. *Whether* a person can be autonomous under conditions of oppression depends in part on the degree of autonomy sought, the area of activity at issue (i.e., "programmatic" autonomy with respect to one or another aspect of life), and whether the problem touches on global or local autonomy.[33] I do not deny that periods of autonomous choice are found in the lives of oppressed persons or that such persons might wield considerable authority within some domains in their lives. What is decisive for autonomy are the variety of domains and how much authority is had within them. To restate, my concern is global autonomy or autonomy as a property over domains that are significant for the person's agency. A person can be self-determining (and self-governing) under conditions of oppression only if the circumstances preserve an adequate degree of authority over affairs in those realms that are of consequence. Such domains include choice of partner, the decision to have children, employment, religious expression, and so on. Notably, all of these are domains of life that enjoy explicit or implicit protection under common law and the United States Constitution. Embattled African-American civil rights activists wielded little authority in any of these domains, legal protections notwithstanding.

4. SUBSTANTIVE ACCOUNTS ARE EMPIRICALLY UNTENABLE

The third worry, the worry about empirical tenability, is premised on the general objection that the social-relational account expects persons to possess *de facto* control of a sort that is "so strong that it's not realistically possible to satisfy."[34] To claim global autonomy is to claim that a person has the power to determine how she shall live. This mandates *counterfactual* power over the management of one's choices, actions, and goals. Absent counterfactual power, autonomy is compromised where certain impediments to self-determination are merely likely, and even where it is possible although unlikely they will be put into effect. Or so it would appear the account maintains.

It should be noncontroversial that truly coercive mechanisms, be they of a human, a military, a legal, a political, a cultural, or a socioeconomic variety, are by definition able to appropriate the reins of control from the actor. But surely not everyone who confronts a possible risk to social and psychological security is lacking autonomy. Nor does it seem correct that a person's autonomy is compromised every time she faces a challenge in executing her will or when executing her will costs her great effort. If this were true, then many of the circumstances that truncate autonomy on my account would seem to be of a noncoercive variety. The bizarre result is that very few persons would count as autonomous.

Fortunately, this result does not follow from my account. Executing my will to present a paper before an audience of philosophers calls for great psychic effort. The same is true of my effort to swim an IM (individual medley) during a Master's workout. The latter effort hardly rises to the level of defeating my autonomy, though the former might well do so if I developed a fear of the public sufficient to prevent me from engaging in philosophical discourse. But other quite commonplace challenges have far graver implications. Take the question of financial security. It is a well-supported fact that persons require a minimum level of economic self-sufficiency "to rule out the possibility that others might gain control over them through their needs."[35] Consider someone who is one paycheck away from homelessness. This person occupies a state of vulnerability that, fortunately, is not a feature of the actual situation of persons such as myself. Most people in my position— well-educated academics—are autonomous. We have control over affairs of importance to agency *just because* we are not living hand to mouth.

Mere financial dependency need not yield an absence of autonomy unless it produces an imbalance of agential authority among the financial partners.

The account I defend does not demand that a person be financially self-sufficient in order to have control over the direction of his life. It is not it the case, as Meyers has charged, that my view would entail that "no stay-at-home parent who isn't independently wealthy is autonomous."[36] The devil is in the details. Suppose Rahm chooses to be a stay-at-home dad rather than a Wall Street financial consultant, with the result that he is now dependent on his partner for financial security. But suppose, too, that Rahm's role as stay-at-home dad, subjectively valued though it may be, yields the result that he has little *de facto* power and authority over discretionary spending of money and of leisure time. As a result, he *would* fail to be autonomous in the sense I maintain amounts to self-determination. This does not seem to me an absurd result. Self-sufficiency is not incumbent upon wealth, and to represent it as such is to present a caricature. But financial insecurity frequently means that a person is in no position to challenge potential encroachments on the part of those who have power over him. Financial insecurity means that whatever ability the person has to determine the shape of life will be limited.

Not one to concede the point, James Rocha has argued that accounts of autonomy such as mine "are overly severed from ordinary life, which requires much subservience."[37] Many careers and work-related activities, Rocha alleges, count as subservient since they involve "constant oversight, order following, or a preponderance of mindless tasks that the agent has no independent reason to perform. Such a career seems to endanger autonomy by removing the worker's ability to control the day to day aspects of her life."[38] In addition, Rocha worries that given my insistence that we focus on autonomy as a global condition, "were we to examine the subservient worker's life globally, we would find that she spends roughly eight hours a day, five days a week, fifty weeks a year, for over forty years of her life acting subserviently. Certainly this much subservience rules out workers for Oshana's version of autonomy."[39] The result is an empirically untenable notion of autonomy that "relegate[s] the term to philosophical fantasy" (315). Impediments to autonomy, so understood, are ubiquitous.

If these are truly features characteristic of the average worker's life, then I for one have no problem sticking to my assertion that these are not autonomous lives. I cannot pursue the details of Rocha's argument in this space, but I will say that I am not persuaded by his depiction of ordinary working life writ large. Not *all* wage labor is coercive, involving "a threat used to make someone carry out a task that the person would not otherwise have independent reason to act upon"[40]; nor is it true that all wage labor makes it difficult for a person to manage her affairs in a way that is significant for her agency. My profession affords me considerable latitude to do just this, and I count myself fortunate as a result. Too much wage labor undeniably does have a coercive component and produces agential-undermining effects.[41] Of course, genuine threats to autonomy should not be so "fanciful" as to include the "bare possibility" that "the fact that I live in a society with a national military makes it possible, albeit unlikely, that I'll be drafted into the U.S. Army with the result that either my autonomy will disappear or I'll be forced to exercise my autonomy to resist."[42] The account I defend need not construe threats to autonomy in so catholic a fashion. Threats of a sort I have in mind are not ubiquitous, but neither are they fanciful. Nor does the account I defend charge that *any* limitation on libertarian freedom reduces autonomy. We can sensibly qualify the parameters of threats to autonomy at the same time we hold that autonomy necessitates counterfactual power and authority. In the case of potentially coercive labor, we would do so by appealing to the three-prong assessment of the type of labor involved (what does it challenge in the actor's life?), the extent of subservience it involved, and cost of combating the subservience.

Rocha raises another complaint, which is that "[T]reating all subservient workers similarly misses out on key differences with respect to whether they sufficiently control their lives, *on their terms*. It is strange, after all, for the agent's own opinion of how much subservience she can tolerate to be irrelevant to autonomous legislation, which is supposed to derive from the agent herself."[43] In response, let me say that while the fact that a person has an unusually high tolerance for subservience is significant for her state of mind, it seems less decisive of the question of her autonomy and her practical agency. I may be a housecleaner who voices pride in being the first worker in her firm not to lose her job due to pregnancy, but this doesn't elevate my autonomy an iota. Rocha's remark recalls Andrea Westlund's attempt to preserve the relational dimension of autonomy absent the substantivist baggage. Westlund charges "there is no contradiction between self-responsibility and self-subordination." Speaking directly to the "Taliban woman" case I have developed, Westlund writes:

> [If] (*ex hypothesi*) a fundamentalist woman *does* freely and authentically accept a condition of social and personal subordination, it seems equally problematic to assume that her condition as subordinate, in and of itself, undermines her status as self-governing agent. [. . .] We should not assume that all individuals who willingly embrace subordinate roles will be psychologically similar to one another. [. . .] Responsiveness to critical perspectives on one's action-guiding commitments . . . should, I think, make a difference to our intuitions about relative autonomy. A "Taliban woman" who is prepared to take up and respond to the critical perspectives of others . . . is strikingly different from one who is not. [. . .] [To] treat her as non-autonomous *even as she speaks* on behalf of her self-subordinating commitments is to refuse to take the possibility of such dialogue with her at face value: not only does this women lack authority over her social circumstances, our treatment implies, she lacks authority over her own voice. And this flies in the face of the evidence she gives of such authority in engaging in just the kind of critical dialogue in which one might expect reflective, self-governing agents to engage.[44]

As Westlund tells it, persons who answer for their commitments by displaying an appropriate level of dialogical engagement will count as self-responsible and so autonomous, even if their commitments are self-subordinating and even if they manifest a lack of self-respect, assuming they have not internalized whatever social expectations might force this commitment. Certainly, the dialogically fluent, critically attuned "Taliban woman" is patently unlike her less engaged counterpart; I have no quarrel with that. It is true that my account demands that the individual not forsake her independence of thought and action in the process of developing her motives for choice and action. But this strikes me as a weak constraint that any account of autonomy should adopt. My point is simply that authority over one's voice is something other than autonomy. Perhaps such persons are aptly described as responsible for their choices and actions and accountable for these. But accountability is a very different notion and is dependent on quite different practical arrangements than is autonomy.[45]

Certainly, I believe it would be a mistake to redescribe the Taliban Woman as an autonomous woman who supports *Sharia*—the law of Allah that regulates all aspects of religious as well as secular life, including the social, political, economic, and domestic spheres—even if she is an adept and impassioned defender of that body of law. Taliban Woman is not, for example, a politically empowered member of the Afghan legislature. Conservative women who are members of the Afghan legislature are not themselves operating under the Talibanic model of *Sharia*, for that model would forbid them from occupying this political role.[46]

As an example of someone whose autonomy was at risk although she clearly met the criteria for dialogical answerability, consider the case of Shirin Ebadi. Ebadi was awarded the Nobel Peace Prize in 2003, the first Muslim woman laureate. She was born in 1947 to a fairly well-off, academic family and, like her father, took a degree in law. She began working for the Department of Justice in Tehran in 1969, serving as a judge while pursuing and subsequently obtaining a doctorate with honors in private law from Tehran University two years later. In 1975, Ebadi became the president of a bench of the Tehran City Court. Here is how she describes her experiences from that point:

> I am the first woman in the history of Iranian justice to have served as a judge. Following the victory of the Islamic Revolution in February 1979, since the belief was that Islam forbids women to serve as judges, I and other female judges were dismissed from our posts and given clerical duties. They made me a clerk in the very court I once presided over. We all protested. As a result, they promoted all former female judges, including myself, to the position of "experts" in the Justice Department. I could not tolerate the situation any longer, and so put in a request for early retirement. My request was accepted. Since the Bar Association had remained closed for some time since the revolution and was being

managed by the Judiciary, my application for practising law was turned down. I was, in effect, housebound for many years. Finally, in 1992 I succeeded in obtaining a lawyer's licence and set up my own practice.[47]

Diana Meyers contends Ebadi "has a high degree of autonomy," having "snatched *de facto* autonomy from the teeth of the mullahs by protesting and publicizing the Iranian state's oppression of women."[48] This statement is belied by Ebadi's own description of her situation. Certainly Ebadi protested her dismissal from the court, and she is to be lauded for this. But the result, as she notes, was forced resignation and years of unemployment. For a period of thirteen years, from 1979 to 1992, Ebadi was not permitted to practice law. Her profession was denied her, and it was denied her because of her gender and an egregious political situation. If this counts as "snatching *de facto* autonomy," it is *de facto* autonomy I could do without. Being disposed to speak for yourself and to be accountable for your choices may go some distance to signaling autonomy as a capacity for self-authorization and may be especially admirable in the lives of persons, such as Ebadi, for whom autonomy was hard earned, only to be snatched away. But this disposition is hardly sufficient for autonomy as practical self-determination and self-governance, just as finding ways to cope with a loss of autonomy is hardly a substitute for autonomy. The plain fact is that, as a Muslim woman, Ebadi fell below the threshold for autonomous agency. She lacked *de jure* autonomy and she lacked *de facto* autonomy. (She had a fair degree of negative and positive freedom, but not where it counted—perhaps having freedom *where it counts* is what makes freedom approach autonomy.) Ebadi made the best out of her situation, noting that she devoted much of her unemployment to writing books and articles.[49] But the moral right to autonomy Ebadi claimed was not enough to sustain a political right of the sort demanded for involvement in the democratic process. Even if Ebadi had enjoyed *de jure* autonomy of the sort that might substantiate a claim to a voice in the democratic process, this claim would be of minute significance. By virtue of her position as a woman in a conservative theocracy, Ebadi was divested of the authority to act for herself.

Worries of the sort raised by Rocha, Westlund, Meyers, and others may reflect the belief that imposing constitutively social-relational constraints upon autonomous agents is inimical to the comprehensiveness of chosen lifestyles found among persons in a pluralist society. To respect autonomy is to permit persons to fashion and pursue their own conceptions of the good. If the theory of autonomy I defend is correct, lives in which a person's status and circumstances are marked by constraint, voluntarily or not, will be irreconcilable with autonomy. But this is a feature of the lives of many adult persons. The account I offer may appear troublingly perfectionist.

This is a legitimate concern. To address it, we might note that power and authority can be compromised in (at least) two ways. One way is in the presence of phenomena that impede agency. These are grave impediments, phenomena that imperil physical, psychological, or social freedom and security either because they are present or are so likely to occur that a person must tailor her behavior and plan her life to accommodate them. If autonomy defines the state a person is in when she is able to act on fundamentally self-defining interests by means of her own agency, and if autonomy defines the state a person is in when she has the authority to manage affairs of significance to her agency, then a grave impediment is one the presence or likelihood of which makes these states improbable.

A second way in which a loss of power and authority occurs is where a person has control, but her control is restricted to activities that are of little value and significance. A constitutive account of autonomy does not demand that the agent have power and authority over every element her life, at every moment, and against counterfactual interferences of any variety. The scope of power and authority needed for autonomy will conform to what a person requires so as to supervise her life, with its unique interests and ends, by means of her own authority. The control needed to live the life of an autonomous Taliban woman may appear different from the control needed in order to live the life of an autonomous female philosophy professor or an autonomous stay-at-home parent or an autonomous Wal-Mart employee. But what differs here isn't the content or fact of control but the circumstances in which one wields it. Autonomy is specified as a modal concept, the truth of which depends on the degree to which a given state of affairs is likely to obtain. In addition, autonomy admits of degrees, which vary depending upon the frequency and intensity of intrusions in a person's life. The central truth is that the loss of autonomy is debilitating, even if the loss is restricted to just one significant domain in a person's life and even if the loss occurs in the context of a life in which little self-governance is expected or is the norm.

None of this should lead us to conclude that the conditions for autonomy thereby depend on the subjective psychological profile of the individual. Indeed, one reason to favor a strongly constitutive as opposed to a content-neutral approach is that doing so settles the question of autonomy's content. While it may be impossible to calculate the threshold that must be satisfied in order for a person to be deemed sufficiently autonomous in a way that will satisfy the critic of the constitutive account, a constitutively social-relational account offers objective and universalized criteria that will be met to a more or less satisfying degree depending on exogenous states of affair.

5. CONCLUSION

I agree that autonomy must not be so demanding as to be unattainable. This aspiration is consistent with a call for real-world conditions that make feasible a naturalized and common-sense account of substantive autonomy.

It is a matter of common sense and entirely within the realm of the feasible that an adult citizen of a society whose Constitution allows for mandatory military conscription is a person whose autonomy is compromised to the degree that policy undermines his agency. It is a matter of common sense and entirely within the realm of the feasible that to the degree citizens must take pains to censor their political speech for fear of retribution, their autonomy will be reduced. It is a matter of common sense and entirely within the realm of the feasible that to the degree persons must fashion their lives knowing that the provision of medical care turns on adherence to guidelines governing socially acceptable sexual behavior and that departures from such behavior portend the loss of medical care, autonomy is commensurately reduced. To the degree that women lack the legal resources that protect them from exploitation and violence and must be guarded in their ambitions and behavior, their autonomy will be commensurately circumscribed. Of course, a person will be fortunate where a counterfactually coercive force operates in tandem with her life plans.[50] Some of these might not even strike observers as objectionable losses of autonomy given the urgency of other socially desirable ends. But each of these will count as a diminution of autonomy nonetheless. I embrace this implication as a virtue and vindication of the substantively social-relational account rather than an indication of the absurdly unrealistic extremes to which the account is driven.

Obviously whether an account of autonomy is adequate depends on the success with which the concept can be deployed in practical as well as theoretical contexts. The plausibility of the account rests on the extent to which the concept makes sense of lives of persons like Ebadi and King. What was at stake for each was not autonomy as a characteristic of choices considered individually. What was at stake is autonomy as the general condition of their lives.

However the individual defines herself and whatever the nature of the circumstances she confronts, there must be in place social mechanisms that safeguard the ability to initiate and guide action on one's behalf; this is what the autonomous person essentially does. The successful agent makes up her own mind, achieves her own ends, and so on, despite the various factors that can impede this, such as coercion, manipulation, and oppressive social circumstances. These ideas about autonomous agency are genuinely congruent with common sense and with the tenets of naturalism. The account of autonomy I defend depicts what is at issue for individuals who are situated with others in the real-world context of moral, social, and political exchange. The conditions it states are not ad hoc but pick out what is implied for the lives of persons such as King and Ebadi. Whether one is drawn to weaker or stronger substantive incarnations of autonomy or is satisfied with what content-neutral accounts have to offer, one can hardly disagree that agency is an end of an autonomous life and that autonomy is valued as the means to this end.

ACKNOWLEDGMENTS

Previous versions of this paper were presented at Pomona College in September 2013, at a workshop on Self-Government and Social Transformation, University of California, Davis, March 2, 2012, to the Practical Philosophy Colloquium, Faculty of Philosophy, University of Utrecht, February 7, 2012, and at a Social and Political Thought Workshop, Department of Philosophy, Vanderbilt University, October 28, 2011. I am indebted to the participants and audiences for helping me refine the ideas in this paper. I also thank members of the Philosophy Club at the University of California, Davis, for discussing the concept of relational autonomy with me.

NOTES

1. For a range of relational accounts that have constitutive elements, some of which are explicitly substantivist, see Stoljar (2000), Oshana (1998), Benson (1991) and (1994), Kristinsson (2000), and Charles (2010).
2. Friedman (2002: 21).
3. Benson (2015, Chapter 7, this volume).
4. Westlund (2009).
5. Friedman (2002: 20).
6. Catriona Mackenzie (2014: 15–41) differentiates global autonomy over a person's life overall from programmatic autonomy, which showcases a person's status with respect to various realms of life. I take global autonomy to be assessed in terms of a person's self-determination in the context of areas of strong programmatic concern.
7. Thus it is not quite accurate to claim, as James Rocha does, that the account I defend requires that an agent must act for her values and must possess control sufficient to bring her values about. Success in that regard is not the definitive marker of autonomy. See Rocha (2011: 313–328).
8. The case of the would-be surrendered woman, brought to my attention by Paul Benson, is an instance of this type. The would-be surrendered woman shows every appearance of leading a life rich with autonomy. She is self-supporting and successful. But her life is incongruent with the life of a contented homemaker she desires. See Oshana (2006: 64–7). For an original "surrendered woman" case, see Doyle (1999). A publicity blurb for Doyle's book states, "*The Surrendered Wife* is a step-by-step guide that teaches women how to: Give up unnecessary control and responsibility; Express their needs while also respecting their husband's choices; Resist the temptation to criticize, belittle or dismiss their husbands; Trust their husbands in every aspect of marriage—from sexual to financial . . . and more."
9. I thank Julie Tannenbaum for urging me to make this point explicit.
10. Oshana (1998; 2006).
11. See Oshana (2006).
12. Christman (2004: 143). Also see Meyers (2008).
13. Christman (2009: 175).
14. Christman (2009: 172).
15. I find Mackenzie's distinction among three axes or dimensions of autonomy instructive here. The axes are self-determination, self-government, and self-authorization. "*Self-determination* involves having the freedom and

opportunities to make and enact choices of practical import to one's life; that is, choices about what to value, who to be, and what to do. [. . .] The self-governance axis identifies internal conditions for autonomy, specifically competence and authenticity conditions. *Self-authorization* involves regarding oneself as having the *normative authority* to be self-determining and self-governing." Mackenzie (2014: 25).

16. Westlund (2009: 43).
17. Ibid.
18. This point is also made by Benson (2011).
19. Noggle (May 2011).
20. Seizing on this point, Thomas Fossen has (in conversation) suggested that autonomy requires adverse circumstances that challenge the actor rather than the absence of impediments. The indolent "couch potato" who rarely has cause to test his powers of self-governance is for just that reason less autonomous than, say, the insurgent in Homs, Syria, who must rise up against challenges of this sort on a continual basis. If Fossen is correct, autonomy is much rarer than we imagine it to be. What will count as an impediment to liberty in one case might be treated as a resource of self-mastery in another. (Bernard Berofsky similarly charges that "The same environmental condition can be regarded as a grand opportunity for one person, shrugged off by another as a minor annoyance, and treated by the third as an absolute barrier" (1995: 42–3.) Phenomena such as racism and sexism, wealth and celebrity, privilege and power, and genius and disability can be similarly double edged. Any of these can test a person's strength of character. Depending on how a person responds to their presence in his life, each may fortify a person's character or debilitate it. For someone lacking in healthy self-esteem, guidance, and a network of support, any of these can present an obstacle to self-management. On the other hand, a person who is endowed with healthy self-esteem, social direction, and a system of support will be better positioned to navigate these challenges with relative ease. But I find Fossen's suggestion implausible. For one thing, there is a distinction between being autonomous and being in situations that call upon one to exhibit one's powers of autonomy. Second, why should we believe that autonomy increases commensurate with situations that foster resistance to it? Third, autonomy is not terribly rare; there are abundant examples of people who direct affairs of significance to their lives absent interference, and few of them fit the model of the indolent couch potato. Finally, we mischaracterize the person who faces no challenges as autonomous simply because he faces no challenges. Autonomy is a matter of active agency. Just because the conditions for autonomy might leave a person free to be left alone and free to do nothing does not mean that freedom of this sort is what autonomy amounts to.
21. Oshana (2006: 129).
22. King, Jr. (April 16, 1963).
23. Shelby (2005: 245).
24. This is not to minimize the fact that white Americans engaged in civil-rights activism were also at grave risk of compromised self-determination.
25. I thank Michael Green for helping me articulate this point.
26. As Shelby notes, "[T]he need to overcome the self-contempt produced by anti-black racism is an important justification for black solidarity. Given the widespread internalization of anti-black prejudice, it becomes necessary for black people to be a significant, if not the primary, force behind their liberation from racial subordination. It is not enough for black people to be freed from their subordinate position by their nonblack allies and sympathizers. They must participate, in a meaningful way, in freeing themselves." (2005: 179).

27. King, Jr. (April 3, 1968).
28. Benson (in conversation) has argued that because the three-pronged test is a test of oppression, it begs the question of whether one can live autonomously under conditions of oppression. Perhaps all oppression (by definition "the state of being subject to unjust treatment and control," Oxford English Dictionary) is antithetical to autonomy. If so, it is an analytic truth that social-relational autonomy alone counterbalances oppression. However, the point of the test is not to affirm this truth. The point is to offer a method for discerning the presence or absence of phenomena that might compromise power and authority of a practical sort.
29. The other black persons to receive the prize were Dr. Ralph Johnson Bunche, an American political scientist who was recognized in 1950 for his intercession in Palestine at the end of the 1940s, and Albert John Luthuli, who was president of the African National Congress (ANC). Lithuli received the 1960 Nobel Peace Prize in recognition of his efforts to combat apartheid in South Africa.
30. Watson (1987: 256–86). Reprinted in Fischer and Ravizza (1993:119–48). The quote is from this volume, 148.
31. Paul Benson reminded me of this fact.
32. "Media coverage of these events brought intense scrutiny on racial segregation in the South. [. . .] Scenes of the ensuing mayhem caused an international outcry, leading to federal intervention by the Kennedy administration. [. . .] By the end of the campaign, King's reputation surged, Connor lost his job, the 'Jim Crow' signs in Birmingham came down, and public places became more open to blacks." http://en.wikipedia.org/wiki/Birmingham_campaign
33. I construe oppressive circumstances broadly, including economic instability and institutional injustice. See section four.
34. Meyers (2008: 204).
35. Meyers (1989: 12). Meyers characterizes economic autonomy as a phenomenon distinct from personal autonomy, charging that while the focus of the former is the conditions that constrain the liberty of people, the concern of the latter is positive, amounting to a statement of how people should live.
36. Meyers (2008: 204). Nothing about the demand for financial security entails or even implies that stay-at-home caregivers lack autonomy. A common but misguided criticism is that a theory of agent autonomy that imports substantive conditions will be a theory that will restrict autonomous desires, life-choices, and actions to desires, life-choices, and actions a person formulates and undertakes independently of other persons.
37. Rocha (2011: 314). These are "pure action" accounts in that they treat autonomy as a concept to be analyzed on its own rather than as a means to some goal of the actor.
38. Rocha (2011: 315).
39. Rocha (2011: 318–9).
40. Rocha (2011: 317).
41. The work of the hotel maid, the housecleaner, the waitress, the nursing-home aide, and the Wal-Mart salesperson described in Ehrenreich (2001) are paradigms of labor that is autonomy depriving.
42. Meyers (2008: 204).
43. Rocha (2011: 319).
44. Westlund (2009: 32).
45. See Oshana (2004).
46. Not every model of Sharia is as fundamentalist as that found in Talibanic Afghanistan or in Saudi Arabia or Nigeria. Still, the writer Fatemola, who, in speaking out against a proposal to introduce Islamic law in Ontario, Canada,

asked, "'How Islamic is Sharia?' [Fatemola] said that Sharia violates the Quran again and again and that it is an institution of political Islam (ref. Maudoodi). 'We don't have to denounce Islam or the Prophet Mohammad, peace be upon him, to denounce Sharia.' He cited several verses of the Quran to illustrate his point" (March 7, 2004).
47. Ebadi (2003). Also see Ebadi (2001).
48. Meyers (2008: 205).
49. The fact that these were published in Iran suggests that Ebadi's situation was less thoroughly oppressive than it might otherwise have been. And the fact that it was less oppressive is, I would suggest, due to the fact that she was a highly educated, affluent, and relatively well-connected member of Iranian society.
50. Think of the U.S. military's policy of "don't ask, don't tell." Prior to its revocation, it was *possible* that some gay members of the military welcomed the policy as a needed incentive to keep their sexual orientation under wraps. That, however, does not change the fact that the policy was autonomy undermining.

REFERENCES

Benson, Paul (1991) "Autonomy and Oppressive Socialization," *Social Theory and Practice* 17 (1991): 385–408.
——— (1994) "Free Agency and Self-Worth," *Journal of Philosophy* 91: 650–668.
——— (2011) "Narrative Understanding and Relational Autonomy: Comments on Mackenzie, Poltera, and Westlund," *Symposia on Gender, Race, and Philosophy*, 7 (1). http://sgrp.typepad.com/sgrp/winter-2011-symposium-mackenzie-poltera-and-westlund-on-autonomy.html
——— (2015) "Stereotype Threat, Social Belonging, and Relational Autonomy," in Marina A. L. Oshana, ed., *Personal Autonomy and Social Oppression: Philosophical Perspectives*, New York and London: Routledge.
Berofsky, Bernard (1995) *Liberation from Self: A Theory of Personal Autonomy*, New York: Cambridge University Press.
Charles, Sonya (2010) "How Should Feminist Autonomy Theorists Respond to the Problem of Internalized Oppression?" *Social Theory and Practice* 36 (3): 409–428.
Christman, John (2004) "Relational Autonomy, Liberal Individualism, and the Social Constitution of Selves," *Philosophical Studies*, 117: 143–64.
——— (2009) *The Politics of Persons*, New York: Oxford University Press.
Doyle, Laura (1999) *The Surrendered Wife*, New York: Fireside Press/Simon and Schuster.
Ebadi, Shirin (2001) *Iran Awakening: One Woman's Journey to Reclaim Her Life and Country*, New York: Random House.
——— (2003) http://nobelprize.org/nobel_prizes/peace/laureates/2003/ebadi-auto-bio.html Accessed March 22, 2008.
Ehrenreich, Barbara (2001) *Nickel and Dimed: On (Not) Getting By in America*, New York: Metropolitan Books.
Fatemola (March 2004) "Synopsis of the panel discussion on Sharia tribunals in Canada and Women's Rights," hosted by the International Campaign for Defense of Women's Rights in Iran.
Friedman, Marilyn (2002) *Autonomy, Gender, Politics*, New York: Oxford University Press.
King, Jr., Martin Luther (April 16, 1963) *Letter from Birmingham Jail*.
——— (April 3, 1968) "I've Been to the Mountain Top," at the Bishop Charles Mason Temple, Memphis, Tennessee.

Kristinsson, Sigurður (2000) "Toward a Weakly-Substantive Conception of Autonomy," *Canadian Journal of Philosophy* 30 (2): 257–286.
Mackenzie, Catriona (2014) "Three Dimensions of Autonomy: A Relational Analysis," in Andrea Veltman and Mark Piper, eds., *Autonomy, Oppression and
Gender,* New York: Oxford University Press, pp. 15–41.
Meyers, Diana (1989) *Self, Society, and Personal Choice,* New York: Columbia University Press.
———— (2008) "Review of 'Personal Autonomy in Society,'" *Hypatia,* 23 (2): 202–
206.
Noggle, Robert (May 2011) "Review of 'Personal Autonomy in Society,'" *The Jour-
nal of Value Inquiry,* 45 (2): 233–238.
Oshana, Marina (1998) "Personal Autonomy and Society," *Journal of Social Phi-
losophy* 29 (1): 81–102.
———— (2004) "Moral Accountability," *Philosophical Topics,* special issue on
Agency 32 (1/2): 255–274.
———— (2006) *Personal Autonomy in Society,* Aldershot, Hampshire: Ashgate.
Rocha, James (2011) "Autonomy Within Subservient Careers," *Ethical Theory and
Moral Practice,* 14: 313–328.
Royanian, Simin (2003–06–27; rev. 2005–03–25), *http://women4peace.org/*
Shelby, Tommie (2005) *We Who Are Dark: The Philosophical Foundations of Black
Solidarity,* Cambridge, Mass.: Belknap Press.
Stoljar, Natalie (2000) "Autonomy and the Feminist Intuition," in Catriona Mack-
enzie and Natalie Stoljar (eds.), *Relational Autonomy,* New York: Oxford
University Press, pp. 94–111.
Watson, Gary (1987) "Responsibility and the Limits of Evil: Variations on a Straw-
sonian Theme," in Ferdinand Schoeman, ed., *Responsibility, Character, and the
Emotions: New Essays in Moral Psychology,* New York: Cambridge University
Press: 256–86. Reprinted in Fischer and Ravizza, eds., *Perspectives on Moral
Responsibility,* Ithaca: Cornell University Press, 1993, pp. 119–48. The quote is
from the latter volume, 148.
Westlund, Andrea (2009) "Rethinking Relational Autonomy," *Hypatia* 24 (4):
26–49.

2 Gender Oppression and Weak Substantive Theories of Autonomy

Jennifer Warriner

1. INTRODUCTION: GENDER HIERARCHY AND LIBERAL FEMINISM

Suppose a woman—call her Jane—chooses to live in a community that subscribes to rigid and hierarchical gender roles as a matter of religious faith. While men pursue careers outside the home, women are strictly wives and mothers and are expected to manage the households and bear and raise children as many children as possible. Furthermore, women are also expected to submit without question to their husbands' authority in all important economic, social, familial, and sexual decisions, on the grounds that an authoritative religious text dictates women ought to be subordinate to male authority in every area of life.

While some might think my description of Jane's religious beliefs and her social relations is a far-fetched caricature, I base this example on the women that Kathryn Joyce discusses in her book, *Quiverfull: Inside the Christian Patriarchy Movement*.[1] Joyce spends time with and interviews women who belong to a variety of Evangelical Christian churches in the U.S., all of which uphold beliefs about female inferiority and the rightness of female subordination to male authority.[2] Furthermore, while some might think gender-hierarchical religious communities are part of a fringe movement within Christianity, they are in reality representative of large-scale, mainstream, and powerful Christian organizations, such as Vision Forum, Focus on the Family, Campus Crusade for Christ, and the Southern Baptist Convention (the latter which Joyce notes has 16 million members).[3]

Real-life examples—like the case of Jane—in which women claim to prefer gender hierarchy have generated a lively debate among feminist theorists. What I shall call the standard liberal feminist position on the preference for gender hierarchy is this.[4] First, the preference for gender hierarchy is *oppressive*, because it contains content about the moral inferiority of women and about the rightness of the moral and social subordination of women *as a class*.[5] Second, acting upon value commitments with oppressive content interferes with women's ability to be autonomous, or to be self-governing and act on the basis of values that are one's own.[6] The assumption here seems to be that value commitments with oppressive content are *imposed* upon women, not chosen. Third, leading an autonomous life is important for all individuals, including women.[7] Fourth, feminists should aim at identifying values with oppressive content and dismantling the ideologies and practices that maintain them, in order that women are free to lead autonomous lives.[8]

However, other feminist thinkers have challenged the standard liberal feminist position on the preference for gender hierarchy and autonomy.[9] The line of thinking goes something like this: if women endorse a preference for gender hierarchy, why suppose that women cannot *autonomously choose* to endorse such a preference? It is simply not the case that every woman who upholds these commitments has them *imposed* upon her. Some women engage in practices of gender hierarchy because they belong to cultural or religious groups that endorse such practices. For these women, engaging in practices of gender hierarchy is an integral and important part of their social identities. Given that feminists claim to be committed to listening to women's own self-understandings and acknowledging the diversity of women's social locations, we run the risk of disrespecting the considered choices of women who endorse gender-hierarchical preferences by claiming that such preferences cannot be autonomously chosen.

The idea being floated here by some feminist thinkers—that a person can be autonomous and subordinate at the same time—has caught the attention of autonomy theorists. On the one hand, it seems deeply counterintuitive to say that autonomous living is compatible with subordination. On the other hand, if autonomy is self-governance on the basis of beliefs one deems important, and if one thinks gender-hierarchical beliefs are important, then perhaps autonomy is compatible with living subordinate to another person. If so, we require a clear and intuitively appealing account of autonomy that explains how this is possible.

To shed light on this issue, autonomy theorists have tended to focus upon what I call the content question: does the content of a person's preference for gender hierarchy interfere with her autonomy and, if so, how?[10] Some theorists, referred to as proceduralists, argue that acting on the basis of gender hierarchical preferences need not impede a person's autonomy, provided she subjects her beliefs to the proper kind of critical endorsement.[11] Other theorists, referred to as strong substantivists, argue that acting on the basis of gender hierarchical preferences *always* impairs a person's autonomy, even if she critically endorses them.[12] This means that a person can *never* qualify as autonomous on a strong substantivist view if she endorses these preferences.

In section two, I discuss the debate between proceduralists and strong substantivists. While each view is motivated by compelling intuitions, critics have raised serious concerns about the viability of each of these views. I review these criticisms in more detail, but for now: critics charge that proceduralism is unable to detect adequately impairments in a person's autonomy, while strong substantivism is untenable as a theory of autonomy because it leads to a paradox. This standoff suggests to some theorists that we look elsewhere for a different approach to autonomy to provide a clear account of whether autonomy is compatible with subordination.

Recently, some theorists have offered what they refer to as a weak substantivist account of autonomy.[13] In section three, I introduce and elaborate on Paul Benson's account of weak substantivism because part of his motivation in formulating his theory of autonomy is in response to the stalemate between proceduralism and strong substantivism. Benson's view claims that autonomy and subordination can be compatible, provided a person who endorses gender-hierarchal preferences holds the proper self-regarding attitude toward her agential authority.[14] According to its defenders, weak substantive accounts are attractive because they carve a path between proceduralism and strong substantivism and thus avoid the objections raised against these views while offering an intuitively compelling account of autonomy and its compatibility with subordination.

I set out my argument against Benson's account in section four. While Benson is confident that weak substantive views represent the way forward over the debate about the compatibility between autonomy and subordination, I am less certain. I argue that not only is it possible for subordinated individuals to meet Benson's weak substantivist standards for autonomy, we should *expect* subordinated individuals to meet them. If my line of argument is correct, the upshot is that Benson's view is equally vulnerable to the objection raised against proceduralism, namely that the view cannot adequately detect impairments to autonomy. As a result, Benson's account fails to shed light on whether autonomy and subordination are compatible.

My argument against Benson's weak substantivist account will set the stage for my own view, which I can only state here rather than offer a full defense. My view is this. An individual's autonomy *can be* threatened by the expectations of the social relationships in which she partakes. I maintain that a subordinate individual's autonomy is *in fact* threatened by the socially derived expectations of the dominant/subordinate relationship. So, on my view, autonomy and subordination are not compatible.[15] Here is why. In the context of the dominant/subordinate relationship, subordinated individuals are provided with a "script" to follow. The script outlines for the subordinated individual the kinds of actions she is permitted to engage in *and* provides her with a set of reasons that justifies her engaging in these actions.[16] Furthermore, in the context of the dominant/subordinate relationship, subordinated individuals are neither permitted to engage in behaviors nor to act for reasons *other than those provided by the script*.[17] I maintain that in the context of the dominant/subordinate relationship, a subordinated individual's autonomy is impaired given how *thoroughly* the script determines her actions and the reasons behind them. A person in a dominant/subordinate relationship is not self-governing but is being governed by the script. It is my claim that weak substantive views fail to acknowledge the degree to which the expectations of dominant/subordinate relationships structure the day-to-day lives of subordinated individuals and thus fail to identify a serious impairment to autonomy.[18]

Why is it important to get clear on whether autonomy and subordination are compatible? One reason is that doing so will settle an important and long-standing debate among autonomy theorists. Moreover, settling this issue may provide new avenues of debate for feminist thinkers. The dismantling of gendered hierarchies has been an important goal for feminists because they have regarded these as antithetical to women's autonomy. But, if it can be shown that some women not only genuinely prefer but are able to autonomously choose lives centered on gender hierarchies, this should give feminists pause about whether to continue pursuing this goal.

2. THE AUTONOMY DEBATE OVER OPPRESSIVE VALUES

I noted earlier that the debate over the compatibility of autonomy and subordination has tended to focus on the question of whether the content of a preference impairs a person's autonomy. Another way to frame the debate between proceduralists and strong substantivists is to say that they disagree over whether a theory of autonomy ought to be content neutral. To be content neutral is to take no stand on the kinds of beliefs an individual must hold in order to qualify as autonomous. While proceduralists insist that any reasonable theory of autonomy ought to be content neutral, strong substantivists claim otherwise. In this section, I offer a rough sketch of their debate, and I consider proceduralism first.

The proceduralist commitment to content neutrality is motivated by two very compelling intuitions. The first is this: autonomy seems to require a large space of noninterference in which individuals can identify and pursue their good as they see fit. Proceduralists claim that one way to capture this intuition is to embrace content neutrality and refrain from imposing normative content restrictions on an agent's preferences as a condition for autonomy. After all, requiring autonomous agents to avoid holding value commitments with particular content reduces the space of noninterference because some commitments will be deemed incompatible with autonomous living. If we uphold content neutrality, however, this provides individuals the greatest possible space to self-govern, or to live according to the beliefs they deem valuable.

The second intuition is this: defenders of proceduralism subscribe to the idea that value commitments "are valid for a person when she can autonomously come to see their import."[19] Here is what I take proceduralists to be saying: unless I decide and endorse my values from my own perspective, I will not see the significance of these values for myself. When someone or something external to my perspective determines the values I should endorse, I cannot see the validity of these values for myself. According to defenders, proceduralist views capture this intuition by not imposing normative content restrictions on an autonomous agent's preferences. Proceduralists claim that there is no "right" value framework that an individual must endorse to be autonomous, and any view of autonomy that claims to identify this framework is perfectionist about the good.[20] Proceduralism denies that it has a complete perspective, decided in advance, on the *kinds* of lives an autonomous agent might lead. Instead, it is left up to agents to determine how they might live, and this includes leading one's life on the basis of values that endorse gender hierarchy. Proceduralism simply identifies a decision procedure for autonomy rather than a prescription for the good life, and this will ensure that individuals are living according to values they endorse from their own perspective.

According to proceduralists, our evaluations about a person's autonomy depend solely upon the kinds of psychological states that result (or could result) from engaging in the right sort of critical reflection. For example, many influential views of proceduralism in the literature claim that when an individual engages in (or could engage in) the proper reflective endorsement of her choice-motivating value commitments, this process renders her value commitments her own and thus autonomous with respect to them.[21] What is especially notable about such views, however, is the following: proceduralists argue that psychological standards are both *necessary and sufficient* for autonomy. No other social or normative considerations play a role in establishing whether a person is autonomous, including the content of the value commitments she endorses or the kinds of social relations in which she lives.[22] One important implication of proceduralism is this: because proceduralists are committed to content neutrality, they are committed to the view that a subordinated wife and even a slave can turn out to be autonomous, provided each of them is reflectively competent and would endorse their value commitments in the right way, were they reflect upon them in the way specified by proceduralism. I will discuss this implication shortly.

Strong substantivist theorists are also guided by a very compelling intuition: some ways of living are *incompatible* with autonomy, and living as a subordinated wife and (especially) as a slave seem to be *paradigmatic examples of these ways of living*.[23] For strong substantivists, the incompatibility between autonomy and some ways of living arises because of the content of the value commitments that undergird these ways of living and not because of how these commitments were formed.[24] Being guided by this intuition leads strong substantivists to formulate a theory of autonomy that places normative restrictions on the content of an agent's preferences or, put another way, that rejects content neutrality.

A strong substantivist theory claims that a person is autonomous if she critically reflects upon and endorses value commitments with content that is not incompatible with autonomous living. In other words, defenders of the view claim that the content of a person's value commitments is *constitutive* of her autonomy. So why does a person lack autonomy if she makes a choice on the basis of a value with the "wrong" content? According to strong substantivist theorists, acting on the "wrong" kind of value impairs a person's autonomy because she makes "a special kind of moral mistake."[25] For example, Jane's moral error stems from the fact that she makes a choice that denies her standing as a moral equal. Strong substantivists say that the *reason* Jane makes this error is due to the content of Jane's preference for subordination. The content prevents her psychology from "hooking up" with an objective feature of the world, namely the fact that she *is* morally equal. On the strong substantivist view, then, if a person avoids holding "wrong" value commitments, her psychology will "hook up" to the world in the proper way and so will avoid making moral errors that prevent her from qualifying as autonomous.[26]

2.1. Strong Substantivism and the Paradox Problem

As I have outlined, proceduralists and strong substantivists are both guided by compelling intuitions. Nevertheless, both are subject to serious objections, and I examine them here.

Proceduralist critics raise the following objection against strong substantivism. Call this the paradox objection. Because of its rejection of content neutrality, strong substantivism results in a paradox. Here is why. Strong substantivist theorists claim as a condition of autonomy that individuals are prohibited from endorsing commitments with particular content, for example, values that endorse gender hierarchy. But, by identifying the "wrong" value commitments, strong substantivists in effect stipulate to people the commitments they should endorse (for example, egalitarian relationships), *regardless of whether people see the value in these commitments for themselves.* So we can pose the following question to strong substantivism: how can a person be autonomous, that is, decide her preferences and values from her own perspective, when others decide them for her?[27]

Because strong substantivism is subject to the paradox objection because of its rejection of content neutrality, one might think that this vindicates proceduralism and its endorsement of content neutrality. However, weak substantivist theorists argue that this is not the case. Weak substantivist critics maintain that strong substantivists are correct with respect to their rejection of content neutrality. A reasonable theory of autonomy should incorporate at least one condition with normative substance. The problem with strong substantivism is that it has identified the wrong kind of normative condition; this is why the view leads to a paradox. I will say more about the normative condition that weak substantivist theorists think ought to be included in a view of autonomy in the following section. Right now, I want to examine the reason behind weak substantivists' rejection of content neutrality. This is best explained by considering a long-standing objection against proceduralism.

2.2. Proceduralism and the Impairment Objection

I want now to return to a claim that I raised earlier, namely that it is possible for subordinated wives and even slaves to be autonomous on proceduralist views, provided that they meet the standards for autonomy identified by the proceduralist. This implication of the view has led many critics question whether proceduralist standards for autonomy are sufficient.[28] Call this the impairment objection. It is deeply problematic to say that a subordinated wife such as Jane can turn out to be autonomous, provided she is reflectively competent and would endorse her value commitment in the right way. This is because it seems reasonable to think that oppressive socialization interferes with a person's capacity for autonomy. Given that this capacity plays a central role in establishing autonomy on a proceduralist view, it seems counterintuitive to say that Jane is autonomous.[29] After all, oppressively socialized individuals such as Jane are socially trained not only to value but *to want* to value subordination. Because Jane's social training has led her to *internalize* so deeply ideas about the "rightness" of female subordination, her critical endorsement of her values as her own may not be indicative of her autonomy as proceduralists claim. We cannot be sure whether oppressive socialization has interfered with an agent's critical faculties, such that her endorsement is itself the result of oppressive socialization or whether her endorsement is authentic. In other words, weak substantivist critics have doubts that proceduralist standards alone can detect impairments to a person's autonomy that arise due to oppressive socialization.

In response to the impairment objection, proceduralists acknowledge that it is possible for certain factors, including one's social training, to interfere with a person's critical faculties, in which case a person would not count as autonomous.[30] But proceduralists also maintain that it is possible social training will *not* interfere with a person's reflective capacities, even if she has been socialized to value subordination. On proceduralist views, we cannot assume that a person who wants to choose according to subordinate value commitments has compromised critical capacities. Furthermore, proceduralists point out that because it is possible for a person to genuinely prefer subordination, a reasonable view of autonomy ought to make conceptual room for this possibility by identifying only minimal standards for autonomy. So here is the task set forth for proceduralist theorists: to identify an account of critical reflection fine grained enough to pick out an agent whom it is reasonable to think authentically endorses value commitments with oppressive content and yet at the same time can provide an effective filter to isolate an agent who holds similar commitments but whom it is reasonable to think does not authentically hold those commitments as her own because of some problem with the agent's critical capacities.

To this end, John Christman defends a proceduralist view that claims a person is autonomous if she were to critically reflect on a value commitment, given the historical processes by which it arose, and the person does not feel a sense of alienation toward the commitment.[31] According to Christman, the historical constraint provides a way to identify agents whose endorsement of a preference for gender hierarchy is authentic. An agent's endorsement of a preference is authentic if and only if she does not feel alienated toward the preference in question, were she to reflect upon the historical process by which it arose.[32] Alienation, in the sense Christman intends, picks out a *reaction* to one's value commitment. Alienation involves feeling *constrained* by a value commitment and wanting to reject it.[33] So, if an agent's reflection upon the historical development of her commitment to gender hierarchy were to reveal a sense of alienation, then she lacks autonomy with respect to that commitment. Agents who authentically endorse their preferences do not feel a sense of alienation toward them. In addition, Christman places further constraints on the process of critical reflection in order to ensure that an agent is genuinely competent or to make certain that her critical faculties are not impaired.[34] Christman stipulates that a person's reflections cannot be "the product of social and psychological conditions that prevent adequate appraisal of oneself."[35] This means that one must be free from certain factors (for example, blinding rage, drug or alcohol addiction, depression). In addition, one must have the ability and the freedom to evaluate aspects of one's personality and social conditions, which requires that one has "minimal education" and "exposure to alternatives."[36]

In response, weak substantivist theorists maintain that Christman has not addressed the impairment objection. The line of thinking goes something like this.[37] Suppose that Jane reflects upon her commitment to subordination in the way specified by Christman. Suppose further that someone *tells her* that she has been socially trained to endorse value commitments that maintain oppressive relations of domination and subordination between men and women. The following problem remains for the proceduralist: were Jane to reflect on her value commitment to subordination, she would likely think, "I *should be* subject to the kind of social training that led me to have this value commitment. This is the way things *should be*. So there is good reason why I don't feel alienated from my commitment to subordination." Because Jane has been trained to want to value subordination and accept the "rightness" of gender hierarchy, it is unlikely she *would* feel a sense of alienation toward her commitment. So, weak substantivist critics conclude, even with Christman's fine-grained modifications to the reflective process, we are still not sure whether Jane's critical reflections secure her autonomy or whether she is simply reiterating the terms of her subordination.

3. WEAK SUBSTANTIVISM

Christman has attempted to address the impairment objection against proceduralism by refining the conditions for autonomy. However, defenders of weak substantivism think this strategy is unlikely to work. Even carefully revised proceduralist standards such as Christman's continue to be too weak to adequately detect any impairment to autonomy that arises due to social factors such as oppressive socialization. Weak substantivist theorists take a different approach and argue that the impairment objection and the paradox objection can be avoided by introducing standards for autonomy that incorporate some normative content. Unlike strong substantivism, however, weak substantivism does not claim that such conditions must involve placing direct restrictions on the content of an agent's value commitments. Instead, Paul Benson argues the normative condition requires agents to hold the right kind of self-regarding attitude toward her agential authority.

3.1. Benson's Weak Substantivist Account of Autonomy

According to Benson, a person is autonomous when she meets the following three conditions:

(1) The authority condition: the person authorizes her agency and regards herself as a competent reasons giver.[38]
(2) The social condition: authorization occurs only within a system of social relations.[39]
(3) The discursive condition: the person is able to voice her reasons for her actions, especially to respond to criticism from others in the social world.[40]

I will begin by considering the first condition.

According to Benson, taking ownership or authorizing one's agency is both *active* and *reflexive*. Taking ownership is active because individuals must (in Benson's terminology) *seize* ownership of their authority as agents.[41] Taking ownership is reflexive because individuals who take ownership of their authority must regard themselves *as* having agential authority. Benson explains that this requires individuals to have "no serious doubts about their competence to recognize or construct reasons for their actions or about their authority to speak and answer for their conduct, should others criticize it."[42] Moreover, individuals must not have "attitudes [which] manifest marked disengagement or dissociation from their conduct."[43]

Furthermore, Benson tells us that "occupying a position of authority to speak for one's intentions and acts seems to depend not only on one's objective fitness to play the role of potential answerer, but also one one's regard for one's abilities and social position."[44] I will say more about the social aspect shortly. For now, it is important to note the following. On Benson's view, whether a person is capable of being a reasons giver depends *not* on whether a person *thinks* she is competent but rather on whether she *really is* competent; so a person's competency is an objective fact about the world. Determining one's objective fitness depends in part upon the social relations in which one stands, so let us turn to Benson's second condition for autonomy.

With respect to the social condition, Benson tells us that, "to have the authority of owning one's acts is to stand in a certain position with respect to others' potential expectations for one's conduct."[45] What Benson is claiming here is that a person's social relations are partly constitutive of her autonomy.[46] That is, Benson thinks that it is a defining condition of autonomy that a person is embedded in social relations in which she can acquire the proper regard for her agential authority *and* in which others recognize her as having this authority. So a person lacks autonomy if other agents in her social world fail to acknowledge her agential authority or if her social relations prevent her from acquiring the proper attitude toward her agential authority.[47] Furthermore, an agent's authority to speak for her actions, especially in light of critical challenges from others, must be in terms of the normative standards *she* regards as important, which standards other agents in the social world may bring to bear critically on her conduct.[48] This leads to Benson's third discursive condition for autonomy. Autonomous agents take ownership of their actions when they occupy a social position in which they are able to voice their action-guiding reasons "should others call for their reasons."[49]

Benson takes the introduction of the authority condition to avoid the impairment objection and the paradox objection for the following reasons. As we saw with Christman's view, proceduralist conditions cannot adequately identify impairments to a person's autonomy: we are not sure whether an agent's critical endorsement of her preference is authentically her own or whether she is expressing the terms of subordination. On Benson's view, autonomy does not turn on whether an agent's endorsement of her preferences is authentic but whether she is able to authorize her agency. Making this move not only allows Benson's view to sidestep any questions raised about the authenticity of an agent's preferences, it offers a way for Benson to identify clearly when a person's autonomy is impaired, namely when her ability to authorize her agency is impeded.[50] Second, the authority condition introduces a normative dimension to autonomy and yet avoids the paradox objection raised against strong substantivist views. This is because Benson's view does not stipulate that agents hold (or avoid holding) preferences with particular content, although his view does require that agents hold the right self-regarding attitude toward their authority as agents.

Furthermore, the introduction of the social condition allows Benson's view to avoid the impairment objection in the following way. Proceduralist views claims that social conditions *may* impair a person's autonomy, for example, by compromising a person's critical faculties, but this need not be the case. However, as we discussed earlier, proceduralist views are unable to pick out those agents whose critical faculties have been compromised from agents whose faculties are intact. According to Benson, the constitutive social condition provides a way to explain, in a clear and intuitive way, how social factors impair a person's autonomy, namely by preventing an agent from developing the proper self-regard for her agential authority or by preventing others from regarding the agent as having this authority. In addition, the constitutive social condition allows Benson's view to avoid what many theorists regard as a deeply counterintuitive implication of proceduralism, namely that it is possible for slaves to qualify as autonomous, provided they meet the conditions for autonomy as specified by proceduralism. However, on Benson's account of autonomy, the constitutive social condition prevents slaves, once they have become slaves, from counting as autonomous. Slaves cannot be recognized as having agential authority because they cannot occupy a social position in which they are able to speak for their actions.

What about subordinated wives such as Jane? Would she count as autonomous on Benson's view? As Joyce testifies in her book, subordinated women in the Evangelical Christian community identify deeply with their religious faith as an integral part of their identity and endorse preferences for gender hierarchy as an expression of this faith. On Benson's view of autonomy, even if Jane has been socially trained to accept these kinds of beliefs, this certainly does not preclude her from taking ownership of her actions and regarding herself as a reasons giver. It is clear that Jane and other women within the Evangelical Christian communities regard themselves as reasons givers and can confidently offer to us a coherent set of reasons for their choice to submit unquestioningly to male authority. In addition, women like Jane seem to *seize* their agential authority, by publishing books outlining their reasons for adhering to strict gender roles (as well as, of course, explaining what this role requires of women, in terms of attitude and action.)[51] In fact, if a person could not identify *any* reasons for her choice, we might wonder if she is an agent in the first place.[52]

Furthermore, even though Jane stands in oppressive social relations in her religious community, these relations still allow her to be a reasons giver. After all, while Jane is required to be subordinate, she is not required to be silent, at least with respect to her reasons for her choice. We can imagine other agents, whether in her own community or outsiders, asking Jane to give reasons for her choice to be a subservient wife. That Joyce was able to interview dozens of women in the Evangelical Christian communities in order to ask them their reasons for adhering to strict gender hierarchy suggests that these women stand in the kind of social relations that allow them to authorize their agential authority and that others regard them as having this kind of authority.

4. WEAK SUBSTANTIVISM AND GENDER-HIERARCHICAL BELIEFS

According to Benson, the introduction of the constitutive social condition and the self-regarding attitude condition allows his view to avoid the impairment objection raised against proceduralism. But is this really the case? It is my contention that Benson's view remains subject to the impairment objection. I want to argue that Benson's weak substantive standards fail to provide an effective filter to pick out those agents who autonomously hold value commitments with oppressive content from agents whose support of the same commitments is not autonomous.

Benson tells us that a person must authorize her agency, that she must be capable of offering reasons for her actions, and that she must be embedded in social relations that allow her to regard herself as a reasons giver and in which others regard her as such. However, I shall argue that to be a reasons giver, to regard oneself as having agential authority, and to stand in social relations in which others regard you as having this authority is compatible with a lack of autonomy because a person who acts upon a deeply inter-nalized preference for subordination is still able to meet these conditions. I argue that a person is able to meet these conditions because of the social expectations of a dominant/slave relationship. To understand what these expectations are and to understand why they allow a subordinate agent to meet weak substantive standards, it will be helpful to begin by comparing the expectations of a master/slave relationship with the expectations of a dominant/subordinate relationship.[53]

In the context of the master/slave relationship, one of the expectations of the "master" is this: once he becomes a master, he is expected to regard the slave as lacking agential authority, or as being a competent reasons giver. Along the same lines, the slave, once he becomes a slave, is expected to view *himself* as lacking agential authority in the way specified by Benson. This is not to say that a slave *in fact* regards himself as lacking this authority or that a slave *in fact* lacks this authority, although the latter case might be true if the slave is subject to particularly brutal treatment.[54] However, it seems more likely that slaves, after they become slaves, view themselves as having agential authority but are unable or unwilling to exercise it as a result of the expectations of the master/slave relationship. The slave narrative of Freder-ick Douglass provides support for this line of thinking.[55]

Douglass describes an incident in his early life in which Mrs. Auld, the kind wife of one of his masters, teaches him the alphabet. When Mr. Auld discovers this, he forbids his wife from teaching Douglass any further. According to Douglass, Mr. Auld said a slave cannot become literate because

> A nigger should know nothing but to obey his master—to do as he is told to do . . . if you teach that nigger . . . how to read, there would be no keeping him. It would forever unfit him to be a slave. He would at once become unmanageable, and of no value to his master. As to him-self, it could do him no good, but a great deal of harm. It would make him discontented and unhappy.[56]

I want to suggest that Auld's reaction expresses clearly the expectations of the master/slave relationship.[57] As a master, Auld knows he is expected to view a slave *only* as someone who *obeys*, that is, as someone who cannot act for his own reasons. Furthermore, Auld knows slaves are not expected to view themselves as having agential authority or as individuals who are able to identify and act for their own reasons. This is why it Auld thinks it is so dangerous to teach Douglass to read, even though he is a seven-year old boy. A literate slave is likely to begin to see himself as someone who wants to act for his own reasons and not simply obey the master.

In contrast, the dominated/subordinated relationship is conceptually different from the master/slave relationship, and so the expectations of the relationship are also different. Subordinated individuals are not slaves. I argue that subordinated individuals are expected to regard themselves as having agential authority and are expected to authorize their agency. This is because subordinate individuals have an interest in seeing themselves—and having others see them—not as slaves who cannot act for their own reasons but as individuals who authorize and exercise their will for their own reasons. It is equally the case that dominant individuals have an interest in ensuring the ongoing continuation of a set of social relations in which they are dominant and therefore reap a lot of benefits. As such, dominant individuals also have an interest in ensuring that the subordinated individuals view themselves as having agential authority. This is because oppressive social relations are best maintained and have the best possibility of continuing not when subordinated individuals are *forced* to accept a subordinate status but when subordinated individuals exercise (and view themselves as exercising) their agency to willingly accept their subordinate status. Such relationships survive when the subordinate party says, "This is what *I* prefer and here are *my* reasons for preferring it." In order for this to happen, subordinated individuals have see themselves as having agential authority and thus be able to offer reasons for their actions to others in the social world, especially dominant individuals.

But notice: subordinated individuals are expected to act for *particular* reasons, that is, reasons scripted by the dominant/subordinate relationship. Furthermore, subordinated individuals cannot choose to act for reasons *other than* those provided by this script.[58] For example, a woman in the Evangelical Christian church cannot offer the following reason: "I choose to be a subordinate wife on feminist grounds that women ought to freely determine their conception of the good." It is the wrong kind of reason for her to offer in her position because it is not a reason supplied by the script and it is not open to her as a subordinated individual to appeal to reasons beyond what the script supplies. However, she is not only *permitted* but *expected* to say something along the following lines: "I choose to be a subordinate wife on the grounds that this is God's plan."

If I am correct about the expectation of the dominant/subordinate relationship, the upshot for Benson's view is this. If someone like Jane is expected authorize her agency and act on the basis of reasons "scripted" by the dominant/subordinate relationship, why think her self-professed reasons for acting on the basis of this value commitment are *her own* rather than the reasons dictated by the script?[59] The problem is that the process of reasons giving does not reveal whether the reasons given are an agent's own reasons or whether she is merely reciting the terms of her subordination. If this is correct, then it seems that having a sense of one's agential authority as conceptualized by Benson is not doing the work it should be doing. Individuals whom we intuitively think are non-autonomous can still meet the weak substantivist's criteria for autonomy. Even with the addition of more normatively robust conditions, Benson's account is still subject to the impairment objection: the view cannot identify in a clear and intuitive way those cases in which a person's autonomy is impaired by social factors.

My final concern is to address two objections that may be raised against my argument. First, Benson might object that I have exaggerated the nature of the dominant/subordinate relationship and its expectations. If I have mischaracterized the dominant/subordinate relationship, then my objection against his view fails. He might claim that I have painted a picture in which subordinated individuals mechanically parrot the values and perspective of the dominant party. It seems as though my view implies that in any instance in which a subordinated person speaks, she is merely expressing what is expected of her as a subordinate. Some feminists, such as Uma Narayan, may agree with Benson and charge that I may be seeing women in the Evangelical Christian church as "dupes" of patriarchy, that is, as women who have "completely subscribed to the patriarchal norms and practices of [their] culture" and who are unaware of the limitations imposed by these norms and practices.[60] Narayan might argue that I wrongly characterize those in dominant positions as scheming manipulators who want nothing more than to "dupe" the subordinate. The second objection is that Benson may argue that my view is problematic because it regards autonomy and subordination as incompatible. It leaves no room for the possibility for individuals to autonomously endorse a preference for gender hierarchy.

In response to the first objection, I do not think all dominant individuals are manipulators or that all subordinate individuals are duped. I reject the simplistic notion that dominant individuals endorse a gender-hierarchical framework *only* because it allows them to successfully manipulate others or that dominant individuals are committed to this framework *only because* others have manipulated them into accepting it. I think most of the individuals in the Evangelical churches subscribe to their beliefs out of the sincere conviction that this is the only way to achieve salvation.[61] Furthermore, I agree with Narayan that subordinated individuals are more or less *aware* of the limitations imposed upon them.[62] However, we have to acknowledge all of the lived realities of the lives of subordinate individuals, and this is what I take my view to be doing. Subordinated individuals, once in a subordinate position, are not permitted to *challenge* these limitations or to act for reasons other than those prescribed by the script. Within the context of the dominant/subordinate relationship, subordinate individuals are not permitted to question the "givenness" of the expectations involved in the relationship.[63] Whether they personally agree with every aspect of that script or not, subordinate individuals are expected to authorize their agency on the basis of reasons provided by that script. Because subordinate individuals are subject to this expectation, I argue that this impairs their autonomy. Subordinated individuals, once they are subordinate, cannot be autonomous.

My response to the second objection is this. I take it that one of the overarching concerns in claiming that autonomy and subordination are not compatible is this. My view seems not only to disrespect the considered views of those individuals who endorse gender-hierarchical preferences, it perhaps paves the way for state paternalism. Some may point out that the state grants social and political rights only to autonomous individuals; if we deem subordinated individuals to be lacking autonomy, it seems to follow that the state is justified in denying them rights. However, to claim (as I do) that subordinated individuals lack autonomy is not a failure of respect but a frank acknowledgement of the reality of the expectations to which subordinated individuals are subject and the constraints these expectations impose on their ability to self-govern. Moreover, I maintain that we should continue to respect the considered choices of the women in the Evangelical church, even if these choices are not autonomous. My view does not demand paternalistic intervention in the lives of subordinate individuals to "save" them from their beliefs or deny political rights to subordinated individuals. Individuals should be able to lead non-autonomous lives, free from interference.[64]

5. CONCLUDING REMARKS

I have argued that the standards introduced by weak substantivism are not doing what proponents say they do, which is to provide a way to pick out individuals who genuinely endorse oppressive values and qualify as autonomous. As a result, weak substantivism remains subject to the same long-standing impairment objection against proceduralism. My discussion here suggests that autonomy theorists should rethink the idea that the standards for autonomy are exclusively or even primarily psychological. Instead, I think that conceptualizing autonomy as primarily a social phenomenon will help theorists move beyond the impairment objection I have discussed here.

ACKNOWLEDGMENTS

I thank Evan Tiffany and Chuck Hudgins for their comments and criticisms of this version of my paper. I owe special thanks to Marina Oshana for her incisive and helpful comments and criticisms of this version of my paper. I also thank Cindy Stark and the participants of the UC Davis Autonomy Workshop, March 2012, for their criticisms of an earlier version.

NOTES

1. In framing this example, I am appealing a real community as documented by Joyce (2009).
2. When I refer to the "Evangelical Christian church," this is merely an umbrella term I use for brevity's sake. Following Joyce, I acknowledge that there are different Evangelical Christian churches, some of which are more doctrinally rigorous than others.
3. Joyce (2009: 7, 13).
4. I take Susan Moller Okin and Martha C. Nussbaum to be representative of this position. See Okin (1989) and (1999). See Nussbaum's "The Feminist Critique of Liberalism" in (1999) and Nussbaum (2001).
5. For example, Okin critiques what she refers to as the "functional" view of women. This view claims that *all* women are metaphysically different from men and that biology determines women's social role to be wives and mothers only. According to Okin, this view of women permeates the canon of political theory, and it structures our daily lives. However, Okin argues that accepting this view of women as valuable only in terms of the "functions" they fulfill is inconsistent with regarding women as equals. See Okin (1979: 10–11).
6. For Okin's critique of how the "gender system" impairs women's autonomy because of the norms and expectations imposed upon women, see "Justice as Fairness: For Whom?" (1989: 89–109).
7. As Okin writes, feminists hold "the belief that women should not be disadvantaged by their sex, that they should be recognized as having dignity equal to that of men, and that they should have the opportunity to live as fulfilling and as freely chosen lives as men can" (1999: 10).
8. This is why Okin argues that "a consistent and wholehearted application of Rawls's liberal principles of justice can lead us to challenge fundamentally the gender system of our society" (1989: 89).
9. I take Uma Narayan and Saba Mahmood to be representative of this position. Narayan argues that women in the Sufi Pirzada community in India are autonomous with their choice to live in *purdah*, even though it is an oppressive practice, which greatly limits their mobility and options. See Narayan (2002), especially 420–421. Mahmood argues (in part) that women in Egypt who choose to accept orthodox views of Islam are not straightforwardly oppressed or non-autonomous but may be actually exercising a form of agency that differs from Western, liberal conceptions of autonomy and for reasons that cannot be captured by Western feminist liberatory discourses. See Mahmood (2005).
10. Natalie Stoljar phrases the content question along similar lines (2013, section 2).
11. Here is a partial list of the most prominent defenders of proceduralism and their most recent or well-known work: Christman (2009), Dworkin (1988), Friedman (2003), Meyers (2002).
12. Among those who defend strong substantive views are Babbitt (1993), Stoljar (2000), and Wolf (1980).
13. Paul Benson is the most prominent defender of a weak substantivist account (2005a, 2005b). See also Kristinsson (2000).
14. Andrea Westlund defends a view of autonomy that is similar to Benson's account. Westlund argues for a constitutively relational proceduralist view. She claims that autonomy is dialogical. This means that a person's autonomy in part depends upon whether she has the proper attitude toward her "*responsibility for self*," where this is "a matter of holding oneself *answerable*, for one's endorsements, to external critical perspectives" (2003: 494–5). Westlund tells us that a person who is self-responsible is "willing to be engaged in a form of potentially open-ended

justificatory dialogue about one's action-guiding commitments" (2003: 495). So, like Benson, Westlund claims that autonomy in part depends upon having the right kind of attitude toward one's agency. However, unlike Benson, Westlund claims that her view is *content neutral*. Individuals are not required to endorse "specific value commitments" as a condition of autonomy (2009: 28). So, because Westlund does not classify her account as weak substantivist view (even if it shares certain insights about autonomy with such views), I do not consider her view here for that reason. That said, Benson questions whether Westlund can consistently maintain a content-neutral position while claiming that the proper self-regarding attitude toward one's answerability to others is a necessary condition of autonomy. If it turns out that Benson is correct and Westlund's view of autonomy is weakly substantive, then I take it that Westlund's account would be subject to the same objections I raise against Benson's view. For Benson's critique of Westlund, see Benson (2011).

15. To be clear, I do not regard autonomy and subordination as incompatible because of the content of the preferences of a subordinated person. This is the strong substantivist view, and I agree with proceduralist critics that this line of reasoning as untenable. I expand upon this in section 3.

16. To motivate my claim, consider one of the couples whom Joyce interviews. Jennifer and Mark Epstein joined the Boerne Christian Assembly (or BCA), a fundamentalist Christian church founded and run by Doug Phillips, the founder of Vision Forum, in San Antonio in 2000, because Jennifer Epstein was dissatisfied by (what she thought were) doctrinally lax Christian churches that her family attended previously. Joyce reports that the Epsteins were happy during their first year in BCA. But, after the first year, Jennifer Epstein began to express displeasure with the leadership style and doctrinal direction of the organization. For example, church elders published an article in 2001 explaining the "Tenets of Biblical Patriarchy." Jennifer Epstein objected against this, though not because she was required to submit but due to what she believed to be the "legalistic direction" in which BCA was heading (113). Specifically, Epstein protested that submitting to male authority "increasingly meant observing a list of proscribed behaviors" (114.) Epstein also criticized Doug Phillips, for example, sending him an email to challenge his claim that "true Christians should vote neither Democratic nor Republican but instead for the candidate of his father's Constitution Party" (117).

17. The example of the Epsteins again provides support for this idea. Around the time Jennifer Epstein was protesting the direction of BCA, the Epsteins began to have marital problems, and they went to Doug Phillips and his wife Beall for marriage counseling. The Phillipses told Jennifer Epstein that any marital problems were the result of her failure to follow the fourteen guidelines of female submission. Part of Jennifer Epstein's marriage counseling was being instructed by Beall Phillips to live up to the fourteen guidelines, and this included refraining "from teaching or having theological discussions with any other men" (Joyce, 2009: 117). In response, Epstein claimed that "she didn't 'have the conviction' that women mustn't speak of theology to men, but she argued that she was already living out the other thirteen points" (117). Beall Phillips told Epstein that "she [Jennifer] could take them or leave [the guidelines for female submission] . . . but if she wanted to remain at BCA, she was 'bound to live by [her] covenant. This means being under authority, and resisting the temptation to bring a false witness against other brothers, or seek to build a private case to justify such behavior" (116–117). Beall Phillips's statement captures the idea I am presenting here, namely that subordinated individuals in a dominant/subordinate relationship cannot choose to act in ways other than the actions approved by the script.

The BCA eventually excommunicated the Epsteins on the grounds that Jennifer was not a submissive woman and that this was the direct cause of the Epsteins' marital problems.

18. If I am correct that the expectations of the dominant/subordinate relationship threaten a person's autonomy, my view may have the following, interesting implication. That is, it might be the case that the autonomy of *dominant* individuals is impaired because of the expectations of a dominant/subordinate relationship. After all, just like subordinate individuals, dominant individuals are expected to follow a script outlining acceptable actions and acceptable reasons for these actions. If the autonomy of subordinated individuals is impaired because they are required to follow a script and dominant individuals are also expected to follow a script, then it seems that the autonomy of dominant individuals would be impaired.

19. Christman (2005: 281).

20. Christman (2004: 151–152).

21. However, proceduralist theorists disagree over what is involved in adequate critical reflection. Benson points out that proceduralists characterize critical reflection roughly along four lines: (1) critical identification, wherein agents are autonomous provided they reflect upon and endorse their value commitments at the second-order level; (2) "evaluative" self-disclosure", in which agents secure autonomy when they act on the basis of their ends; (3) "identity-based theories", in which agents are autonomous just in case they act on the basis of value commitments integrated in agents' personalities; and (4) "reflective non-alienation", in which agents are autonomous when they reflect upon the historical processes by which their value commitments arose and would not resist this history (2005b: 103–104).

22. Put another way, proceduralist theorists deny that "living in the 'right' social conditions" or "holding the 'right' values" is part of the *definition* of autonomy or partly *constitutive* of autonomy.

23. I owe the following formulation of the strong substantivist view to Stoljar (2013, section 8). I should note that Stoljar attributes the argument above to Thomas Hill and suggests in this entry that Hill is a strong substantivist theorist on the basis of his arguments about the Deferential Wife in his paper "Servility and Self-Respect" (in 1991: 15). However, it's not clear to me that this is an accurate interpretation of his view. For one thing, Hill argues in this paper that the Deferential Wife is *servile* because she fails to respect herself as a moral agent, but he says nothing about whether she lacks autonomy. For another, Hill's own view identifies seven conditions for autonomy, none of which say anything about avoiding the "wrong" preferences. In fact, given that his seventh condition is that individuals "have ample opportunities to make use of these [other six] conditions in living a life over which they have a high degree of control," I think there is an argument to be made that Hill's view is socio-relational, not strong substantivist. A socio-relational view of autonomy claims that a person's social conditions are mainly constitutive of her autonomy. Note that, on Hill's view of autonomy, the seventh condition requires that certain social conditions obtain in order for a person to be autonomous. I leave this line of reasoning for another paper. For Hill's account of autonomy, see "Autonomy and Benevolent Lies" (in 1991: 36). For a defense of socio-relational autonomy, see Oshana (2006).

24. For example, strong substantivists do not claim that the incompatibility between autonomy and subordination arises because individuals arrive at these values through oppressive socialization. For strong substantivists, it is never possible to be autonomous and subordinate at the same time, even if a person makes the choice under what I will say are "optimal conditions," for example, she lives in

a liberal state, is raised in a gender-egalitarian home, receives a decent education, knows her options, and chooses gender hierarchy after careful reflection.
25. Stoljar (2013, section 8).
26. Ibid.
27. The "others" I refer to in this case are strong substantivist theorists.
28. Benson (2005b: 104).
29. As Benson notes, "The processes or states of identification, evaluation, psychological integration, or (hypothetical) reflective scrutiny that are supposed to cement the connection between persons' wills and their practical identities can themselves come about through histories of brainwashing, trauma, pervasive social control, psychosis, and so on that intuitively undermine autonomy" (2005b: 104).
30. Christman (2007: 6). See also Friedman (2003: 97).
31. While there are a number of proceduralist views in the literature, I focus upon Christman's for the following reasons. First, theorists consider his account to be one of the most sophisticated defenses of proceduralism. Second, Christman has refined his view largely in response to the criticisms related to proceduralism's inability to identify adequately impairments to autonomy. Last, it is important to note that Christman's view is *hypothetical*, in the sense that it does not require actual reflection to occur in order for a person to qualify as autonomous (2007:13).
32. It is important to emphasize on Christman's view that a person reflects (or would reflect) on the *preference* in question, not the process itself. Christman stipulates this in order to avoid an objection raised against his view by Al Mele. Mele (1995) argues that a person could be raised to hold particular religious commitments in a very restrictive social environment and accept her commitments while rejecting the kind of upbringing to which she was subject. Christman acknowledges this point, and this is why he changes his view of autonomy to place more importance on reflection upon the value itself given its historical development rather than merely the development itself.
33. Christman (2009: 143). Christman emphasizes a page later that "the key element of such alienation is this resistance, the anxious sense that the fact in question is constraining" (144).
34. Christman (2009: 146).
35. Christman (2009:146–147).
36. Christman (2009: 147).
37. Benson (1991: 393–394).
38. Benson (2005b: 107).
39. Benson (2005b: 108).
40. Benson (2005b: 108–109).
41. Benson (2005b: 110).
42. Benson (2005a: 128).
43. Ibid.
44. Benson (2005b: 110–111).
45. Benson (2005b: 108).
46. Benson argues that there is an "inherent, constitutive connection between agential ownership and persons' social relations" (2005b: 108).
47. To illustrate his point, Benson appeals to Ralph Ellison's novel *The Invisible Man*, in which the narrator has internalized his "social invisibility" as an African-American man in the Jim Crow era. According to Benson, the protagonist cannot answer for his actions because (1) he is unable to regard himself as a competent, reasons-giving agent due to internalizing his invisibility and (2) his social conditions prevent him from occupying a position of agential authority. In other words, the protagonist not only fails to have the right sort of self-regarding

attitude toward his authority as an agent, other agents in the social world also fail to recognize him as having agential authority due to institutionalized racism (2005b: 111–112).

48. The idea that a person is subject to the normative standards that are important from her "own evaluative standpoint" is important because it serves to distinguish Benson's weak substantive view from a normative competence view of autonomy. This latter view (which Benson himself defended at one point) is more normatively robust than a weak substantive view because it requires an individual to speak for his actions in response to an evaluative framework that he may not regard as important from his own standpoint . See Benson (2005b: 112–113).

49. Benson (2005b: 108). Benson notes further that being able to provide reasons for one's actions does not require one to have "privileged access to the conditions that best explain their behavior. Nor must autonomous agents be more proficient than others at constructing reasons that could justify their acts. Rather, the special authority conveyed in local autonomy concerns who is properly situated to face and answer potential criticism" (2005b:109).

50. Benson (2005b: 107).

51. Some examples of women who publish books in the Evangelical Christian community and who also engage in popular speaking tours to promote their ideas and books are P. B. "Bunny" Wilson, author of *Liberated Through Submission*; Martha Peace, *The Excellent Wife*; Nancy Cobb and Connie Grisby, *The Politically Incorrect Wife*; Shannon Ethridge, *Every Woman's Battle*, Joyce (2009: 50, 51, 55).

52. Perhaps such a being would count as a "wanton" in the Frankfurtian sense. See Frankfurt (1971: 11).

53. I thank Evan Tiffany for helping clarify this point for me.

54. For example, consider the following scene from the popular *Game of Thrones* series. One of the main characters, Daenerys Targaryen, is attempting to form an army in order to fight for the Iron Throne, which she regards as rightfully hers. She is considering buying an army of slaves, called the Unsullied, who have been subject to intense and harsh physical and psychological training. For example, male slaves are eunuchs, so that they aren't interested in "plunder or rape." Moreover, the slaves have been trained to refer to themselves as "this one." So, when a male slave is asked what his name is, he replies, "This one's name is Red Flea, your Worship" (Martin, 2000: 327). I take this to be an example of a slave failing to regard himself as having agential authority at all, given that the slaves do not even think of themselves in terms of "I" and are trained not to form their own preferences. I thank Evan Tiffany and Jason Scott for pointing me toward this reference.

55. Douglass (1845).

56. Douglass (1845, chapter VI).

57. I say in part because it seems likely there are other reasons driving Mr. Auld's response to his wife's actions, for example, having racist beliefs about African Americans.

58. See footnotes 14–15.

59. Another example may help support my claim. Recently, the British Columbia (B.C.) Supreme Court had a hearing on the legitimacy of antipolygamy laws in Canada. This hearing directly affects the Fundamentalist Latter-Day Saints church in Bountiful, B.C., Canada, because this religious sect practices polygamy. One of the women from the community voluntarily testified that she preferred polygamy because engaging in this practice will secure her salvation, even if there are trials and hardships involved in a polygamist marriage. To my mind, this is an example of a person who is non-autonomous in a clear and intuitive

way. She has been raised since birth and has received education only within the community, and she subjects herself to male authority (whether religious leaders or her husband). Nevertheless, she can offer reasons for her action, and she clearly stands in social relations with others that allow her to have agential authority, given that she is testifying in court. I would argue that if this woman can meet weak substantivist standards for autonomy, then these standards aren't robust enough to meet the impairment objection raised against proceduralism. See Brian Hutchinson, "Polygamous Life Takes 'Faith and Determination,' Bountiful Woman Testifies," *The National Post*, January 25, 2011, national edition. www.nationalpost.com/news/Polygamist+life+takes+faith+determination+Bountiful+woman+testifies/4166970/story.html#ixzz1CAQB8r2W

60. Narayan (2002: 419). Of course, Evangelical Christianity isn't a culture in the sense that Narayan has in mind in her paper when she discusses the Sufi Pirzada women in India.

61. For example, Joyce tells us that "The payoff for women who obey properly is described . . . as a deeply sensual, almost erotic union with Jesus: the fulfillment of all their stifled and postponed emotions and longings as they finally meet the man whose emissaries, their husbands, they've long served" (2009: 55).

62. For example, Joyce explains that the BCA church required all female members to ask their husbands for permission for any day-to-day activity, including helping new mothers by cooking meals for them. Joyce writes that "the meal sign-ups . . . became a bureaucratic ordeal on the scale of organizing a public school field day, as a church full of women had to seek their husbands' permission before signing up for meal duty" (Joyce, *Quiverfull*, 114). I take it that the women in the BCA would be aware of the "bureaucratic ordeal" and coordination problems that arise as a result of needing their husbands' permission.

63. The case of Jennifer Epstein again provides support for this claim. Epstein challenged the expectations of the dominant/subordinate relationship and was punished for doing so, that is, by being excommunicated by the BCA (Joyce, 2009: 114).

64. That said, I think we can still make judgments about the lack of *goodness* of non-autonomous lives relative to the lives of autonomous agents, without claiming this lack of goodness justifies paternalistic state intervention in the lives of non-autonomous agents. In making this claim, I follow *Kymlicka (1989)*.

REFERENCES

Babbitt, Susan (1993) "Feminism and Objective Interests: The Role of Transformation Experiences in Rational Deliberation," in Linda Alcoff and Elizabeth Potter (eds.), *Feminist Epistemologies*, New York: Routledge, pp. 245–264.

Benson, Paul (1991) "Autonomy and Oppressive Socialization," *Social Theory and Practice* 17 (3): 385–408.

Benson, Paul (2005a) "Feminist Intuitions and the Normative Substance of Autonomy," in James Stacey Taylor (ed.), *Personal Autonomy: New Essays on Personal Autonomy and Its Role in Contemporary Moral Philosophy*, Cambridge: Cambridge University Press, pp. 128–142.

Benson, Paul (2005b) "Taking Ownership: Authority and Voice in Autonomous Agency," in John Christman and Joel Anderson (eds.), *Autonomy and the Challenges to Liberalism: New Essays*, Cambridge: Cambridge University Press, pp. 101–126.

Benson, Paul (2011) "Narrative Self-Understanding and Relational Autonomy: Comments on Catriona Mackenzie and Jacqui Poltera, 'Narrative Integration,

Fragmented Selves, and Autonomy,' and Andrea C. Westlund, 'Rethinking Relational Autonomy,'" *Symposia on Gender, Race and Philosophy* 7 (1), http://web.mit.edu/sgrp/2011/no1/SGRPvol7no12011.pdf.

Christman, John (2004) "Relational Autonomy, Liberal Individualism, and the Social Constitution of Selves," *Philosophical Studies* 117: 143–164.

Christman, John (2005) "Procedural Autonomy and Liberal Legitimacy," in James Stacey Taylor (ed.), *Personal Autonomy: New Essays on Personal Autonomy and Its Role in Contemporary Moral Philosophy*, Cambridge: Cambridge University Press, pp. 277–298.

Christman, John (2007) "Autonomy, History, and the Subject of Justice," *Social Theory and Practice* 33 (1): 1–26.

Christman, John (2009) *The Politics of Persons: Individual Autonomy and Socio-Historical Selves*, Cambridge: Cambridge University Press.

Douglass, Frederick (1845) *Narrative of the Life of Frederick Douglass: An American Slave*, www.gutenberg.org/files/23/23-h/23-h.htm.

Dworkin, Gerald (1988) *The Theory and Practice of Autonomy*, Cambridge: Cambridge University Press.

Frankfurt, Harry (1971) "Freedom of the Will and the Concept of a Person," *The Journal of Philosophy* 68 (1): 5–20.

Friedman, Marilyn (2003) *Autonomy, Gender, Politics*, Oxford: Oxford University Press.

Hill, Thomas (1991) *Autonomy and Self-Respect*, Cambridge: Cambridge University Press.

Hutchinson, Brian (2011, January 25) "Polygamous Life Takes 'Faith and Determination,' Bountiful Woman Testifies," *The National Post*, national edition, www.nationalpost.com/news/Polygamist+life+takes+faith+determination+Bountiful+woman+testifies/4166970/story.html#ixzz1CAQB8r2W

Joyce, Kathryn (2009) *Quiverfull: Inside the Christian Patriarchy Movement*, Boston: Beacon Press.

Kristinsson, Sigurdur (2000) "The Limits of Neutrality: Toward a Weakly Substantive Account of Autonomy," *Canadian Journal of Philosophy* 30 (2): 257–286.

Kymlicka, Will (1989) *Liberalism, Community, and Culture*, Oxford: Clarendon Press.

Mahmood, Saba (2005) *The Politics of Piety: The Islamic Revival and the Feminist Subject*, Princeton, NJ: Princeton University Press.

Martin, George R.R. (2000) *A Storm of Swords*, New York: Bantam Books.

Mele, Alfred (1995) *Autonomous Agency: From Self-Control to Autonomy*, Oxford: Oxford University Press.

Meyers, Diana T. (2002) *Gender in the Mirror: Cultural Imagery and Women's Agency*, Oxford: Oxford University Press.

Narayan, Uma (2002) "Minds of Their Own: Choices, Autonomy, Cultural Practices and Other Women," in Louise Antony and Charlotte Witt (eds.), *A Mind of One's Own: Feminist Essays on Reason and Objectivity*, Second Edition, Boulder, CO: Westview, pp. 418–432.

Nussbaum, Martha C. (1999) *Sex and Social Justice*, Oxford: Oxford University Press.

Nussbaum, Martha C. (2001) *Women and Human Development: The Capabilities Approach*, Cambridge: Cambridge University Press.

Okin, Susan Moller (1979) *Women in Western Political Thought*, Princeton: Princeton University Press.

Okin, Susan Moller (1989) *Justice, Gender, and the Family*, New York: Basic Books.

Okin, Susan Moller (1999) *Is Multiculturalism Bad for Women?* Edited by Joshua Cohen, Matthew Howard, and Martha C. Nussbaum, Princeton: Princeton University Press.

Oshana, Marina (2006) *Personal Autonomy in Society*, Burlington, VT: Ashgate Publishing.

Stoljar, Natalie (2000) "Autonomy and the Feminist Intuition," in Catriona Mackenzie and Natalie Stoljar (eds.), *Relational Autonomy: Feminist Perspectives on Autonomy, Agency, and the Social Self*, Oxford: Oxford University Press, pp. 94–111.

Stoljar, Natalie (2013) "Feminist Perspectives on Autonomy," *Stanford Encyclopedia of Philosophy*, http://plato.stanford.edu/entries/feminism-autonomy/.

Westlund, Andrea (2003) "Selflessness and Responsibility for Self: Is Deference Compatible with Autonomy?" *The Philosophical Review* 112 (4): 493–523.

Westlund, Andrea (2009) "Rethinking Relational Autonomy," *Hypatia* 24: 26–49.

Wolf, Susan (1980) "Asymmetrical Freedom," *The Journal of Philosophy* 77: 151–166.

3 Responding to the Agency Dilemma
Autonomy, Adaptive Preferences, and Internalized Oppression

Catriona Mackenzie

INTRODUCTION

Feminist efforts to theorize the impact of social oppression on autonomy must negotiate what Serene Khader (2011) refers to as the "agency dilemma." This is the challenge of recognizing and analyzing the vulnerabilities of persons subject to social oppression or deprivation while also acknowledging and respecting their agency. In particular, since the effects of social oppression can run deep and can shape people's practical identities or self-concepts, responding to the challenge posed by the agency dilemma requires explaining how social oppression can be simultaneously identity constituting yet identity fracturing and agency constituting yet autonomy impairing—at least in certain domains or with respect to certain aspects of agents' practical identities.

Relational theories of autonomy have been criticized for failing adequately to respond to this challenge. Relational theorists argue that personal autonomy is a relationally constituted capacity requiring extensive interpersonal, social, and institutional scaffolding. Relational theorists also seek to analyze how social oppression can impair the development and exercise of autonomy.[1] However, several critics have charged that the explanations proffered by some relational theorists of the autonomy-impairing effects of social oppression risk impugning the agency of oppressed persons and opening the door to objectionably paternalistic and coercive forms of intervention in their lives.[2]

Khader develops an important variant of this kind of criticism in her book *Adaptive Preferences and Women's Empowerment* (2011). Khader's own response to the agency dilemma involves a subtle and instructive analysis of the concept of adaptive preferences, with which I am broadly sympathetic. However, she argues that it is a mistake to understand adaptive preferences as autonomy deficits and cautions that doing so implies that oppressed and deprived persons are not rational and cannot make their own decisions, thus inviting illiberal and coercive forms of intervention into their lives.

In this chapter, I seek to show that although Khader's criticisms should be taken seriously, her argument is mistaken insofar as it equates autonomy with choice and instrumental rationality.³ I also argue that an adequately nuanced relational theory of autonomy can meet the challenge of the agency dilemma. In the first section, I outline Khader's analysis of adaptive preferences and her critique of the idea that adaptive preferences should be understood as autonomy deficits. In the second section, I outline a multidimensional and relational analysis of the concept of autonomy as involving three distinct but causally interconnected axes: self-determination, self-governance, and self-authorization. In doing so, I critically appraise Khader's account of autonomy and show how her analysis of adaptive preferences is actually consistent with and draws on the conceptual vocabulary of autonomy thus understood.

1. KHADER'S ANALYSIS OF ADAPTIVE PREFERENCES

Khader presents her analysis of adaptive preferences as a response to three dilemmas of transnational feminist theory and activism: the global justice, agency, and cultural diversity dilemmas. The global justice dilemma concerns the challenge of how to theorize about the causes of third-world women's deprivation and promote local-level, nonsystemic interventions to alleviate deprivation without occluding the systemic nature of global injustice or assuming that third-world women's oppression is primarily the result of local cultural practices (2011, 25). The cultural diversity dilemma concerns the challenge of how to oppose oppressive cultural practices while also supporting people's right to live according to culturally specific values (37). Although my discussion in this chapter mentions aspects of Khader's responses to the global justice and cultural diversity dilemmas, its main focus is her response to the agency dilemma.

Khader argues that an adequate response to these dilemmas requires what she refers to as a "deliberative perfectionist" account of adaptive preferences. To explain her account and to clarify the sense in which it is both deliberative and perfectionist, I will use her definition of adaptive preferences to tease out some of its central features. Khader defines adaptive preferences, or what she prefers to refer to as "inappropriately adaptive preferences" (IAPs), as: "(1) preferences inconsistent with basic flourishing that (2) are formed under conditions nonconducive to basic flourishing and (3) that we believe people might be persuaded to transform upon normative scrutiny of their preferences and exposure to conditions more conducive to basic flourishing" (2011, 41). Examples of IAPs that are discussed extensively by Khader include preferences relating to gendered norms and practices with which those subject to them seem to be complicit, such as female genital cutting, severe restrictions on women's mobility, female illiteracy, restricted educational and employment opportunities for women, placing women's needs for nourishment secondary to the needs of men, or accepting abusive marriages. A crucial characteristic of IAPs, therefore, is that people who have them seem to be complicit in perpetuating their own oppression and deprivation.

Khader's tripartite definition makes salient four important features of her analysis of IAPs. I outline these four features, although I postpone discussion of the fourth feature—her explanation of what constitute morally justifiable forms of intervention to transform people's IAPs and why such interventions must involve collaborative deliberation—until after I have explained Khader's views on autonomy.

First, IAPs are characterized both by their substantive content (claim 1: IAPs are preferences the content of which is inconsistent with basic flourishing) and by the processes of their formation (claim 2: IAPs are preferences that are formed under conditions nonconducive to basic flourishing). Thus the definition of IAPs appeals to both substantive and procedural criteria (2011, 52).

Second, this analysis is perfectionist for two reasons. The substantive content claim (claim 1) appeals to a conception of well-being or flourishing as distinct from pleasure or desire satisfaction, assuming that not everything a person may desire or find pleasurable promotes her well-being. Thus it assumes that IAPs are unreliable indicators of well-being. Further, the notion of preference transformation (claim 3) appeals to what Khader calls the Flourishing Claim. This is the claim that "people tend to pursue their basic flourishing, and preferences that impede people's basic flourishing are unlikely to be their deep preferences," that is, "preferences they would retain under conditions conducive to flourishing" (51).

It is important to note that Khader's Flourishing Claim appeals to a conception of flourishing that she claims is substantively and justificatorily minimal and hence more likely to be cross-culturally acceptable. It is substantively minimal, in her view, because she understands flourishing in terms of achievement with respect to basic levels of functioning across a range of dimensions of well-being rather than in terms of human excellence. Khader does not attempt to specify the various components or dimensions of basic flourishing on the grounds that a vague account of flourishing articulated in terms of basic human needs described at a high level of generality (e.g., mobility, adequate nutrition and shelter, education, bodily integrity) is more likely to be the subject of cross-cultural agreement (2011, 21). She does, however, refer to the list of human rights and the various lists of central human capabilities developed by theorists such as Martha Nussbaum (2001) and Sabina Alkire (2005) as examples of the kinds of components that might be included in a multidimensional account of flourishing. Such a conception of flourishing, she claims, is justificatorily minimal because it requires only cross-cultural agreement *that* these functionings are important rather than agreement about *why* they are important (2011, 61). This means that the question of why specific functionings are important and what flourishing means in practice can be specified at the level of local deliberation.[4]

Third, all three claims within this definition, along with the Flourishing Claim, assume that IAPs are imposed on agents in some sense by their oppressive or deprived circumstances rather than being an endorsed expression of their authentic or deep preferences. By "deep" preferences, Khader seems to mean preferences that are not only consistent with flourishing but also embody or express a person's sense of what matters to her—her deepest cares and values. One of her central claims is that the sense in which IAPs are "imposed" should not be understood in terms of the contrast between "chosen" and "unchosen" preferences but in terms of the contrast between "deep" and "shallow" preferences, where shallow preferences are those that would not persist or be endorsed under conditions that are more conducive to flourishing (2011, 147). This claim is important for understanding the grounds on which Khader argues against understanding IAPs as autonomy deficits. It is also important for understanding why she thinks her deliberative perfectionist analysis of IAPs can meet the challenge of the agency dilemma while charging that many feminist theories of autonomy fail to meet this challenge. For this reason, it is important at this point to pause my exposition of the four central features of Khader's analysis of IAPs to explain her position on autonomy.

Khader surveys a range of (feminist and nonfeminist) procedural conceptions of autonomy—as informed and rationally competent deliberation, as higher-order reflection, or as the capacity to develop a life plan or to represent one's own interests—and argues that it is a mistake to understand adaptive preferences as procedural autonomy deficits for two reasons. First, doing so yields "conceptions of adaptive preference that are intuitively implausible, unsuited for use in development practice, and/or morally objectionable" (2011, 75) because such conceptions imply that people with adaptive preferences are irrational, unreflective, and incapable of developing a life plan or representing their own interests. Second, to explain why adaptive preferences are problematic, any candidate procedural theory of autonomy needs to be supplemented by a conception of the good, that is, a normative conception of what people *should* desire. Substantive conceptions of autonomy are not susceptible to this second criticism, because they specify that only preferences with certain contents or consistent with certain norms or conducive to flourishing count as autonomous. However, Khader also objects to understanding adaptive preferences as substantive autonomy deficits on the grounds that such conceptions encourage "condescension towards people with IAPs" (105), "lead[s] us towards policies that are decidedly illiberal" (105), and open the door to coercive interference with people's choices (104).

Without rehearsing the details of Khader's arguments, I think some of her specific criticisms of certain procedural and substantive theories of autonomy may be justified while others are mistaken.[5] However, I want to focus here on Khader's more general arguments against understanding IAPs as autonomy deficits. These arguments seem to be structured by three central (and questionable) assumptions about autonomy. First, that autonomy is equivalent to choice and instrumental rationality. Thus, to conceive of adaptive preferences as autonomy deficits is to think of adaptive preferences as unchosen, rationally deficient, and unreflective. Second, autonomy (or non-autonomy) is an all-or-nothing matter rather than a matter of degree and domain. Third, since "the role of autonomy in a political philosophy is typically to sort persons whose decisions are worthy of respect from those who are not" (2011, 146), to deem a person's preferences or decisions non-autonomous is to sanction coercive and paternalistic interference with that person's life. In what follows, I raise some questions about the first assumption. My response to the second and third assumptions is developed in the second section of the chapter.

With respect to the first assumption, whereas Khader understands adaptive preferences in terms of the deep/shallow contrast, she understands autonomy and non-autonomy in terms of the contrast "chosen"/"unchosen." Thus she equates being autonomous with making (or having the capacity to make) "true" or "real" choices and being non-autonomous with being incapable of making one's own choices. She links this characterization of autonomy to the way empowerment is understood in much development discourse as a process of enabling people to make "real" or "true" choices, as distinct from choices that are imposed upon them by their social conditions, where "imposed" is understood as unchosen (2011, 76). It is on the basis of this assumption that Khader says: "Claiming that APs [adaptive preferences] are characterized by a lack of autonomy—either procedural or substantive—suggests that people with APs have had their capacities to make choices impaired" (105). Khader argues, however, that not only does this imply disrespectful attitudes toward people with IAPs, it confuses an important distinction between making and having choices: "To have a choice is to have acceptable options; to make a choice is to go through a particular type of deliberative process. A person needs to *have* some options to make a choice, but a person can make choices without having a range of *acceptable* options" (183). What characterizes oppression and deprivation, she argues, is not a lack of capacity to make choices but rather a lack of meaningful or significant opportunities for flourishing.[6] Moreover, in contexts in which people's option sets are constrained and their circumstances make it impossible to flourish in all domains or to live their lives in a way that fully embodies their conceptions of the good, people may trade off flourishing in one domain for flourishing in other domains. For example, women whose husbands restrict their mobility with threats of violence may trade off mobility for bodily safety and self-preservation. Women who do not avoid HIV exposure out of fear that their husbands will leave them, resulting in financial destitution for themselves and their children, trade off risks to their own health for the well-being of their children. Khader argues that such trade-offs are autonomous because they are rational and may be the best means to achieving the person's higher-order preferences (bodily safety, self-preservation, the well-being of their children) in constrained circumstances—even if these choices do not express the person's deep preferences, are causally related to nonflourishing conditions, and are inconsistent with her flourishing (147–48).

I agree with Khader that it is a mistake to understand IAPs in terms of the chosen/unchosen contrast. I also agree that it is important to distinguish between the capacity for deliberation (making choices) and opportunities for flourishing (having choices). And I agree that oppression and deprivation are often characterized by the lack of meaningful opportunities for flourishing and force people into situations in which they are required to sacrifice flourishing in one domain in order to achieve it in another. However, I think Khader is mistaken, first, in interpreting the concept of autonomy in terms of the chosen/unchosen distinction and, second, in characterizing such trade-offs as autonomous because they are rational responses to highly constrained circumstances. These mistakes arise from conflating instrumentally rational choice with autonomy. Furthermore, although Khader claims that the deep/shallow distinction is different from the autonomously chosen/nonchosen distinction, the deep/shallow distinction implicitly invokes the vocabulary of autonomy, as is evident in Khader's appeals to a person's deepest cares and values and to the notion of authenticity. I return to some of these issues in the following section.

At this point, however, I want to return to Khader's definition of IAPs to draw out the fourth salient feature of her analysis of IAPs. The fourth feature is that claim 3 of this definition, the preference transformation claim, is based on two assumptions: first, that the principle of respect for persons does not simply require uncritical acceptance of a person's existing lower-order expressed preferences where these are inconsistent with basic flourishing, for example, an expressed preference for restricted mobility, inadequate nutrition, or not to be educated; and second, that interventions to transform IAPs need be neither paternalistic nor coercive. Rather, if IAPs are preferences that perpetuate oppression or deprivation and undermine agents' flourishing, then some interventions by public institutions (e.g., nongovernment and government organizations) that seek to transform these preferences are not only morally justifiable but consistent with liberalism. I agree with both assumptions. Indeed, Khader's analysis of morally justifiable forms of intervention is nuanced, attentive to the hazards of intervention, and informed by relevant examples of collaborative interventions from development practice.

Khader is sanguine about the epistemic difficulties faced by practitioners both in making judgments that a person's preferences are inappropriately adaptive and in developing morally justifiable interventions. She identifies three significant epistemic hazards that result in interventions that are ineffective or actually reduce well-being: psychologizing the structural—mistaking preferences that are due to structural causes, such as economic conditions or social and political structures, as the result of people's beliefs, attitudes, or cultural practices; misidentifying trade-offs—assuming that "failing to flourish in one domain reveals a global lack of desire for flourishing" (2011, 57); and confusing difference with deprivation—arising from failure to understand others' different life contexts and values.

The deliberative aspect of Khader's deliberative perfectionism, which requires practitioners to develop interventions in collaborative deliberation with persons with IAPs, aims to address these hazards. Genuinely deliberative collaboration, she argues, involves epistemic humility on the part of practitioners, deep contextual knowledge, and attention to people's first-person narratives to ensure that interventions engage their values, religious beliefs, or conceptions of the good and are framed in a language and conceptual vocabulary that makes sense to them. This does not mean that deliberative IAP interventions must take people's existing values and beliefs as given. Rather, it means that such interventions "should be conceived as attempts to help people clarify and evaluate their conceptions of the good rather than as attempts to replace their conceptions of the good with external ones" (2011, 153). Only IAP interventions that are genuinely collaborative in this sense are properly deliberative. Further, it is the collaborative aspect of deliberative IAP interventions that, in Khader's view, makes the perfectionist aspect morally permissible.

Khader's deliberative perfectionist account of adaptive preferences, particularly its perfectionist elements, will seem controversial to many liberals. In contrast, I have considerable sympathy for this account. Where I disagree with Khader is with respect to her understanding of autonomy. In the following section, I propose a multidimensional and relational conception of autonomy and seek to show that autonomy thus understood is quite consistent with Khader's analysis of adaptive preferences.

2. AUTONOMY AS MULTIDIMENSIONAL AND RELATIONAL

Much of the debate in the feminist literature on autonomy and social oppression has focused on identifying necessary and sufficient conditions for a preference, decision, or value to count as autonomous. The debate has also been structured around examples and counterexamples designed to test the necessity and sufficiency of rival claims.[7] The focus on identifying necessary and sufficient conditions for autonomy may seem to lend credence to Khader's second assumption that autonomy is an all-or-nothing matter rather than a matter of degree and domain. Further, because the examples and counterexamples deployed in the literature are philosophical thought experiments rather than engaging with the contextual detail of real people's lives, Khader's worry that both procedural and substantive accounts of autonomy seem to encourage condescending attitudes toward oppressed and deprived persons should be taken seriously.

   In my view, the project of identifying necessary and sufficient conditions for autonomy is mistaken on two grounds. First, the concept of autonomy is employed for different purposes in different social and normative contexts, and in these different contexts, some dimensions of the concept will be more salient than in others. Autonomy is thus not the kind of concept that is best analyzed in terms of necessary and sufficient conditions for its correct application. Second, a necessary-and-sufficient-conditions analysis assumes that autonomy is a unitary concept, the kernel of which is the notion of self-governance. In contrast, I think autonomy is better understood as a multidimensional concept involving three distinct but causally interdependent dimensions: self-determination, self-governance, and self-authorization.[8] *Self-determination* involves having the freedom and opportunities necessary to make and enact decisions of practical import to one's life, concerning what matters, who to be, and what to do. *Self-governance* involves having the skills and capacities necessary to make and enact decisions and to live one's life in a way that expresses or coheres with one's reflectively constituted diachronic practical identity. *Self-authorization* involves regarding oneself as having the *normative authority* to be self-determining and self-governing. In other words, it involves regarding oneself as authorized to exercise practical control over one's life, to determine one's own reasons for action, and to define one's values and identity-shaping practical commitments.

   In what follows, I outline these three dimensions more fully and explicate their links with Khader's analysis of IAPs. Before doing so, I want to preface this discussion by highlighting two important features of my analysis. First, each of these dimensions can and should be understood as a matter of degree and domain. A person can be self-determining, self-governing, and self-authorizing to differing degrees, both at a time and over the course of her life. Autonomy is thus not an all-or-nothing matter. Although the different dimensions of autonomy are causally interdependent to a certain extent, the benefit of a multidimensional analysis is that it accords better with our intuitions about autonomy, enabling us to acknowledge that it is possible, even if difficult, for a person with limited freedom and opportunities nevertheless to be highly self-governing and have a strong sense of herself as a self-authorizing agent.

   It also makes sense of the way that people may be more or less autonomous in different domains of their lives. It is certainly the case that, if the concept of autonomy is to retain its meaning, there must be a threshold for each dimension below which a person no longer counts as self-determining, self-governing, or self-authorizing. But exactly where such thresholds should be drawn is inevitably a matter of social and political contestation and deliberation. I will seek to show that Khader's analysis of basic flourishing implicitly appeals to the normative and practical importance for a flourishing life of threshold levels of self-determination, self-governance, and self-authorization. That is, her analysis appeals to our intuitions that it is bad for people if deprivation or oppressive social structures do not enable them to exercise a significant degree of self-determination, to live in a way that expresses their practical identities and accords with their deepest values, or to regard themselves as self-authorizing agents.

Second, my analysis of each dimension is social and relational. Insofar as I value personal autonomy, I am committed to a form of normative individualism, that is, to the view that the rights, welfare, dignity, freedom, and autonomy of individuals impose normative constraints on the claims of collectives. However, I hold that an adequate conception of personal autonomy must be grounded in a social ontology of persons, that is, a conception of persons that emphasizes the role of embodied social practices (linguistic and cultural), social group identities, and historical contingencies in the constitution of individual identity. It must also be able to account for the way that social oppression can impair—to varying degrees—agents' abilities to be self-determining, self-governing, and self-authorizing.

2.1. Self-Determination

One of the roles that the notion of autonomy plays in our moral and political discourse is to delimit what constitutes unwarranted interference (either by the state or by other agents) with agents' freedom of action and to ground social and political obligations to provide the opportunities necessary for persons to live self-determining lives. The notion of *self-determination* captures this dimension of autonomy, identifying external, structural conditions for personal autonomy, specifically *freedom* conditions and *opportunity* conditions. This dimension of autonomy, I claim, is distinct from the notion of *self-governance*, which specifies internal conditions for autonomy relating to the structure of agents' will, or practical identities, and to the skills and competences needed to govern oneself. One problem with failing to distinguish self-determination from self-governance and with analyzing autonomy in terms of necessary and sufficient conditions for self-governance is that it makes it difficult to explain how constraints on freedom or inadequate opportunities due to social oppression can compromise autonomy other than in terms of the incompetence or inauthenticity of oppressed persons.[9] As a result, such analyses run the risk of what Khader refers to as "psychologizing the structural."

Freedom conditions specify the liberties, both political and personal, that are necessary for leading a self-determining life. The political liberties include, among others, freedom of thought and expression, freedom of association, freedom of conscience and religious exercise, and freedom to engage in political participation. The personal liberties include freedom of movement, freedom of sexual expression, and freedom from all forms of coercion, manipulation, exploitation, and violence, including sexual exploitation and assault. The importance of these personal and political liberties for individual self-determination is reflected in their inclusion in important human rights documents and in the various lists of the capabilities required for flourishing endorsed by Khader—specified at a level that is sufficiently general as to leave scope for local-level deliberation about their interpretation and application.[10] Moreover, these liberties are frequently violated in social contexts marked by oppression and deprivation. It is noteworthy that many of the examples of gender-based IAPs nonconducive to flourishing that are discussed by Khader involve deprivations of freedoms, such as freedom of movement, freedom of sexual expression, and freedom from gender-based violence. Khader's notion of basic flourishing thus seems to appeal to our intuitions about the importance of self-determination for flourishing.

Opportunity conditions specify the personal, social, and political opportunities that need to be available to agents in their social environments in order to give substance to the freedom conditions and hence in order for agents to make and enact decisions of practical import to their lives, concerning what matters, who to be, and what to do. Among theorists of autonomy, Joseph Raz (1986) is the most prominent exponent of the view that self-determination, as I have defined it, requires not only political and personal liberties but also access to an adequate array of significant or feasible opportunities, or what he refers to as options. Raz argues that access to an adequate array of feasible options is crucial for being able to determine and live one's life in accordance with one's conception of the good and hence for autonomy. If, due to deprivation or oppression, agents' social environments do not provide access to an adequate array of feasible options, their autonomy (in the self-determination sense) is thereby impaired.

Khader acknowledges the conceptual connections between her account of IAPs and Raz's account of the importance of significant options for autonomy. She nevertheless resists analyzing IAPs as autonomy deficits on the grounds that to do so "leads us towards policies that are decidedly illiberal" (2011, 103). Since autonomy, she claims, is a feature of people's subjective states, to characterize IAPs as autonomy deficits is to suggest that people with IAPs lack the capacity to make their own decisions. It is also to ignore the causal relationship between IAPs and deprivation or oppression. However, this argument is problematic on a number of grounds. First, it conflates self-determination and self-governance. To claim that a person's autonomy in the self-determination sense is compromised because she lacks access to adequate options due to oppression or deprivation need not imply that she thereby lacks either the capacity for self-governance or the capacity to make instrumentally rational decisions. Second, as I have already argued, Khader conflates autonomous deliberation with the capacity to make instrumentally rational decisions. Third, there is no justification for claiming that referring to IAPs as autonomy deficits opens the door to coercive and illiberal forms of intervention. With respect to Raz's view, rather than justifying coercive and illiberal forms of intervention, his concern is to show that public institutions have a social justice obligation to support the opportunity conditions for self-determination. The kind of deliberative IAP interventions that Khader supports seem to be just the kind of interventions that Raz would support.

Moreover, I would suggest that the alternative vocabulary on which Khader prefers to draw, the vocabulary of capabilities theory, is also centrally concerned with articulating the importance of the opportunity conditions for self-determination, insofar as capabilities are opportunities to achieve valuable functionings, that is, functionings that are conducive to flourishing.

The importance of opportunity conditions for Khader's analysis of basic flourishing is evident in her discussion of the difference between "tactical" and "strategic" choices. Tactical choices are "choices by which a person manages and responds to contingency and limited options" (2011, 189). For example, an uneducated young woman in Nigeria might make a series of tactical choices about what to do to scrape a living together, such as switching from trading to soap making to selling shoes, where these choices are driven by limited options and changes to the woman's contingent circumstances. Strategic choices, in contrast, are higher-level choices that involve "long-term goal setting and the deliberate weighing of alternative paths for achieving one's goals. They are choices about the path a person wants her life to take" (2011, 189–90). Khader argues that the notion of strategic choice serves to identify domains in which it is particularly important for a person to have a range of *acceptable* choices in order to lead a flourishing life—domains such as choice of career, spouse, or use of one's body (191), although exactly which domains are important for flourishing will vary according to sociocultural context and should be the focus of local-level deliberation. Having strategic choices thus "means the presence of opportunities to *flourish* in certain domains" (191). It seems to me that Khader's claims about the importance for flourishing of having acceptable choices within certain crucial domains of one's life points to the importance of the opportunity conditions for self-determination. In other words, the reason strategic choices or opportunities are crucial for flourishing is because without them, it is difficult for a person to lead a self-determining and self-governing life. The notion of strategic choice thus appeals implicitly to the vocabulary of autonomy.

The virtue of an analysis that distinguishes self-determination from self-governance is therefore that it accounts for the importance of freedom and opportunity (and the structural social and political conditions that enable them) for autonomy, thereby averting the risk of psychologizing the structural. Contra Khader, it also shows why autonomy is not solely a matter of a person's subjective states and capacities.

2.2. Self-Governance

Self-governance, as I understand it, involves having the skills and capacities necessary to make choices and enact decisions that express or cohere with one's reflectively constituted diachronic practical identity. Whereas the self-determination axis identifies external, structural conditions for autonomy, the self-governance dimension identifies conditions that are internal to the person, specifically competence and authenticity. However, from a relational perspective, the distinction between internal and external conditions is complicated. If persons are socially constituted, then external conditions, including our social relations with others, shape the process of practical identity formation—the *self* of self-governance—and the development of the skills and competences required for *governing* the self. On the one hand, this is not necessarily problematic from a relational perspective—it points to the facts of developmental and ongoing dependency and to the extensive interpersonal, social, and institutional scaffolding necessary for self-governance. On the other hand, in contexts of social oppression or deprivation, the internalization of restrictions on a person's ability to lead a self-determining life can shape a person's practical identity—her sense of who she is, what matters, and what she can be and do—in a way that impedes her flourishing. It is this phenomenon that Khader's account of adaptive preference formation seeks to analyze.

Competence conditions specify the range of competences or skills a person must possess, to some degree at least, in order to be self-governing. These include cognitive skills, ranging from minimally specified capacities to understand and process information to more complex capacities for critical reflection and reasons-responsiveness, as well as volitional skills, such as self-control, and decisiveness. Relational autonomy theorists have also drawn attention to the importance for self-governance of a range of other skills, including emotional skills, such as emotional responsiveness and being able to interpret one's own and others' emotions; imaginative skills, which are necessary for envisaging alternative possible courses of action, or "imagining oneself otherwise" and engaging in self-transformative activities; and social or dialogical skills required for self-understanding or self-knowledge.[11] Khader insists that, except in cases involving extreme physical or psychological abuse, social oppression and deprivation do not typically impair agents' cognitive or volitional skills.[12] She does recognize, however, that the imaginative horizons and skills of persons with IAPs may be quite restricted as a result of social oppression or lack of opportunity (2011, introduction, chapters 1, 5). One of the aims of deliberative IAP intervention, she argues, is to expand agents' imaginative horizons and to use dialogical interaction to promote self-understanding. I would suggest, therefore, that Khader's analysis of IAPs and of appropriate IAP interventions draws on the vocabulary of the competence conditions for self-governance, at least insofar as these conditions are conceptualized by relational autonomy theorists.

Authenticity conditions specify what it means to be self-governing with respect to one's motivational structure, that is, what it means for a choice, value, commitment, or reason to be one's own. In articulating authenticity conditions, relational autonomy theorists have highlighted the importance of attending to both the historical and social processes of practical identity formation and thus the way that social oppression and deprivation can lead to inauthenticity or self-alienation. John Christman provides a succinct account of authenticity, thus understood, as "non-alienation upon (historically sensi-tive, adequate) self-reflection, given one's diachronic practical identity and one's position in the world" (2009, 155), or as reflective self-acceptance. As we have seen, Khader's analysis of adaptive preferences appeals to a related if somewhat stronger notion of authenticity as endorsement (rather than nonalienation). She suggests that one of the central intuitions to which the notion of adaptive preferences is a response is that "people with adaptive preferences have developed them for reasons that have more to do with circumstances than authentic endorsement" (2011, 47). She also suggests that opportunities, life projects, or interventions that are endorsed are more likely to be conducive to flourishing. Her analysis of IAPs and her account of basic flourishing thus seem to appeal once again to the vocabulary of autonomy.

One reason that Khader seems to want to distance her understanding of authenticity from the vocabulary of autonomy is because she wants to distance her position from what she refers to as the "Adaptive Self" view, which she regards as prevalent in feminist work on autonomy and social oppression. This is a tendency to think of adaptive preferences as somehow affecting oppressed or deprived persons' entire self, resulting in diminished desires for one's own well-being, generalized lack of aspiration, and impaired self-worth; in sum, generalized negative self-entitlement or a distorted sense of one's self as not deserving or worthy of flourishing (2011, 109–114). The problem with the Adaptive Self view, Khader charges, is that it suggests people with IAPs cannot form authentic desires and therefore might lead development practitioners to regard them as "unreliable sources of judg-ment about their well-being" (115) and to seek to impose on them coercive forms of intervention. Khader does not deny that some forms of abuse and severe social oppression can result in generalized negative self-entitlement. However, she argues that typically IAPs result in selective rather than gener-alized self-entitlement deficits.

Khader's account of selective self-entitlement is based on several assump-tions. First, people's concepts of self-entitlement are multiple, comparative, and vary across contexts and domains. For example, with respect to her need for nourishment, a woman might regard herself as less worthy than her husband but as more worthy than her daughter-in-law. And she might have a strong sense of self-entitlement in one domain, for example with respect to being a good wife and mother, but not in another domain, for example with respect to sexual satisfaction or bodily health. Second, the internalization of social oppression is not typically global but rather par-tial, resulting in degrees of internal conflict, struggle and resistance, and fractured self-concepts: "People with fractured self-images identify partly with the negative views about their worth; they judge themselves according to oppressive standards. Yet their identification with these negative views is incomplete" (2011, 123).[13] Thus they can actively defend the importance of their flourishing while simultaneously endorsing negative views about themselves. Third, a person's preferences may be internally inconsistent and express a range of different attitudes about herself, both negative and positive. This is because a single preference may differentially affect well-being in different domains of life, leading to positive outcomes in one domain and negative outcomes in another. Further, in contexts of social oppression, there may be strong social incentives for people to make self-harming lower-order choices in order to achieve higher-order goals. As a result, people may misperceive their interests and make choices that diminish their overall flourishing. For example, a young American woman might decide to have breast implants because she thinks this will increase her chances of becoming a television star; a young North African woman might decide to undergo genital cutting because she thinks this will improve her marriage prospects.[14]

Khader is correct to criticize a global deficit analysis of adaptive preferences, and her notion of selective self-entitlement deficits provides a nuanced account of the complex effects of social oppression on agents' identities. While she acknowledges, rightly in my view, that "having a somewhat coherent self-concept that allows a person to feel authentically herself is a good thing" (2011, 117), she also recognizes that coherence is an achievement and one that is particularly fraught in contexts of social oppression. Next I identify the resonances between Khader's notion of selective self-entitlement and the third dimension of autonomy, which I refer to as self-authorization.

2.3. Self-Authorization

Self-authorization involves regarding oneself as authorized to exercise practical control over one's life and to determine one's own values and identity-defining commitments. Self-authorization, as I understand it, encompasses three conditions: that a person regards herself as a moral agent, that is, as accountable and answerable for her reasons and her conduct—call this the *accountability* condition; that a person stands in certain self-affective relations to herself, in particular relations of self-respect, self-trust, and self-esteem—call this the *self-evaluative attitudes* condition; and that such attitudes in turn presuppose that the person is regarded by others as having the social standing of an autonomous agent—call this the *social recognition* condition.

Self-authorization is sometimes understood as requiring substantive epistemic and normative independence from authority. That is, the self-authorizing person does not look to any external authority—whether another person or God—in defining her beliefs, values, and commitments. In my view, this is a mistaken interpretation of the requirements for self-authorization. What the accountability condition requires is rather that a person regards herself as responsible to herself and as answerable and accountable to others for her beliefs, values, commitments, and actions. To regard oneself as accountable does not require being accountable to certain specific others. Nor does it mean being held to account for each and every belief, value, commitment, or action. What it requires is what Westlund (2009) refers to as a "disposition" to regard oneself as answerable. Self-authorization, however, also involves having a reciprocal sense of being entitled to call others into account. The accountability condition is thus fundamentally social and dialogical, not only because its structure is dyadic or second personal but also because as agents, our reasons, values, and commitments, indeed our sense of our selves, only emerge through this kind of dialogical interaction. Thus understood, accountability is not inconsistent per se with religious commitment. However, it is inconsistent with dogmatic forms of religious commitment, or any other form of dogmatism, for that matter, which involve appeals to authority that bypass a person's reflective agency.

To regard oneself not only as accountable to others but also as entitled to call others into account involves having a sense of one's epistemic and normative authority with regard to one's life and one's practical commitments. Some relational autonomy theorists, myself included, have argued that this in turn requires that an agent has certain self-evaluative attitudes, in particular attitudes of appropriate self-respect (regarding oneself as the moral equal of others and hence entitled to call them into account), self-trust (a sense of basic self-confidence in one's judgment), and self-esteem or self-worth.[15] Relational theorists have also argued that internalized social oppression can impair or erode appropriate self-regarding attitudes—to varying degrees and across a range of domains. Now it is always possible to find or think up examples of heroic persons who hold appropriate self-evaluating attitudes even in situations in which they are despised and humiliated by others. However, psychologically, these self-evaluative attitudes are typically dependent on intersubjective social relations. They are also constituted within normative structures and practices of *social recognition* that determine the extent to which a person is regarded by others as a respect-worthy agent who is entitled to participate in reciprocal accountability relations.[16]

These claims resonate with Khader's claim that a sense of "positive self-entitlement" is a condition for agency (2011, 113) and that internalized social oppression results in selective self-entitlement deficits.[17] However, the notion of self-authorization is normatively more robust than the notion of positive self-entitlement insofar it is underpinned by an explicit conception of persons as moral equals who are entitled to be recognized as such in reciprocal accountability relations. It also highlights how internalized oppression is an effect of normative social structures and practices characterized by misrecognition. In contexts of social oppression or deprivation, misrecognition by others can result in feeling that one is not the moral equal of (certain) others and that one is not worthy of participating fully in reciprocal accountability relations.

Khader's normative justification for her deliberative approach to IAP identification and intervention also appeals to something akin to the notion of self-authorization. First, deliberative IAP intervention is a dialogical process involving reciprocal relations of accountability. On the one hand, public deliberation gives people "opportunities to interrogate and clarify their desires in light of their deeply held values and the values and desires of others" and to "voice, explain, and analyze their inchoate dissatisfaction" with their situation (2011, 133–4). On the other hand, public deliberation gives people with IAPs the opportunity to interrogate and hold development practitioners to account for their values and assumptions and to reject proposed interventions that are not meaningful for them and that they do not endorse.

Second, respectful deliberative IAP interventions "can help people develop agential capacities" and "more robust senses of who they are and what they care about" (68), thereby enhancing their sense of self-entitlement. Khader gives the example of an empowerment project in rural Honduras with women whose husbands severely restricted their mobility and who prior to the project had severely diminished senses of self-worth and self-entitlement. The interventions developed by practitioners with the women, and based on their cultural values, aimed to empower women through educational programs, income- and food-generation programs, and confidence-building programs designed to assist them to renegotiate their relationships with their husbands.[18] Successful programs of this kind could thus be characterized as aiming to enhance the women's sense of self-worth and of themselves as self-authorizing agents entitled to engage in reciprocal accountability relations with their husbands. In doing so, such programs might begin to transform (even if only partially) gendered normative structures and practices of social (mis)recognition that impair women's flourishing and their autonomy.

CONCLUSION

In this chapter, I have argued that while Khader is right to draw attention to the dangers of a global deficit analysis of IAPs, she is mistaken to reject the relevance of the concept of autonomy for understanding the phenomenon of adaptive preference formation. Her analysis of IAPs is not only consistent with a multidimensional and relational analysis of autonomy but implicitly appeals to these different dimensions of autonomy. The benefit of a multidimensional analysis is that it enables a nuanced identification of the different sources and kinds of autonomy deficit and thereby assists in the process of developing appropriate interventions. Restrictions on self-determination caused by violations of freedom or limited opportunities require structural social and political change. Very different kinds of personalized intervention are required, however, if a person's capacities for self-governance are impaired due to cognitive and/or volitional deficits. If a person's imaginative horizons are limited or her sense of herself as a self-authorizing agent is diminished due to social oppression or deprivation, a combination of structural change and targeted IAP intervention may be required. Contra Khader's assumption that autonomy is an all-or-nothing matter, this analysis shows that autonomy is a matter of degree and domain. Further, far from sanctioning objectionable coercive and paternalistic forms of intervention, a multidimensional and relational approach to autonomy lends support to Khader's deliberative approach to IAP intervention. An adequately nuanced relational and multidimensional account of autonomy can thus respond to the agency dilemma.

ACKNOWLEDGMENTS

Many thanks to Marina Oshana for her constructive and insightful editorial comments on an earlier version of this chapter.

NOTES

1. Relational autonomy is an "umbrella term" encompassing a variety of feminist accounts of autonomy, both procedural and substantive. Although I do not explicitly address the procedural/substantive distinction in any detail in this chapter, the account of autonomy that I outline in the second section incorporates both procedural and weakly substantive elements. For an overview of the difference between procedural and substantive approaches, see Mackenzie and Stoljar (2000).
2. Most of these criticisms are addressed to what are referred to in the literature as "strong substantive" relational theories, such as those of Oshana (1998, 2006), Stoljar (2000), and Superson (2005). For different versions of this basic criticism, see, for example, Christman (2004), Holroyd (2009), and Sperry (2013). It should be noted, however, that criticisms of strong substantive approaches to autonomy sometimes conflate two quite different kinds of theory: theories that require autonomous agents to hold particular autonomy-affirming values and theories that maintain agents cannot be autonomous if they are subject to social relations of oppression, subordination, or domination. Stoljar and Superson's views are arguably theories of the first kind, while Oshana's view is a theory of the second kind.
3. Natalie Stoljar criticizes Khader's account of autonomy on related grounds in Stoljar (2014).
4. Khader's notion of basic flourishing and the claim that people tend to pursue their basic flourishing, may, however, be more substantive than she acknowledges, especially insofar as it seems to require achievement with respect to basic levels of functioning rather than the capability for achievement.
5. For a more detailed analysis of some of the problems with Khader's critique of procedural and substantive theories of autonomy, see Stoljar (2014).
6. Khader refers to these as "strategic" as opposed to "tactical" choices (2011, 189–90). I discuss this distinction in the following section.
7. For a sample of these examples and counterexamples see, for example, Benson (1991, 2000, 2005), Friedman (1986), Mackenzie (2002, 2008), Oshana (1998, 2006), Superson (2005), and Stoljar (2000).
8. The multidimensional analysis of autonomy on which I draw in this section of the chapter is developed in more detail in Mackenzie (2014).
9. Khader also fails to make this distinction and presumes that autonomy refers solely to agents' subjective states (2011, 91, 105), as I discuss in the text below.

10. Note that genuinely collaborative local-level deliberation (of the kind endorsed by Khader) about the interpretation and application of the political and personal liberties can also play an important role in strengthening and developing people's capacities for self-governance (e.g., by helping them to clarify their values) and their sense of themselves as self-authorizing agents—I discuss this more fully toward the end of the chapter.

11. On the importance of emotional and imaginative skills for autonomy competence, see, for example, Mackenzie (2000, 2002) and Meyers (1989).

12. Whether or not Khader is accurate about this is to some extent an empirical claim. For empirical evidence suggesting that deprivation can have seriously detrimental impacts on people's cognitive and volitional capacities, see Mani and colleagues (2013). Thanks to Marina Oshana for drawing my attention to this empirical evidence.

13. I agree with Khader that self-integration is a matter of degree and that most people experience some degree of internal conflict, fragmentation, ambivalence, discontinuity, or alienation with respect to some aspects of their identities (see, e.g., Mackenzie and Poltera 2010.) I also agree that this kind of internal conflict and fracturing is particularly characteristic of agents' self-identities and self-narratives in situations of social oppression or disadvantage due to limited opportunities or prevailing cultural narratives and practices (on this point, see, e.g., Mackenzie 2000, Oshana 2005). IAP interventions must therefore aim to transform those aspects of agents' self-narratives that sustain adaptive preferences. This is particularly challenging in contexts in which people's self-narratives are shaped by powerful and oppressive cultural narratives. Hence the importance of what Lindemann Nelson (2001) refers to as "counter-stories" and of what Khader refers to as "resistant social spaces" (2011, 125) in which counter-stories can be narrated.

14. Khader's account equivocates about how to characterize such choices. On the one hand, she thinks they are clearly IAPs that are nonconducive to flourishing and as such are appropriate targets of intervention. On the other hand, she says they are often instrumentally rational (and hence, in her view, procedurally autonomous) responses to oppressive circumstances.

15. See, for example, Anderson and Honneth (2005), Benson (1994, 2000, 2005), Govier (2003), Mackenzie (2008), and McLeod (2002).

16. For a developed argument in support of this claim, see Anderson (2014).

17. For example, Khader says: "A person who is an agent identifies with her chosen courses of action rather than regarding them as instances of mere subjection—to another's will or the uncontrollable tides of fortune. She has a sense of what matters to her and attempts to act in a way that reveals this. In order to make choices according to her own sense of what matters, a person must regard her own projects as worth pursuing" (2011, 113).

18. See Khader (2011, introduction and chapter 4) for detailed discussion of the Programa Educativo de La Mujer (Women's Educational Project, PAEM) in rural Honduras during the 1980s and 1990s.

REFERENCES

Alkire, Sabina (2005) *Valuing Freedoms: Sen's Capability Approach and Poverty Reduction*. Oxford: Oxford University Press.

Anderson, Joel and Honneth, Axel (2005) "Autonomy, Vulnerability, Recognition and Justice," in J. Christman and J. Anderson (eds.), *Autonomy and the Challenges to Liberalism*. Cambridge: Cambridge University Press, pp. 127–149.

Anderson, Joel (2014) "Vulnerability and Autonomy Intertwined," in C. Mackenzie, W. Rogers, and S. Dodds (eds.), *Vulnerability: New Essays in Ethics and Feminist Philosophy*. New York: Oxford University Press, pp. 134–161.

Benson, Paul (1991) "Autonomy and Oppressive Socialization," *Social Theory and Practice* 17: 385–408.

——— (1994) "Free Agency and Self-Worth," *Journal of Philosophy* 91: 650–668.

——— (2000) "Feeling Crazy: Self-Worth and the Social Character of Responsibility," in C. Mackenzie and N. Stoljar (eds.), *Relational Autonomy: Feminist Perspectives on Autonomy, Agency and the Social Self*. New York: Oxford University Press, pp. 72–93.

——— (2005) "Taking Ownership: Authority and Voice in Autonomous Agency," in J. Christman and J. Anderson (eds.), *Autonomy and the Challenges to Liberalism*. Cambridge: Cambridge University Press, pp. 101–126.

Christman, John (2004) "Relational Autonomy, Liberal Individualism and the Social Constitution of Selves," *Philosophical Studies* 117: 143–164.

——— (2009) *The Politics of Persons: Individual Autonomy and Socio-Historical Selves*. Cambridge: Cambridge University Press.

Friedman, Marilyn (1986) "Autonomy and the Split-Level Self," *Southern Journal of Philosophy* 24(1): 19–35.

Govier, Trudy (2003) "Self-Trust, Autonomy, and Self-Esteem," *Hypatia* 8(x): 99–120.

Holroyd, Jules (2009) "Relational Autonomy and Paternalistic Interventions," *Res Publica* 15(4): 321–336.

Khader, Serene (2011) *Adaptive Preferences and Women's Empowerment*. New York: Oxford University Press.

Mackenzie, Catriona (2000) "Imagining Oneself Otherwise," in C. Mackenzie and N. Stoljar (eds.), *Relational Autonomy: Feminist Perspectives on Autonomy, Agency and the Social Self*. New York: Oxford University Press, pp. 124–150.

——— (2002) "Critical Reflection, Self-Knowledge, and the Emotions," *Philosophical Explorations* 5(2): 186–206.

——— (2008) "Relational Autonomy, Normative Authority, and Perfectionism," *Journal of Social Philosophy* 39: 512–533.

——— (2014) "Three Dimensions of Autonomy: A Relational Analysis," in A. Veltman & M. Piper (eds.), *Autonomy, Oppression and Gender*. New York: Oxford University Press, pp. 15–41.

Mackenzie, Catriona and Stoljar, Natalie (2000) "Introduction: Autonomy Refigured," in C. Mackenzie and N. Stoljar (eds.), *Relational Autonomy: Feminist Perspectives on Autonomy, Agency and the Social Self*. New York: Oxford University Press, pp. 3–31.

Mackenzie, Catriona and Jacqui Poltera (2010) "Narrative Integration, Fragmented Selves and Autonomy," *Hypatia* 25(1), 2010: 31–54.

McLeod, Carolyn (2002) *Self-Trust and Reproductive Autonomy*. Cambridge, MA: MIT Press.

Mani, Anandi et. al. (2013) "Poverty Impedes Cognitive Function," *Science* 341(6149): 976–980.

Meyers, Diana (1989) *Self, Society and Personal Choice*. New York: Columbia University Press.

Nelson, Hilde Lindemann (2001) *Damaged Identities, Narrative Repair*. Ithaca: Cornell University Press.

Nussbaum, Martha (2001) *Women and Human Development: The Capabilities Approach*. Cambridge: Cambridge University Press.

Oshana, Marina (1998) "Personal Autonomy and Society," *Journal of Social Philosophy* 29(1): 81–102.

———— (2005) "Autonomy and Self-Identity," in J. Christman and J. Anderson (eds.), *Autonomy and the Challenges to Liberalism*. Cambridge: Cambridge University Press, pp. 77–99.

———— (2006) *Personal Autonomy in Society*. Aldershot, UK: Ashgate.

Raz, Joseph (1986) *The Morality of Freedom*. Oxford: Clarendon Press.

Sperry, Elizabeth (2013) "Dupes of Patriarchy: Feminist Strong Substantive Autonomy's Epistemological Weaknesses," *Hypatia* 28(4): 887–904.

Stoljar, Natalie (2000) "Autonomy and the Feminist Intuition," in C. Mackenzie and N. Stoljar (eds.), *Relational Autonomy: Feminist Perspectives on Autonomy, Agency and the Social Self*. New York: Oxford University Press, pp. 94–111.

———— (2014) "Autonomy and Adaptive Preference Formation," in A. Veltman & M. Piper (eds.), *Autonomy, Oppression and Gender*. New York: Oxford University Press, pp. 227–252.

Superson, Anita (2005) "Deformed Desires and Informed Desire Tests," *Hypatia* 20(4): 109–126.

Westlund, Andrea (2009) "Rethinking Relational Autonomy," *Hypatia* 24(4): 26–49.

4 Autonomy, Self-Knowledge, and Oppression

Beate Roessler

1. INTRODUCTION: EPISTEMIC INJUSTICE AND AUTONOMY

In this chapter, I focus on the problem of epistemic injustice as a form of oppression and how this kind of injustice can form obstacles to autonomous action. I shall argue that if a person is the victim of epistemic injustice, she is thereby impaired in her ability to act autonomously: to make autonomous decisions and follow autonomous projects in her life. More specifically, I shall argue that the link between epistemic injustice and autonomy is to be found in the fact that epistemic injustice damages and unsettles a person's relation to herself—to her self-worth as well as her self-knowledge, both of which are prerequisites for autonomous action.

Epistemic injustice, as Miranda Fricker famously argues, affects a subject in her capacity as a knower and in her capacity as a giver of knowledge. I shall be mostly concerned with what she calls "testimonial injustice": "A speaker suffers a *testimonial injustice* (. . .) if prejudice on the hearer's part causes him to give the speaker less credibility than he would otherwise have given" (2007, 4). The person is not believed because of prejudices that prevent that person's utterances from being heard as those of an equal among equals. I think it is fair to say that Fricker analyzes epistemic injustice primarily from the perspective of the person committing the injustice. She works mainly within the framework of virtue epistemology and discusses the necessary epistemic virtues on the side of the hearer; it is only in a secondary sense that she is interested in the harmful consequences for the victim of epistemic injustice (Fricker 2007, 43ff. 129ff). However, this is precisely what I want to focus on: what precisely is the harm that is done to the suffering subject? The person who suffers this form of injustice often experiences uncertainty and self-doubt—and it is the analysis and explanation of these uncertainties and their consequences for autonomy that will be the topic of this chapter.

The assumption underlying my argument is a rather broad and uncontested concept of personal autonomy: a person is autonomous when she can, in principle, rationally reflect and knows, in principle, what she thinks, intends, and wants (i.e., she is competent) and when she acts for her own reasons (i.e., she is authentic).[1] This means that an autonomous person can deliberate and reflect on her aims—short-term aims and longer-term aims—and then (if there are no further obstacles) do what she has decided to do. A person is autonomous when she lives in an environment (or in a social context) that, in principle, encourages her autonomy and supports the idea of autonomy in general.

Why is this general concept of autonomy sufficient for the following arguments and considerations? The reason is that I am interested in two specific aspects of this idea of autonomy: for a person to be autonomous, she needs to have a sense of self-worth and she needs to have self-knowledge. She has to fundamentally value her projects, which must also be recognized by (significant) others—this is what self-worth means. And she has to know in broad terms what she wants, believes, intends, desires in order to be able to reflect on her beliefs and desires in order to find out what she autonomously believes and wants to do—this is what self-knowledge involves. As will be noted, the capacity to act autonomously on reasons of one's own is dependent on self-knowledge and self-worth. Both of these aspects play at least some role in all of the different and more substantial concepts of autonomy. That does not mean that the arguments I am going to develop in the following will have to be accepted by every single theory of autonomy, but it does mean that the simple relationship between autonomy, self-respect, and self-knowledge is relevant for all of them.

Accordingly, the goal of this article is, starting with examples that provide us with a rough phenomenology of epistemic injustice, to ask how the various possible forms of self-doubt, uncertainty, insecurity that a subject suffers—or at least can suffer—in a situation of testimonial injustice can be explained. I shall argue that in order to be able to answer this central question, we have to acknowledge that the harm that is done by epistemic injustice can be understood only within the normative framework of autonomy and practical rationality. However, I have more than one reason to write this chapter. The first is, as I just explained, the wish to analyze the consequences of epistemic injustice as a form of oppression of personal autonomy. The second reason complements this first one: it is my long-standing suspicion that a theory of autonomy is in need of a theory of self-knowledge, since it is plausible to assume that if self-knowledge is necessary in order for a person to be autonomous, then the theory of autonomy must at least be able to explain its underlying concept of self-knowledge.

In the following section, I shall explain the problem with the help of two examples. I shall then present Fricker's ideas in greater detail in section 3. In sections 4 and 5, I shall go on to explain why I think that epistemic injustice is of central concern for the relationship between the subject and herself, focusing first briefly on epistemic injustice and its impact on self-worth (in section 4) and secondly its impact on self-knowledge (in section 5). Since this last problem will be the central topic of my chapter, I shall dedicate more space to a discussion of the concepts of knowledge and self-knowledge and the ways in which both concepts play a role in the analysis of epistemic injustice in sections 6 and 7, respectively. By way of conclusion, in section 8 I shall explain why epistemic injustice can impair the conditions for rational agency and personal autonomy.

2. TWO EXAMPLES

Testimonial injustice, in the way Fricker has coined the concept, refers to "cases of telling," so predominantly to cases where a person utters propositions of the form p, and so forth. However, the term "testimonial injustice" can be extended to people who tell stories and give "judgements, views, opinions" (Fricker 2007, 50 fn 22). I would like to first give a rather simple example of the plain "telling" form and then a more substantial example which goes beyond the paradigm case (p) of testimonial injustice.

The first example concerns the case of a speaker at an English conference discussion in which the speaker has quite a heavy Cockney accent. Let us imagine that he is the only person with a very clear class-related accent attending the conference. When he speaks, consequently, people tend to listen to the accent much more than to the actual content of his contribution. They react nicely and talk to him in a friendly way, but they do not actually react to *what* he is saying. The other participants in the conference do not take the speaker's contribution as seriously as they would have had he spoken without an accent. He is being treated with a little condescendence, and with sympathy, but not as an equal among equals.

Although this is rather a simple example of testimonial injustice, it still can serve to make the point in a preliminary way and to raise the question: what is happening to the subject in the example? We can assume that he will have feelings of uncertainty, embarrassment, and self-doubt—maybe leaving aside the anger he might also feel in the face of not being taken seriously by his colleagues. He perceives that they are less inclined to believe what he is saying, and this seems to have consequences for the way he thinks about *what* he was saying and for the way he thinks about *himself*.

Let us turn to my second, more substantial example. In a famous passage in her diary reporting a crucial discussion with Jean-Paul Sartre, Simone de Beauvoir writes, "I struggled with him for three hours. In the end, I had to admit I was beaten; besides, I had realized, in the course of our discussion, that many of my opinions were based only on prejudice, bad faith or thoughtlessness, that my reasoning was shaky and my ideas confused. '*I'm no longer sure what I think, or even if I think at all*,' I noted, completely thrown."[2]

What is happening here and why are these examples so interesting for the questions I want to raise? The setting of de Beauvoir's story and analysis clearly shows that Sartre did not take her seriously as an equal conversational partner—this becomes even more obvious when we read a little more about the context and the background of the passage quoted.[3] It therefore seems fair to say that Beauvoir not only doubts whether she does or does not know or believe that p; Sartre's remarks and reaction apparently cut so deep that she even starts to doubt her very capacity to think and reflect. She is being undermined as a person and not only as a credible source of knowledge.

Both of the examples suggest an investigation into the possible consequences of epistemic injustice for the self-attitudes of the subject. I think we should differentiate between two aspects of the person's relationship to herself that can be upset by the injustice: the aspect of self-respect or self-worth and the aspect of self-knowledge. If the feelings of insecurity threaten the person's self-respect or self-worth, the person may ask herself, "Am I worth joining this discussion? Are my views worth communicating?" The insecurity also threatens self-knowledge, as it prompts a person to ask herself, "Do I really believe *that p*? Am I really certain that I want to defend *that p*?"

Before I argue this in greater detail, let me make some conceptual clarifications that will be relevant throughout the article. If I maintain that p, and the listener does not believe me, then it can *either* be the case that p is wrong *or* that p is true (or at least its falsity has not yet been shown), but the listener has "bad reasons" for not believing me. If we pursue the second option, then "he does not believe me" can have different forms: he can either very strongly believe that not-p and therefore not be listening to me, or he can reject my utterance, or he can ignore it. In the latter two cases, he does not take what I say seriously and does not treat me as an equal knower among equal knowers. These "bad reasons" for not believing me are the ones that make it a case of epistemic injustice (they may be structural prejudices, for instance). Before I return to these "bad reasons," let me introduce two further distinctions: if I *feel* that I am being treated in an epistemically unjust manner, then it can either be the case that I am in fact being treated in this way or that I am a rather neurotic, insecure person who always assumes people ignore her or don't take her seriously. If I am in fact being treated in an epistemically unjust manner, then I can feel either anger and rage (and maybe even take these feelings as a source of self-worth), or I can start doubting that p but try to shake off the doubt, or I can be unsettled in my belief that p, and experience severe self-doubts and uncertainty. In all of these three cases I do not have to be conscious of the fact that I am a victim of epistemic injustice—de Beauvoir, for instance, was certainly not aware of it at the time (and realized it, if at all, only much later). It is the very last case that I am mostly going to focus on in this chapter. I shall return shortly to the meaning of epistemic injustice, to the question "what precisely is the wrong of epistemic injustice?" and to its precise consequences for the person.

In the following, when I am analyzing testimonial epistemic injustice, I shall assume that "that p" is true (or its falsity has not yet been proven), that the listeners reject or ignore the claim the subject is raising, and that the subject does not have to be conscious of the injustice as an injustice. I shall assume that the cases I am talking about are *in fact* cases of epistemic injustice: so, to put it rather bluntly, Sartre acted wrongly and de Beauvoir had to bear the consequences. The problem of how precisely to differentiate empirically between cases of epistemic injustice and other cases is certainly interesting, but it is not the topic of my chapter.[4]

Both the threat to self-respect and the threat to self-knowledge have to be understood as moral harms caused by the epistemically unjust treatment by others. Other examples abound, and we will discuss some of these in following sections. Here it should suffice to have given initial plausibility to the interpretation that the harm of epistemic injustice has or can have these different aspects.

3. FRICKER'S THEORY OF EPISTEMIC INJUSTICE

Let us first take a closer look at Fricker's theory. According to Fricker, epistemic, and, more specifically, testimonial injustice is done to a person and in a certain situation when knowledge and testimony are central: "A speaker suffers a *testimonial injustice* . . . if prejudice on the hearer's part causes him to give the speaker less credibility than he would otherwise have given."[5] This form of injustice is epistemic if and because, as Fricker writes, "someone is wronged in their capacity as a giver of knowledge" (Fricker, 2007, 7). The reason for this form of epistemic justice is, in most cases, "identity prejudice" (7): the hearer has a deeply rooted prejudice vis-a-vis the social identity of the speaker—her gender, race, cultural background, class, and accent. Therefore, "The central case of testimonial injustice is identity-prejudicial credibility deficit" (28). Thus, it is obvious why the two examples presented are examples for testimonial epistemic injustice. In the simpler case of the Cockney accent, the hearers apparently exhibit "identity-prejudicial credibility deficit" vis-a-vis the speaker because of his class. The second case involving de Beauvoir and Sartre has to be interpreted as a case of sexism and therefore also as an "identity-prejudicial credibility deficit."

As I mentioned, Fricker is first of all interested in the person or persons *committing* epistemic injustice. She develops a theory of epistemic virtues that aims to provide a normative account of the "responsible hearer," of the virtues of understanding, and embeds her account in virtue epistemology, demonstrating that the virtue of epistemic justice is an ethical as well as epistemic virtue.[6] In her theory, she focuses on the structure and pervasiveness of prejudices. However, Fricker is also interested in understanding more specifically the harm that is done to the victim of epistemic injustice. On one hand, she develops a rather broad approach and describes the harm being done as "intrinsic": "To be wronged in one's capacity as a knower is to be wronged in a capacity essential to human value. When one is undermined or otherwise wronged in a capacity essential to human value, one suffers an intrinsic injustice."[7] Since knowledge and the capacity as a knower or a "giver of knowledge" is so closely linked to reason and to our capacity to reason, which is in turn fundamental for our self-understanding as human beings, epistemic injustice "cuts deep" and can undermine subjects "in their very humanity" (44).

On the other hand, Fricker argues more specifically that, due to the loss of "epistemic confidence," the subject "literally loses knowledge" (133). She writes that "testimonial injustice (. . .) wrongfully deprives the subject of a certain fundamental sort of respect and [Fricker's analysis] . . . helps reveal this as a form of objectification. The subject is wrongfully excluded from the community of trusted informants, and that means that he is unable to be a participant in the sharing of knowledge" (132). This is essential: if one does not appear "fit" to participate in the practice of knowledge, to be part of the "pool of informants," one is "denied the very status of a knower." This, in turn, Fricker argues, has consequences for the subject's identity and identity formation, at least in cases in which the epistemic injustice takes structural and persistent forms: "[W]henever someone suffers testimonial injustice they are thereby inhibited (. . .) in the formation of their identity" (54).

Although Fricker refers to and discusses the consequences epistemic injustice has for the suffering subject, I want to argue that she does not go deep enough in her discussion and that she tends to keep to the third-person perspective and does not focus on the first-person perspective of the person who is suffering the injustice. I think, however, that the problem needs to be considered from a participant's point of view, from that of the victim of epistemic injustice: in order to understand the relevant connection between injustice or harm on the one hand and knowledge claims on the other, we have to understand the problem of epistemic injustice by reference to autonomy, self-worth, and self-knowledge, or so I will argue. The harm that is being done changes the subject and her relationship to herself, which is the central reason the subject's status as a rational agent and ultimately her autonomy is undermined. I am therefore interested in a yet closer and more detailed analysis of what it means for someone to be "undermined in their status as a knower."[8]

4. EPISTEMIC INJUSTICE AND SELF-WORTH

As I have argued, it might be helpful to follow up on the question as to what it is precisely within rational agency and in being a "knower" that is harmed when one is treated in an epistemically unjust way by linking this question to the self-relationship of the suffering subject. I asserted earlier that what the subject experiences in a situation of epistemic injustice can be severe self-doubt, embarrassment, or shame and that this self-doubt can take two directions: it can take the form of a lack of self-worth or, alternatively, uncertainty as to the subject's self-knowledge. Both aspects can be differentiated from one another by separating the questions the subject might ask herself: "Am I worthy of joining this discussion?" on one hand and "Do I really believe that p, do I want to defend it?" on the other.

Let me first focus on the relationship between epistemic injustice and self-respect or self-worth before I discuss at greater length the consequences of epistemic injustice for a person's self-knowledge.[9] Testimonial injustice is a paradigm of denial of the credibility of the subject and respect for the subject. Why is the self-worth of the subject at stake in cases of testimonial injustice?

We can illustrate this form of injustice and its implications for a person's autonomy with the help of the film *Gaslight* by George Cukor and Paul Benson's analysis of it. Benson is among the authors who have pointed out different ways in which autonomy, or rational agency, is dependent on self-evaluative attitudes: without some sense of self-worth or self-respect, rational and free agency is not possible. Damaging—through testimonial injustice—the self-evaluative attitudes therefore directly undermines the subject's agency, Benson argues convincingly. In the film, the female protagonist, Paula, played by Ingrid Bergman, is systematically misled and deceived regarding her perceptions, beliefs, and the truth of her utterances by her husband Gregory, who is played by Charles Boyer. For Gregory, the only way to get the jewels of the character played by Bergman is to declare her deranged and psychopathic. The Bergman character, in the end, herself believes that she is mad, since her husband has systematically called into question what she said and what she believed: she herself does not know any longer what to believe and what to think. She is completely bereft of any sense of self-worth and self-confidence: "The gaslighted woman doubts her mental competence to meet the expectations that others might have of her" (Benson 1994, 660). Although the case of the "gaslighting" is slightly different from the cases we have discussed as examples of epistemic injustice—since Gregory commits epistemic injustice explicitly and intentionally—it still seems fair to say that the consequences for the subject being harmed are comparable. Not being taken seriously as a knower, she starts doubting her own competences and is ultimately unable to act as a free and rational agent. Benson makes it clear in his interpretation of the film how the ability to act, the need to be believed, and the sense of self-worth are tied up with one another.

Following Benson, I would like to argue that without a sense of self-worth, a person cannot act autonomously; if she is not able, in her *own* view, to follow the normative rational standards necessary for social interaction, she then is not in a position to participate rationally and autonomously in social interaction. If her beliefs are systematically rejected as either irrelevant or false, she then is prevented from taking her own reasons as possibly the right—and valuable—ones that she could endorse. This means that she is no longer in a position to act autonomously. Thus, self-worth or self-respect is a precondition for autonomous action, and it is dependent on social circumstances and contexts that are amenable for autonomous persons.[10]

Quite a few authors have conceptualized this link between self-respect or self-worth and autonomy on one hand and the social conditions that are necessary in order for a person to gain and to develop self-worth or self-respect on the other. Rawls, for instance, although not a theoretician of autonomy, argues that self-respect is "the most important primary good" and that a "person's sense of his own value" is necessary for his freedom. In the same vein, he states that "without self-respect nothing may seem worth doing."[11] Although Rawls is talking about projects in general, I think it is helpful to apply his thoughts to the contexts of epistemic injustice we are discussing. It "may not seem worth doing" to maintain that *p* when one is epistemically discriminated against, when people reject or ignore what one is saying. The same point could be argued with reference to recognition theory (such as that proposed by Honneth and Anderson) or by theories of relational autonomy.[12] I do not think that the differences between these approaches are important here: my point is only to argue that because epistemic injustice affects and undermines the self-respect of a person, it thus also undermines her autonomy. This is most evident, of course, in examples of structural discrimination or oppression (as in the case of racism, for instance, in Harper Lee's Tom Robinson[13]), and the next step—which I do not have to take here—would be to work out the exact conceptualization of autonomy on this basis and thereby to take a stance on the question over how strong, substantial, and precise the social conditions of autonomy have to be.

5. EPISTEMIC INJUSTICE AND SELF-KNOWLEDGE

Although there is already quite a lot of research on the relationship between self-respect or self-worth and autonomy, the relationship between self-knowledge and autonomy is rather unexplored.[14] I have argued that epistemic injustice undermines the possibility of rational or autonomous agency in undermining the self-worth and self-knowledge of the subject. The question now is how to explain the possibility of self-doubt, of doubt whether one is "thinking at all," as a consequence of epistemic injustice. Let us return again to de Beauvoir: "I struggled with him for three hours. In the end, I had to admit I was beaten; besides, I had realized, in the course of our discussion, that many of my opinions were based only on prejudice, bad faith or thoughtlessness, that my reasoning was shaky and my ideas confused. *'I'm no longer sure what I think, or even if I think at all,'* I noted, completely thrown" (Fricker (2007, 50). Fricker, as we have seen, interprets this case as a case of "losing knowledge": ". . . the implications for someone who meets with persistent testimonial injustice are grim: not only is he repeatedly subject to the intrinsic epistemic insult that is the primary injustice, but where this persistent intellectual undermining causes him to lose confidence in his beliefs and/or his justification for them, he literally *loses knowledge*" (Fricker (2007, 49). But "loss of knowledge" would mean only that one does not believe that p any longer or that one is no longer confident in believing that p.[15] However, the passage in de Beauvoir seems to imply a more fundamental unsettledness than this: it seems to imply that she has lost a sense of her own reasons for her own beliefs, because her beliefs were systematically thrown into doubt. In order to explain the deep insecurity to which victims of epistemic injustice seem to be subject, I have to make a small excursus and discuss in greater detail the relationship between knowledge and self-knowledge.

6. KNOWLEDGE AND SELF-KNOWLEDGE

My aim is to look for the reasons the uncertainty of believing or knowing that p can undermine the certainty of self-knowledge, and I shall try to explain this by referring to the rationality of self-knowledge.[16] In order to understand the scenario of epistemic injustice, it is important to realize that there is a connection between knowledge and self-knowledge: in order (genuinely) to believe that p, I have to be in a position to know that I believe that p. This is different from the situation in which I doubt that p but am certain that I doubt that p—for instance, when I still have to find the right reasons for or against p. If I am not in a position to know that I believe that p, then I cannot maintain my belief. My epistemic standing, so to speak, is undermined if I am not in a position to endorse my first-order beliefs. What does this mean? When I maintain that p and other people do not believe me or ignore or reject me, then it seems to be helpful to distinguish between two possibilities.[17] One possibility is that I imperturbably keep believing that p but do not dare to argue it any longer; this scenario certainly is plausible, since epistemic injustice does not always have to lead to doubt and self-doubt, and even if it does lead to doubt, it does not always lead to the fundamental self-doubt we are discussing here.[18] Alternatively, I start doubting that p and subsequently start doubting what I believe. How do we explain this latter possibility? Let us start by explaining the link between p and "believing that p." What do I do when I am asked "Do you believe that p?" I reflect, and I deliberate about p. The classical passage in this context is, of course, from Gareth Evans: "If someone asks me 'Do you think there is going to be a Third World War?', I must attend, in answering him, to precisely the same outward phenomena as I would attend to if I were answering 'Will there be a Third World War?'" (Evans 1982, 225). The idea is, as Moran explains, that I get to answer the question "How do I know what I believe?" by deliberating on p (on "will there be a third world war?"). This is what is called "transparency": the first-person question of what I believe gets to be answered by giving precisely the same reasons that would be given to answer the corresponding question about the world.[19]

   At this point, we are confronted with a central parting of the ways, with introspection as the one way and transparency as the other one: if asked what I believe, I do not turn to "look inside" but rather turn to the world and deliberate on p—which seems to be phenomenologically more adequate than the introspective view. The transparency condition shows that it is not plausible to conceive of self-knowledge as monitoring an internal condition; it is more plausible to conceive of it as the ability to reflect on the possible reasons to believe that p. Thus, if one doubts whether p, one doubts whether one has the right reasons to believe that p.[20] This is the link between the belief "that p" and "p": as a consequence, self-knowledge plausibly has to be analyzed as *making up one's mind* as opposed to ascribing, after introspection, a belief to oneself. As the transparency condition shows, it is up to each person to make their mind up about what to believe. So we can already tentatively say that, as the passage quoted demonstrates, something has apparently gone wrong in the process of de Beauvoir's "making up her mind": not only was her confidence in her beliefs undermined, but also her confidence in her ability to make up her mind in the first place. I shall return to this point in what follows.

Self-knowledge, I argue, is misunderstood if it is understood in terms of "inner looking." Beliefs are not objects of possible introspection and observation but are rather constituted through rational deliberation on their content.[21] However, if it is up to me whether I believe that p, then in endorsing a belief, I commit myself to having this belief, after deliberation and on the basis of reasons. It is precisely this rational deliberative stance toward our own mental life that makes us rational agents and that establishes, according to Moran, the genuine form of self-knowledge (2001, 59f). Thus, it is more plausible and more explanatory to conceptualize the stance of a person toward herself and her mental states not as the theoretical observer but as the rational deliberator. We can see now why situations of epistemic injustice impair not only knowledge but also self-knowledge: if a person is ignored or rejected in her belief that p, then she starts to doubt her reasons for p. However, in order to be able to commit herself to a belief, she has to be in a position actually to be able to deliberate on the reasons and, hence, to have a sense of her own reasons and to endorse them. Epistemic injustice prevents precisely that: if people ignore or reject what a person says and what her reasons are for believing that p, she starts doubting her own reasons for p and at the same time starts doubting—might start doubting—that she is able to believe anything at all. Thus, if people deny to a person that she knows that p, then they deny her the possibility to make up her mind as an equal (knower) among equals (equal knowers), and they deny her the ability to commit herself to a belief on the basis of her own reasons; they deny her self-knowledge and the freedom to make up her mind.

7. SELF-KNOWLEDGE, RATIONAL AGENCY, AUTONOMY

So where do we stand? We started by suggesting that in order to be able to explain the consequences of epistemic injustice, we have to assume a link between a person believing that p and her knowing that she believes that p, as I said earlier: in order to believe that p, a person has to be in the position to know that she believes that p. The assumption suggested that if one is unsettled in one's belief that p, one is at the same time—somehow—unsettled in one's belief that one believes that p. In a first step to explaining what is going on here, I suggested following rationalist theories of self-knowledge, such as Moran's, and analyzing the question "do I believe that p?" not by turning inside to have a good inner look but by turning to the world in order to see whether p is the case. The next step was: in order to see whether I believe that p, I have to deliberate. Given that I have turned to the world, are my reasons good enough to support my belief in p? Can I really say that I believe that p? This second step already encompasses rational agency, since deliberation and the weighing of reasons is, of course, a form of rational agency.

The third step brings this to the center: in deliberating whether I believe that p, I eventually have to *make up my mind*: I have to commit myself to believing that p, as the result of my deliberation. This "avowal" (as opposed to a sheer observation of myself) constitutes a cognitive achievement, not because I have successfully observed myself but because I have deliberated and am therefore legitimized in committing myself to a certain belief.[22] The link among knowledge, self-knowledge, and rational agency is stated very clearly by Moran:

> It would not . . . make sense to answer a question about my state of mind (e.g., my belief about the weather) by attending to a logically independent matter (the weather itself) unless it were legitimate for me to see myself as playing a role in the determination of what I believe generally, . . . in the sense that . . . the responsiveness to reasons that belongs to beliefs is an expression of the person's rational agency (2012, 213).

It is essential for the person making up her mind that she knows that it is up to her and her own reasons, that she has the authority as well as the obligation to reflect and deliberate and to make up her mind *for herself*. This is exactly where knowledge, self-knowledge, and rational agency come together in forming a plausible theory of what it means to know that one knows that p.

From the viewpoint of someone trying to understand the wrong of epistemic injustice, this is the crucial link: self-knowledge and the freedom to deliberate and to make up one's mind cannot be separated from one another. It is the freedom to be able to weigh reasons, to react to reasons, and to commit oneself to a certain assertion that is necessary in order for a person to be able to say that she knows that she believes that p. Making up one's mind means that it is up to me what I believe, although, obviously, it is not entirely up to me if one wants, as I do, to reject voluntarism. Rational agents have to ground their beliefs and to endorse them according to standards of rationality.[23] Their beliefs are up to them in the sense that they have the authority and the obligation to make up their own minds: this is the bottom line of the critique of the introspection view that argues in favor of the theoretical and observational stance toward our mental life. It is this freedom that is being violated or restricted in situations of epistemic injustice: here, deliberation, making up one's mind, and self-commitment are no longer possible.[24]

It has to be legitimate for the person to see herself as playing a role in what she believes—if we read this from the perspective of epistemic injustice, we can see that the possible harm for the person lies in her not being able or not being allowed to see and recognize herself as legitimized to make up her mind and to determine what she believes. This is precisely how we should interpret the de Beauvoir example. She is harmed not only because Sartre does not believe her and does not take her seriously as an equal conversational partner but also because she is unjustly prevented from making up her own mind. If other people ignore, reject, or do not listen to what one says, one can come to believe and experience that what one believes is not up to oneself.

It is now possible to see more clearly the damage that is done to the self-relationship of the subject by epistemic injustice. If we consider that one aspect of this harm lies in the distortion of the self-relations or self-attitudes of the subject (self-worth and self-knowledge) and in the severe self-doubts a subject might suffer as a consequence of testimonial injustice, then it seems plausible to discern a direct link between the person who is not believed by others and her doubting and uncertainty over how she knows what she believes at all. This is explained and clarified by a rationalist theory of self-knowledge.

8. EPISTEMIC INJUSTICE AND AUTONOMY

Epistemic injustice is a wrong because it is a form of exclusion, of denying respect, and of restricting freedom, including the freedom to be treated as equal among equals. However, I have argued that there can be a more subtle and more substantial reason why epistemic injustice is a wrong and why it restricts a person's autonomy: epistemic injustice can undermine or destroy the basis of autonomy in undermining the self-knowledge and the self-worth of a person, which are constitutive for her autonomy. Without self-worth or self-respect and without "knowing herself," a person cannot act autonomously as a rational agent, cannot reflect on what she wants to do, and cannot follow her projects in the necessary self-confident way. As I pointed out, not every case of epistemic injustice has to cut so deep as to disturb a person's fundamental self-attitudes—sometimes it might be possible to shake off the injustice. However, if it does cut deep, we have to be able to understand exactly why this is the case. The excursus into the analysis of what it means to lose one's self-worth and the excursus into the analysis of what it means to believe that *p* were both necessary in order to show how precisely epistemic injustice can affect the rational and autonomous agency of a person. It should be noted that this links in to what I explained in the introduction as the general concept of autonomy: a person has to be rational, to be able to reflect, and to be sufficiently confident and trustful of herself—in short, she must have the cognitive and emotional competencies necessary for autonomous agency. She must also be able to act on reasons of her own—and therefore to be able to reflect on and endorse these reasons as her own. Furthermore, we can see how a person's autonomy is also dependent on the social circumstances that enable her to live autonomously. Both conditions of autonomy are impaired by epistemic injustice.

Let me briefly discuss two objections. First, one could argue that in the way I conceptualize self-knowledge, I am not completely clear about the relation between autonomy and self-knowledge: is self-knowledge a precondition for autonomy or the other way round? In the discussion of what it means to have self-knowledge, we could see that a theory of self-knowledge for which the transparency of beliefs, the rationality of agents, and their commitment to their beliefs is central, does indeed rely on an idea of autonomy or individual freedom. But I would like to argue that personal autonomy in the broader sense I sketched needs more than these rational reflective capacities—therefore, self-knowledge in the sense I described is necessary for personal autonomy (and not the other way round). It certainly is not wrong to say that one could have the autonomy necessary for self-knowledge without being able to lead an autonomous life in the more general sense.

However, this leads to a second objection. This second objection claims that it is not really self-knowledge that is necessary for autonomy, but it is the *abilities* that are at stake, for self-knowledge as well as for autonomy: being able to make up one's mind, deliberation, reason-responsiveness. What this objection brings to light is, first, that there is indeed an analogy between autonomy in the more general sense and the autonomy that is necessary for self-knowledge since both rely on and exhibit the same set of abilities. This only strengthens my point, I think, that the rationalist theory of self-knowledge is the most plausible one precisely because it essentially links the idea of autonomy and freedom with an explanation of what it means to have self-knowledge. But the reason the objection misses its target is, again, the claim that the concept of personal autonomy is much broader than the concept of autonomy that is being used to explain self-knowledge. We need more—abilities, social conditions—than the abilities that are necessary for self-knowledge if we want to lead an autonomous life. Therefore, what this objection also brings to light is that there is a certain disanalogy between the relation of self-worth and autonomy on one hand and the relation of self-knowledge and autonomy on the other. Both, self-worth and self-knowledge are necessary for the autonomous agent, and both can be damaged by epistemic injustice, but the ways in which they constitute the autonomy of a person have to be analyzed differently.

The two reasons for writing this contribution, which I mentioned in the introduction, were, first, to understand the wrong of epistemic injustice and, second, to understand why a theory of self-knowledge could contribute to a theory of autonomy. I hope to have shown that the rationalist theory of self-knowledge I presented is the most plausible not only for understanding the self-knowledge of rational agents but also for understanding epistemic injustice. Epistemic injustice is a form of oppression because it prevents people from being autonomous, in subtle as well as in not-so-subtle ways.

ACKNOWLEDGMENTS

I am very grateful to audiences at the philosophy departments at Utrecht University, Free University Berlin, and Konstanz University for helpful debates on earlier versions of the paper. I also profited enormously from the discussions in the reading group on self-knowledge at my department: thanks to Julian Kiverstein, Naomi Kloosterboer, Thomas Nys, and Christian Skirke. I am very grateful to Monika Betzler, Johannes Roessler, and Katrin Schaubroeck, as well as, again, to Christian, Thomas, and Naomi for their helpful and thoughtful comments. Many thanks also to Marina Oshana for her comments and questions.

NOTES

1. See Christman (2009), Oshana (2006), Bratman (2007), and Taylor (2005); differences between the approaches will be pointed out where they are relevant; for more on my view on autonomy, see Roessler (2012a) and (2012b).
2. Fricker (2007, 51); Fricker claims to quote de Beauvoir (1959, 344), but she changes (without pointing this out) the English translation of the originally French passage (de Beauvoir 1958, 343) and is completely right to so change it. Fricker's translation from the French is far more literal and adequate than Kirkup's; I only mention these philological issues because the de Beauvoir quote plays a central role in my argument.
3. "'From now on, I'm going to take you under my wing,' Sartre told me when he had brought me the news that I had passed" (de Beauvoir 1959, 339). This illustrates rather clearly de Beauvoir's experience of and perspective on the relationship: she does not mention that she passed second after Sartre, that she was a brilliant philosophy student, that she thought of giving up philosophy under Sartre's influence; see Fricker (2007, 50ff).
4. See Wanderer (2012, 160ff) and Fricker (2007, 17ff), although neither of them makes precisely these distinctions.
5. Fricker (2007, 4); her central case is the well-known example of Tom Robinson (the black victim of a racist all-white jury in Harper Lee's *To Kill a Mockingbird* (1960), and she provides a brilliant discussion of this example; see 22ff; see also her interesting difference between testimonial and hermeneutic injustice (2007,

147ff), which I do not discuss here. It should be noted that her definition of testimonial injustice is given from the perspective of the doer and does not make any reference to the autonomy of the victim, which, if my argument is right, renders it incomplete.

6. For more on the framework of virtue epistemology, see Zagzebski (1996) and Brady & Pritchard (2003).

7. Fricker (2007, 43 ff); see Wanderer (2012, 152f).

8. Fricker endorses two different forms of rationality, which are "closely intertwined": "The sort of epistemic objectification that we are concerned with is the cognitive counterpart to Kant's practical rationality conception of what constitutes immoral treatment of another person (. .). In testimonial injustice, one person undermines another's status as a subject of knowledge; in Kant's conception of immorality, one person undermines another's person status as rational agent" (136). "The undermining of someone as a knower is, conceptually and historically, closely related to their being undermined as a practical reasoner" (137). If my argument is right, this talk of two different forms of rationality is misleading.

9. I use the concepts "self-worth" and "self-respect" interchangeably, although in some theories—but not in mine—the difference is significant; see, for instance, Anderson and Honneth (2005) and Oshana (2006, 81ff).

10. See Benson (1994, 661) "The sense of worthiness to act that is necessary for free agency incorporates a social dimension (. . .)."

11. All citations come from Rawls (1971, 440); see for more detail 440ff.

12. Anderson and Honneth (2005); Mackenzie and Stoljar (2000); Christman (2009); the strongest social account is arguably Oshana (2006).

13. See Fricker (2007, 23): "The trial proceedings enact what is in one sense a straightforward struggle between the power of evidence and the power of racial prejudice, with the all-white jury's judgement ultimately succumbing to the latter."

14. But see for instance Christman (2005).

15. I am simplifying here: of course, there are gradations in beliefs (between being convinced by the truth of a proposition and being doubtful about it), but this simplification does not, I hope, impair my argument.

16. See for the following Moran (2001, 2012); also McGeer (2007), Gertler (2011, 166ff), and Byrne (2011).

17. It should be remembered that we are only talking here about genuine cases of epistemic injustice (see above p. 71) and also that I do not need to know that I am being epistemically discriminated against (it simply being sufficient that I am in fact discriminated against); see Wanderer for the difference between rejecting and ignoring (2012).

18. The first scenario is what Fricker calls the "freedom of speech problem" (43): if I keep believing that "*p*" though under the prevailing conditions cannot maintain it publicly, then the problem is not so much that people do not believe me, but that "*p*" cannot become part of the "pool of knowledge."

19. For more detail on the transparency condition, see Moran (2001, 60ff), Roessler (2013), Gertler (2011, 190ff), and Byrne (2011). See Evans: Wittgenstein was "forcing us to look more closely at the nature of our knowledge of our own mental properties, and, in particular, by forcing us to abandon the idea that it always involves an *inward* glance at the states and doings of something to which only the person himself has access. . . . in making a self-ascription of belief, one's eyes are, so to speak, or occasionally literally, directed outward—upon the world. (. . .) We continue to have no need for the inward glance" Evans (1982, 225, 226).

20. This is a very rough summary of a rather sophisticated debate; on the introspection view and its discussion, see, for instance Cassam (1994), Gertler (2011, 129ff), and Bilgrami (1998).
21. See Moran (2012, 219ff. 233f) on the difference between "active" and "passive" beliefs.
22. See Moran (2001, 83ff. 134ff); see also Williams (2002, 191ff) on the idea of cognitive achievement.
23. See Hieronymi (2006); Moran (2001, 38ff).
24. See Moran (2001, 145): The deliberative question is "answered by a decision or commitment of oneself rather than a discovery of some antecedent truth about oneself. This is a perfectly homely assertion of one's freedom. It is what is exercised in the undramatic situations of making up one's mind about some matter . . . " See Moran (2001, 138ff) on the relation between rational freedom and self-knowledge.

REFERENCES

Anderson, Joel & Honneth, Axel (2005) "Autonomy, Vulnerability, Recognition, and Justice," in Christman, John & Anderson, Joel (eds.), *Autonomy and the Challenges to Liberalism: New Essays*. Cambridge University Press, pp. 127–149.
Beauvoir, Simone de (1958) *Memoires d'une jeune fille rangee*. Paris: Gallimard.
Beauvoir, Simone de (1959) *Memoirs of a Dutiful Daughter*, translated from the French by James Kirkup. London: Penguin.
Benson, Paul (1994) "Autonomy and Self-Worth," *Journal of Political Philosophy* 91 (12): 650–686.
Bilgrami, Akeel (1998). "Self-Knowledge and Resentment," in Wright, Crispin, Smith, Barry C. & MacDonald, Cynthia (eds.) *Knowing Our Own Minds*. Clarendon Press: Oxford, pp. 207–242.
Bratman, Michael (2007) *Structures of Agency*. New York: Oxford University Press.
Brady, Michael & Pritchard, Duncan (eds.) (2003) *Moral and Epistemic Virtues*. Oxford: Blackwell.
Byrne, Alex (2011) "Transparency, Belief, Intention," in *Proceedings of the Aristotelian Society* 85 (1): 201–221, Suppl. Volume.
Cassam, Quassim (ed.) (1994) *Self-Knowledge*. Oxford: Oxford University Press.
Christman, John (2005) "Autonomy, Self-Knowledge and Liberal Legitimacy," in Christman, John & Anderson, Joel (eds.), *Autonomy and the Challenges to Liberalism: New Essays*. Cambridge University Press, pp. 330–357.
Christman, John (2009) *The Politics of Persons: Individual Autonomy and Socio-Historical Selves*. New York: Cambridge University Press.
Evans, Gareth (1982) *The Varieties of Reference*, ed. John McDowell. Oxford: Clarendon Press.
Fricker, Miranda (2007) *Epistemic Injustice. Power and the Ethics of Knowing*. Oxford University Press.
Gertler, Brie (2011) *Self-Knowledge*. London: Routledge.
Hieronymi, Pamela (2006) "Controlling Attitudes," *Pacific Philosophical Quarterly* 87 (1): 45–74.
Lee, Harper (1960) *To Kill a Mockingbird*. London: Heinemann.
Mackenzie, Catriona & Stoljar, Natalie (eds.) (2000) *Relational Autonomy: Feminist Perspectives on Autonomy, Agency, and the Social Self*. Oxford: Oxford University Press.
McGeer, Victoria (2007) "The Moral Development of First-Person Authority," *European Journal of Philosophy* 16 (1): 81–108.

Moran, Richard (2001) *Authority and Estrangement: An Essay on Self-Knowledge.* Princeton, NJ: Princeton University Press.

Moran, Richard (2012) "Self-Knowledge, 'Transparency,' and the Forms of Activity," in Smithies, D. and Stoljar, D. (eds.), *Introspection and Consciousness.* Oxford: Oxford University Press, pp. 211–236.

Oshana, Marina (2006) *Personal Autonomy in Society.* Aldershot, UK: Ashgate.

Rawls, John (1971) *A Theory of Justice.* Cambridge, MA: Harvard University Press.

Roessler, Beate (2012a) "Meaningful Work: Arguments from Autonomy," *Journal of Political Philosophy* 20 (1): 71–93.

Roessler, Beate (2012b) "Authenticity of Cultures and of Persons," *Philosophy and Social Criticism* 38 (4–5): 445–455.

Roessler, Johannes (2013) "The Silence of Self-Knowledge," *Philosophical Explorations* 16 (1): 1–17.

Taylor, James Stacey (ed.) (2005) *Personal Autonomy. New Essays on Personal Autonomy and Its Role in Contemporary Moral Philosophy.* Cambridge University Press.

Wanderer, Jeremy (2012) "Addressing Testimonial Injustice: Being Ignored and Being Rejected," *Philosophical Quarterly* 62: 148–169.

Williams, Bernard (2002) *Truth and Truthfulness.* Princeton, NJ: Princeton University Press.

Zagzebski, Linda (1996) *Virtues of the Mind: An Inquiry Into the Nature of Virtue and the Ethical Foundations of Knowledge.* Cambridge: Cambridge University Press.

5 Autonomy and the Autobiographical Perspective

Andrea C. Westlund

Everyone has a story but me. What's *my* story!

So wonders the protagonist of *A Book* by children's author Mordicai
Gerstein. *A Book* tells the story of a young girl who lives in a book (indeed,
she lives in *A Book*) with her family. She finds that all the other members of
her family, right down to the pets, know what their stories are—but she does
not know her own. So she sets out to find it, traipsing page by page through
a familiar set of literary genres: fairytales, mysteries, historical novels,
science fiction, and more. None of it feels quite right. So at dinner, when
all the members of her family have returned from their own adventures, she
declares: "My story is that of a young girl who doesn't know what her story
is, and so . . . and so she writes her *own* story; I shall become an *author*!"
We leave her lying on her bedroom rug, scribbling out the opening words of
what appears to be an autobiographical fiction (the very story we have just
read, no less): "Once, in a book, there lived a young girl, who did not know
what her story was . . ."

It has become something of a commonplace, in the literature on narrative
agency, to think of ourselves as narrators of our own lives, engaged in a kind
of ongoing autobiographical self-interpretation. Self-narration, moreover, is
often taken to play an important role in free, autonomous, or responsible
agency.[1] There are many variations on this theme, but here I focus primarily
on the idea (metaphorically expressed) that we manifest a special, morally
important form of freedom when we "write" the stories of our own lives,
rather than having them "written" for us. John Martin Fischer, for example,
argues that the value of free action is the value of a certain kind of unhindered
or unimpaired artistic self-expression: "In acting freely," he writes, "we are
writing a sentence in the story of our lives" (Fischer 2005, 377). Coerced or
manipulated actions might add to the story of one's life, but not as an exercise
of one's own authorial agency—and this, he argues, makes a difference to our
intuitions about moral responsibility and other related notions.

Taking up a similar theme from a different angle, feminist theorists have
located a distinctive form of unfreedom in oppressed persons' lack of control
over the "master narratives" that are available to structure and interpret

their lives and have touted the liberatory potential of counterstories that challenge those narratives. Hilde Lindemann Nelson defines a counterstory as "a story that contributes to the moral self-definition of its teller by undermining a dominant story, undoing it and retelling it in such a way as to invite new interpretations and conclusions" (Nelson 1995, 23). Whereas Fischer focuses on the contribution a free act makes to one's story, Nelson highlights the fact that, for those subject to oppressive master narratives, retelling the story of one's life may be a prerequisite to free, self-authored action: one cannot, through one's actions, add a sentence to the story of one's life—or at least not the sentence one wants to add—if the kind of sense one wants to make of one's life can receive no uptake under dominant interpretive schemas. To achieve authorial control over the narrative frames through which one's life is made intelligible to others is to overcome at least one important form or "face" of oppression.[2]

But how are we to understand the guiding metaphor of self-authorship? In this chapter, I begin from the idea, embraced by both Fischer and Nelson (as well as Karen Jones, Genevieve Lloyd, J. David Velleman, and others), that the meaning or significance of a particular event or episode in one's life often depends on the place of that event or episode in a narratively structured whole. Once one accepts this idea, it may seem but a short step to the further idea that a valuable form of freedom resides in the activity of exercising authorial control over that meaning. But herein lies a puzzle: as self-narrators, the control we exercise over the meaning of our actions is limited not just by hindrances of the sort Fischer has in mind (coercion, manipulation, and the like), nor even just by these plus the symbolic domination of master narratives, but also by constraints peculiar to the autobiographical perspective itself. We attempt, through self-narration, to fix the meaning of our choices and actions by assigning them a place within a larger narrative, but so long as that narrative has yet fully to unfold, the meaning we assign is at best provisional. Who we are and what we are up to is vulnerable to future contingency, in a way that might seem to threaten the idea that we could ever truly be free to write sentences in the stories of our lives *as* we are living them.

In fact, I do not think that the limits of authorial control undermine the idea that self-narration is connected to a valuable form of freedom, nor do I think they undermine the important idea that counterstories can enhance freedom by challenging dominant master narratives. But I do argue that recognition of the limits of self-narration should shift our understanding of the conceptual terrain. The peculiarities of the autobiographical perspective point to a notion of autonomy that is distinct from the kinds of freedom Fischer and Nelson have in mind. Autonomy, understood as self-governance, cannot *simply* be a matter of freely adding sentences to the story of one's own life, even under conditions of nondomination.[3] We should, instead, think of the autonomous self-narrator as one who recognizes the limitations inherent to the autobiographical perspective and responds to these by holding herself answerable for the stories she tells.

In the first section of this chapter, I identify a problem posed by attempts to narrate one's own life as one lives it and explore responses to this problem in the work of Elisabeth Camp and Genevieve Lloyd. In the second section, I draw on Karen Jones's concepts of trajectory dependence and interpretation sensitivity to argue that we cannot simply avoid or sidestep the problem identified in the first section: to some significant extent, the very selves we express in our choices and actions are indeterminate, but we face distinctive practical pressures to proceed as if that were not so. In the third and fourth sections, I argue that these realities require us to depart from any model of autonomy that relies on the expression of a determinate self in action and opt for a model focused instead on the ability to question and revise the stories through which we understand and present ourselves to others. In the end, I suggest, this picture puts the ability to tell and entertain counterstories even closer to the center of autonomous agency than one might have thought.

1. THE AUTOBIOGRAPHICAL PERSPECTIVE

It is a much-discussed feature of narrative, often taken to distinguish it from mere chronology, that later events can affect the meaning or significance of earlier ones. But as self-narrators, of course, we often do not know how things will turn out. The perspective that autobiographical narration prompts us to take on our lives is thus a perplexing one. Like Gerstein's young protagonist (the girl in *A Book*), we find that is often not terribly clear what story we are a part of. Unlike her, however, we do not have the advantage of being fictional characters. We do not live in a book, our stories have not already been written, and it generally will not do to trail off with a suggestive ellipsis. Deciding that your story is the story of someone who writes her own story will not get you very far if the content of that story is precisely what is in question.[4] We seem to be in need of a more determinate organizing principle.

Elisabeth Camp (2011) notes that the authors of many classical autobiographies solve this problem (at least rhetorically) by appealing to a deity or other external authority that determines the end or goal around which their lives are organized, thereby giving determinate meaning to the events recounted even as they unfold. Her central example is Wordsworth's poetic autobiography, *The Prelude*. In *The Prelude*, Camp points out, Wordsworth casts himself not just as (contingently) a poet but as a "Prophet of Nature" whose choice to become a poet was a response to a calling, the force of which he came to recognize over time. In order to cast the various experiences of his childhood and youth as contributing to the fruition of his destiny, Camp says,

> Wordsworth must cultivate a global, retrospective view of his life . . .
> [that] enables him to conclude that his life is "in the end / All gratulant, if

rightly understood" (XIV.379–387): to conclude, that is, that the result explains and justifies his experiences along the way, by transforming them into means *toward* a significant end.

(Camp 2011, 3)

Here we see the projected end not only fixing the meaning of earlier events but also, in doing so, playing a kind of justificatory role. The narratively projected end saves earlier efforts and episodes in a life from meaninglessness or futility, giving them a kind of value they would not otherwise have.[5]

But Camp argues that the very maneuver that makes *The Prelude* so powerful as autobiography is unavailable to us, as self-narrators, since we must reject as fantastical the teleological ontology on which that maneuver depends. We cannot seriously posit an externally mandated end around which our lives are necessarily organized and that authoritatively gives meaning to all its parts.[6] One might suggest that, like the girl in *A Book*, the best we can do is to adopt our own self-defining ends, without the backing of an external mandate, and allow those to structure our stories. Both Fischer's notion of self-authorship and Nelson's notion of counternarration seem to presume our ability to do something of this sort. The trouble is, this move seems to require a kind of teleological sleight of hand: in choosing to narrate her life in one way rather than another, the autobiographer implicitly projects closure and imposes determinacy on a story that still is, and cannot help but remain, open as long as she continues to live. However useful or necessary such narrative projection might be, in making sense of what we are doing, the stable sense of self it provides seems to rest on little more than an illusion.

Genevieve Lloyd takes up precisely this theme in her fascinating treatment of Sartre's autobiography *Words* (Lloyd 2008). Here, too, we find the idea that the autobiographer writes as though from a future perspective on his own life as a completed whole, in which the contingency of the present is transformed into the fixity of the past and the end is prefigured in the beginning. Sartre, on Lloyd's reading, is fully conscious of the trick he performs and in fact makes it a theme of the work: not only does he project himself into a future perspective from which he can view his life as a whole, Lloyd argues, he represents his childhood self as already taking such a perspective on his life—as choosing for his future self the past of a famous writer, and transforming an accidental feature of himself (his literary talent) into a "mandate" that he write (Lloyd 262). Lloyd points out that the young Sartre's perspective, as represented in *Words*, is a carefully constructed fiction, which mirrors the perspective taken by the later Sartre as autobiographer: in telling the story of his life, he projects an end and reads it back into the present and past, engaging in a kind of "backward living." Sartre's maneuver, Lloyd suggests, is familiar to us as interpreters of our own lives, as we go about "impos[ing] a pattern of necessity on the fragments" (264) that make up our lives, treating them as having a sort of fixity that in fact eludes us as long as we continue to live. We, as self-narrators, dabble in fiction as well.

How ought we to react to this unavoidable element of fiction in teleological autobiography? Camp responds by cautioning us against the dangers of self-confabulation and emphasizing the mistakes we make in identifying our lives or selves too closely with our stories. She cites Louis Mink approvingly, noting that:

> Stories are not lived but told. Life has no beginnings, middles or ends; there are meetings, but the start of an affair belongs to the story we tell ourselves later, and there are partings, but final partings only in the story. There are hopes, plans, battles and ideas, but only in retrospective stories are hopes unfulfilled, plans miscarried, battles decisive, and ideas seminal.
>
> (Mink 1970, 557)

While accepting (and indeed embracing) this point, Lloyd nonetheless takes a more optimistic view of our adventures in backward living. She (like Fischer) suggests that narrative self-interpretation allows us to experience a distinctive form of freedom, connected with its ability to impart meaning to episodes in our lives. Who is right?

I agree with Camp that teleological autobiography exposes us to distinctive risks and that we are all too easily drawn into grandiose (or not-so-grandiose) illusions about who we are and what we are doing. But I suspect that these are risks we cannot entirely avoid and that Lloyd is right that engaging in backward living nonetheless has a special value that is connected with its ability to impart meaning. I attempt to reconcile my pessimism with my optimism about self-narration over the remaining sections of this chapter and to say something about how this reconciliation bears on the concept of autonomy.

2. FREEDOM, MEANING, AND INDETERMINACY

I begin with the claim that the risks of backward living are not entirely avoidable, and I appeal to an argument of Karen Jones's to flesh out this idea. Jones argues convincingly that many of our properties, including many self-ascribed emotions, attributes, and characteristics, are both "trajectory dependent" and "interpretation sensitive" (Jones 2008). A property is trajectory dependent, in Jones's sense, if ascriptions of that property have temporally extended truth makers, such that the correctness of ascribing the property at a particular time depends on what happens at some other time (or, as Jones puts it, on what happens "elsewhen"). Jones takes the property of being in love as her central example, arguing that whether one counts as being in love at a particular time (as opposed, for example, to simply having a stomach ache) depends on the place of certain characteristic thoughts, feelings, and actions within a temporally extended whole. The very same thoughts, feelings, and reactions might count as part of an episode of love on one trajectory but not on another.

Love is also "interpretation sensitive" on Jones's view: conceptualizing one's experience as being in love makes it more likely that the relevant truth-making trajectory will actually unfold by providing one with a set of culturally available scripts to follow. It is not the case that just anything goes when it comes self-interpretation; some interpretations are just too far-fetched to get the right kind of trajectory-shaping purchase in an agent's "motivational and cognitive economy" (283). But Jones argues there is nonetheless a "zone of indeterminacy" (283), within which the meaning of what one does or feels truly is open to interpretation.

The existence of a zone of indeterminacy around a property such as being in love would help to cash out, in less metaphorical terms, Fischer's idea that free actions add a sentence to the story of one's life. A free action may add to or complete a temporally extended sequence in a way that favors one interpretation of one's feelings over another, such that one really is exerting something like authorial control over the significance of those feelings, and over the meaning of related choices and actions. Jones suggests that many properties of interest to moral psychologists, including possibly all practical identities, share the features of trajectory dependence and interpretation sensitivity.[7] If Jones is right, there will be zones of indeterminacy around many of the psychological and characterological properties to which we appeal in explaining our choices and actions, and we will encounter many opportunities to tip the balance in favor of one story rather than another.

One might doubt that *all* practical identities could be trajectory dependent or interpretation sensitive, since some seem far less sensitive to future contingency or interpretation than others do. But some of the properties that make us "who we are" in a practical sense (that structure our first-personal, deliberative perspective) do seem to fit Jones's model. Consider, for example, time-slice twins A and B, both involved in identical youthful efforts to reduce pollution and raise environmental awareness. A and B share, at time *t*, an identical but still partial set of the emotions, desires, and dispositions that would constitute a full-blown commitment to environmental conservation. Twin A goes on to follow a trajectory that leads her to develop the full suite of relevant attitudes, building a life around conservation and environmental activism, whereas for Twin B, the partial set dwindles and withers away, being replaced, ultimately, by other concerns. It seems to me that the author of Twin A's biography might rightly say that the young Twin A already cared about environmental conservation and date her history as activist in such a way as to include that time. Twin B's biographer, on the other hand, would speak very misleadingly if he were to describe the young B as a budding environmentalist. How young Twins A and B themselves understand their identities (and associated reasons for acting) at time *t* will rely on a particular interpretation of their current concerns and priorities and on a projected trajectory that would support that interpretation over time. Likewise, arguably, with a great many other self-ascribed identity properties to which we appeal in explaining our decisions and actions and planning for our futures.

This peculiar feature of our moral psychology helps to explain both why it is risky to go in for self-narration and why it is nonetheless sometimes practically unavoidable. The meaning of any "sentence" we enter into the story, even ones that do not appear to invite competing interpretations at a particular time, will be at least to some degree subject to future contingency. It might sometimes be possible to tell when a meaning-fixing trajectory has more or less run its course, but there will be some lack of certainty even in the clearest cases, and at any given time there will be much about us that remains up in the air. Outside of the context of a wider narrative arc, it will often not be clear exactly what "self" we are expressing in our choices and actions. There will, however, be practical pressures on us to assign at least a provisionally fixed meaning to such feelings and actions, both prospectively, in making decisions and plans, and retrospectively, in providing a justification for what we have done thus far. Proleptically placing them in the context of one story rather than another is a reasonable response to these practical pressures. Opting out of narrative self-interpretation will hardly be possible, at least as a general policy, when we ourselves are partly characterized by trajectory-dependent and interpretation-sensitive properties.

On this picture of selfhood and self-understanding, the risks of confabulation that Camp identifies will be endemic. In fact, they will come in several different flavors. One might be in denial about one's own role in interpreting the raw materials of one's emotional and practical life, taking the significance of these materials simply to be given or found. One might similarly be in denial about the provisionality of the interpretations one provides and fail to take responsibility for revising or reformulating them in response to changing circumstances or new information. One might fail to see that a self-interpretation formulated at one time has come to have less and less plausibility over time, as a meaning-conferring trajectory has unfolded in an unanticipated way. One might also fail to see how one's interpretations conflict with plausible counterinterpretations offered by others or to care adequately about resolving such interpretive disagreements.[8]

So much for the risks. Where is the room for optimism? How much freedom remains in the face of all this uncertainty? Somewhat surprisingly, Lloyd argues that self-narration puts us in touch with a form of freedom that is not captured by the modern notion of autonomy of the will but is instead to be found in the ancient idea, which she traces back to the Stoics, of "the mind's active engagement with necessity" (Lloyd 2008, 258). The core idea is that, through the "joyful acceptance and appropriation" (Lloyd 2008, 257) of that which one cannot control, one transforms it and makes it one's own. Lloyd illustrates this theme through a fascinating discussion of Spinoza's response to the Cherem, or censure, by which he was expelled from his congregation. In his acceptance of the Cherem, Spinoza recasts his past life and identity in terms that favor the separation and render it meaningful from his own point of view. He cannot control the actions of his synagogue, but he *can* transform the contingent and accidental into something like a narrative necessity by embracing it and incorporating it into a meaning-conferring story about himself. As Lloyd puts it, he "mak[es] his future continuous with what he already is" (Lloyd 2008, 256)—not by changing the course of events but by freely interpreting his own identity in a way that redeems them.

Arguably, we see this kind of rapprochement between freedom and necessity whenever a person responds to a setback or unexpected turn of events as though it were "meant to be." People do sometimes seem to find this thought quite liberating—a fact that can be puzzling until one realizes that the attitude does not rely on belief in fate or design but marks the incorporation of an otherwise disruptive event into a sequence that will after all be meaningful to the agent who has experienced it. Where there is (in Jones's terms) a zone of indeterminacy around the question of who one is, adopting a narrative of self-realization or redemption over one of dashed hopes and lost opportunities might actually *allow* one to realize oneself instead of living a life of fragmented or diminished meaning.[9] As for Fischer, the value of self-authorship seems, for Lloyd, to have to do with a form of influence over *meaning* in our lives rather than control over what happens. (As Fischer puts it, it matters that we "make a statement," not that we "make a difference;" 1999, 287.) For one engaged in backward living, Lloyd writes, "freedom resides in the telling of the story, in the narrating, in the appropriating of the details of the life into a coherent whole" (Lloyd 2008, 265).[10]

The idea that there is freedom to be found in the joyful acceptance of necessity strikes me as rich and interesting and certainly worth fleshing out more fully than I can here. But when the necessities in question are *narrative* necessities, generated in large part through our own autobiographical efforts, the joys of self-authorship come intermingled with the risks we have already considered. It is, I think, instructive that we often react with skepticism when others claim that some apparently terrible event or bit of poor treatment was "meant to be." It may look like a dodge or a sign of adaptive preference or of mere acquiescence. Alternatively, it may seem like wishful thinking or self-deception or bad faith. Our stories, after all, are provisional. As Lloyd herself points out, autobiography provides at most a "fragile" and "transient" unity, and the "pieces can always be reassembled into another pattern" (Lloyd 2008, 264). In the question of how to relate to and manage our fragile narrative creations, there is no further necessity to embrace.

But there is, arguably, a role for autonomy. I suggest that autonomy as self-government (in contrast with the Stoic freedom evoked by Lloyd) requires acknowledgment of the provisional nature of the fixity we achieve by narrative means and of the peculiarity of the stance one takes as autobiographer. Because we cannot do without fixity altogether, we must sometimes take the plunge and (provisionally) impose it. But we must also be able to achieve some distance from the narratives we construct, open ourselves to alternative interpretations, and take responsibility for working and reworking our stories as our lives continue to unfold. Being autonomous means living with some uncertainty about meaning in our lives. I will attempt to unpack some of these claims in the remainder of this chapter.

3. AUTONOMY AND SELF-EXPRESSION

First of all, what do I mean by "autonomy?" I will begin by reflecting on Lloyd's use of the term. Her aim is not to fully explicate the notion of autonomy but just to contrast it in general terms with Stoic freedom. It should be noted that she uses the word "autonomy" itself (as opposed to various near synonyms) only once in the paper I've been discussing. But it is nonetheless relatively clear what she has in mind. Lloyd links the concept of autonomy with a broadly speaking Cartesian conception of freedom as freedom of the will, according to which "the limits of human control coincide with the limits of freedom" (Lloyd 2008, 258). Otherwise put, the modern notion of autonomy is for Lloyd most centrally a notion of control over that which we have the power to change through our decisions and actions. That which we cannot control is, on this conception, outside the sphere of possible freedom.

Lloyd is right that this notion is very different from the idea of freedom as the joyful embrace of that which we *cannot* change. Lloyd suggests that insofar as the more ancient notion survives, it survives as "a commendable form of endurance, of patience, of resignation" (Lloyd 2008, 258)—not as a part of our understanding of freedom. While patience and endurance (less so resignation) may still be seen as virtues, I'm not convinced this really is the only form in which the ancient ideal survives. Indeed, I don't think that autonomy, as it is elaborated in recent literature, really is *just* the modern Cartesian notion to which Lloyd contrasts Stoic freedom. In fact, a case could be made that our current notion of autonomy represents a sometimes uncomfortable marriage between *both* ideas of freedom—or, at least, between certain aspects of each.

Here's what I mean. It has become commonplace to draw a distinction between two different components of an account of autonomous agency, namely, between authenticity conditions and competence conditions. Competence conditions concern the cognitive, executive, and other capacities one needs in order to engage in motivationally effective practical deliberation (such as rationality, self-control, imagination, and so on), while authenticity conditions pertain to the question of what makes the desires or values on which one ultimately acts truly "one's own." I would suggest that authenticity conditions are at least thematically connected to the ancient tradition Lloyd highlights, whereas competence conditions are more closely related to its Cartesian successor.

Consider authenticity conditions first. While these conditions are by no means always elaborated in narrative terms, the question of what distinguishes authentic from alien desires or values is often answered by appeal to attitudes that serve to make them the agent's own. According to highly influential accounts that develop ideas in Harry Frankfurt's early work (including Frankfurt's own later account), these are paradigmatically attitudes of either of wholehearted endorsement, care, or love. Depending on how exactly they are elaborated, such attitudes are not such a far cry from the "joyful embrace" described by Lloyd in her discussion of Spinoza. Indeed, in his later work, Frankfurt appeals to Spinoza's declaration that the highest good we can hope for is "*acquiescentia in se ipso*," which Frankfurt translates literally as "acquiescence to oneself," and suggests that the willing acceptance of the motives by which one is moved is "much the same thing as having a free will" (Frankfurt 17).[11]

On Lloyd's refinement of the Stoic ideal, the necessities we accept are necessities only within a narrative structure that we ourselves impose on otherwise ambiguous fragments. After all, Spinoza, Sartre, Wordsworth, and other aficionados of "backward living" *could* have embraced different necessities, just as you and I *could* have ended up endorsing different desires or loving different things. Lloyd notes that Spinoza could, for example, have organized his life around seeking reconciliation with his congregation instead of accepting his separation (Lloyd 2008, 264). But the sense of "could" in play here is not that of Cartesian control: embracing an alternative narrative regarding his expulsion presumably felt unthinkable to Spinoza, just as endorsing different motives or loving different things or people might well feel unthinkable to us. What Frankfurt perceptively describes as "volitional necessities" *could* have been otherwise, but they are not under our direct volitional control.

Now take competence conditions. Unlike authenticity conditions, competence conditions are prima facie connected to questions of Cartesian control over what we do, since they tend to be focused on the development and exercise of our critical and executive capacities. But it is interesting to note that, in recent accounts of autonomy, these capacities often appear subordinate to the ideal of authenticity: for example, on a typical, hierarchical view of autonomy, the competence condition may be satisfied by possession of whatever capacities one needs to engage in motivationally effective reflective endorsement of desires. Cartesian control, on such accounts, becomes a matter of exercising some degree of mastery over the contours of the self, and autonomous action is then defined as action that is determined by or expressive of that self.[12] Autonomous action reflects a "fit" between who we are and what we do, whereas heteronomous action marks a slippage between the two.

This picture of autonomy might seem to be a natural extension of Fischer's thesis, that the value of free action is the value of a kind of self-expression. But I have come to think that both parts of the picture are infected with a (understandable) fantasy. The first facet of the fantasy is that there is generally enough determinacy to who we are for what we do to decisively express or be determined by it. Authenticity, as I've been characterizing it, strikes me as an impossible ideal, for reasons brought to light by Jones's argument: the contours of our own identities are in important respects trajectory dependent. Camp makes a similar point in her discussion of autobiography as teleology: as long as there is more living to be done, the meaning of earlier events remains to that extent indeterminate, and the narrative is not complete. If the self is narratively constituted, and the narrative to be told about a life cannot be finished until the life is over, then we seem forced to conclude that there is no determinate self until life's end. To Camp, this seems unacceptable, but I suspect it contains a kernel of truth. (Actually, there may be reason to doubt there is a determinate self even *at* life's end, since there may still be a plurality of defensible interpretations, but that is another story.)

The second facet of the fantasy is that we can exercise the desired form of control—call it Cartesian control—by *making* ourselves who we are. This is a problematic idea for more or less the same reason: our efforts at self-making are at best provisional. I am comfortable with the thought that we can be *part* authors of our identities, since (as Jones argues) many of our properties are interpretation dependent as well as trajectory dependent: regarding ourselves as having certain properties will often make it more likely that our narratives unfold in ways that substantiate our own self-interpretations. Nonetheless, this is not fully under our control. Temporal trajectories may upend even our most cherished self-interpretations and self-attributions, and they may also be subject to legitimate challenge from other points of view.

I'd like to illustrate these points and work toward an alternative picture of autonomy through consideration of an example I draw from Nelson: Megan O'Brien is a nurse practitioner in a nonprofit family planning clinic described by Nelson in her book *Damaged Identities, Narrative Repair* (2001). Nelson recounts an episode in which O'Brien consults with a high school dropout seeking birth control and ends up giving her Norplant, a long-acting hormonal contraceptive implanted under the skin on the upper arm. Nine months later, the girl asks to have the implants removed: "she was experiencing breakthrough bleeding and her boyfriend didn't like the feel of the strips under her skin" (Nelson 2001, 17). But O'Brien refuses to remove the implants, believing that the girl did not fully appreciate how disastrous an unintended pregnancy would be for her and not trusting her to be responsible with other forms of birth control. As Nelson would have it, O'Brien's refusal reveals something that could not be seen nine months earlier: "that not only for the immediate moment but for the past nine months the contraception has been coercive" (Nelson 2001, 17). I take it that what Nelson means is that the coercive nature of O'Brien's earlier decision could not be seen even by O'Brien herself—and not simply because she was self-deceived but because the meaning of her choice was in fact indeterminate. It would depend, in part, on what she would do and how she would react "elsewhen." To use Jones's terminology, coerciveness is a trajectory-dependent property of O'Brien's act.

Now suppose that, at the time of the initial implant, O'Brien interprets her interaction with the girl in a way that coheres with an overall story quite different from the one that we are (later) in a position to tell: she sees herself as a defender of a young woman's interests, encouraging her autonomy by counseling and deliberating with her about what birth control method to choose. She sees it as part of her calling as a nurse to relate in this way to her patients. In describing herself in these terms, she goes out on something of a limb. Some of the decisions she makes are ambiguous and depend, for their disambiguation, on her later follow-through. She is not being disingenuous; she genuinely takes herself to be a facilitator of her patients' autonomy rather than its enemy. But the fact remains that whether she counts, in the way she optimistically describes herself, as an advocate rather than a manipulator will depend in part on how later events unfold—and we know that they in fact unfold in a way that challenges her own earlier story.[13] O'Brien later makes a decision that, on its face, would be very hard to square with an autobiographical narrative in which she figures as caring advocate rather than paternalistic manipulator.

What can we learn from this hypothetical scenario about selfhood and autonomy? For one thing, it reinforces Camp's cautionary note against taking talk of narrative self-constitution too literally (though for slightly different reasons). If we take O'Brien's self-narrative as decisively self-constituting at any given point, then we lose sight of the fact that her kindness or coerciveness is trajectory dependent and that her meaning- (i.e., trajectory-) fixing narrative proceeds from an imaginatively projected but literally impossible perspective. In the Norplant case, there *is* no determinate fact of the matter about O'Brien's conduct until nine months have elapsed and she confronts the girl's request to have it removed. At that point, things take a new turn, fixing the meaning of what came before in an unanticipated way. It is possible that, even then, its meaning is indeterminate and the "fixing" only provisional. Will O'Brien's refusal turn out to be an isolated slip or part of a pattern of manipulation? Or will still later developments reveal her as (say) a shrewd ally, who gives the girl a safe and welcome way of defusing an overbearing boyfriend's pressure? O'Brien's autobiographical narrative may, at any point in time, proleptically purport to resolve these matters, but it cannot ever quite succeed in doing so. Self-narration is always in part an aspirational matter.

This leads us back to my concern about how authenticity figures into accounts of autonomy. On an account of autonomy that marries authenticity conditions with competence conditions in roughly the way I've described, an autonomous act is one that is determined by or expressive of the agent's true self, and the desires or values that are expressed in the act count as the agent's own because she has exercised due control over the contours of her self—through, for example, the exercise of critical reflection and other related competencies. If O'Brien has adopted (or, better, reflectively endorsed) a narrative in which she is cast as a caring and respectful advocate for young women, it can easily look as though her refusal to remove the Norplant is a classically *non*-autonomous act, precisely because it does not express who she truly is. We might say she is "not herself" when she does it or (less colloquially) that her act is not expressive of her "true self". But one lesson we should draw, both from Jones's work on trajectory dependence and from Nelson's anecdote, is that it would be a mistake to think that even a robustly self-narrating version of O'Brien has a self that is determinate enough, at the time of implantation, to count as "true." The lack of fit between O'Brien's later refusal and her prior self-understanding is not necessarily indicative of a failure of self-expression; it might instead retroactively determine the inaccuracy of her earlier would-be self-constituting narrative. With respect to properties that are trajectory dependent, a narrative self-interpretation does not generally have enough determinacy to serve as the litmus test for the autonomy of an act.

I recognize that defenders of narrative self-constitution do not suppose that just any self-narrative, no matter how fanciful, can successfully constitute a self. Self-narratives must meet various constraints, including "reality" constraints described by Nelson, Marya Schectman, Kim Atkins (2008), and others. But the key point of the foregoing discussion still stands: since reality itself is such that many important properties, including properties of our own acts and characters, are trajectory dependent, reality constraints will not give any particular time-slice of the narratively determined self the kind of stability it needs to ground the "true self" picture of autonomy sketched out earlier. To return to Lloyd's insightful formulations, we might well exercise a special kind of freedom in imposing narrative necessities on ourselves, but (paradoxically) those necessities are only provisional.

Whereas Lloyd wants to mark a contrast between the older, Stoic notion of freedom and the modern notion of freedom as autonomy, I think we can develop a more adequate understanding of autonomy itself by thinking through the implications of this paradox. We need a picture of autonomy that represents a more stable reconciliation of the ancient urge for necessity and the modern desire for control. Such a picture must come to grips with the limitations of both and must be focused squarely on our plight as agents who must come to grips with these same limitations.

4. AUTONOMY AS ANSWERABILITY

Again, my point is not that we should entirely eschew autobiographical narration. On the contrary, I argue that we need to rethink the concept of autonomy in light of the conundrum posed by our practical need to self-narrate. One aim of the chapter has been to suggest that the impulse to autobiography arises from a very real problem about meaning in our lives: sometimes the meaning of what we feel and do is indeterminate on its own, and we cannot make sense of it without putting it into some sort of wider interpretive frame. Self-narration serves both a backward-looking and forward-looking function in our lives. Looking back (like the autobiographer who recounts his childhood with a view to what comes later), we seek to articulate the meaning of past choices and actions in terms of their place in a narratively structured whole. This understanding is something we seem to value for its own sake, quite apart from questions of further actions we might take. We value it, perhaps, because it can help us understand our own lives as meaningful in the sense that Susan Wolf (2010), for example, has recently tried to cash out: it may help us to identify (if only tenuously) ways in which our lives have been organized around positive engagement with things of value.

Taking an autobiographical perspective can also affect our view of things looking forward, since different narrative frames will cast the options before us in different lights. The much-discussed example of Gauguin abandoning his family to paint in Tahiti helps to illustrate this point. It is hard to imagine how we would make major, life-changing decisions at all without imposing some interpretive framework or other, and where we confront trajectory dependence, the framework we impose will naturally be narrative in form.

When Gauguin makes a choice that will only seem sensical in the narrative in which he in fact goes on to paint great works, he takes a leap of faith. He is "following" a script that may or may not come to have any plausible application to his life. On one possible trajectory, what he does will count as positive engagement with things of value, whereas on another, it will simply count as senseless self-indulgence. All we can do, having made such leaps, is to do our best to make things turn out in one way rather than another. We will be more likely to succeed to the extent that we are committed to the narrative in question—if we hold too much back, or keep too keen an eye on our exit options, we will not be doing what we set out to do. But if we allow ourselves to be *too* fully taken in by our own self-narrations, we will lose our ability to respond to mismatches between the narratives we project for ourselves and the ones that actually seem to be unfolding around us. And we may lose our ability to see other ways in which the narratives we draw on are problematic, even when there is no obvious mismatch.

When we engage in autobiographical narration, we commit ourselves to a narrative framework that gives our choices, actions, and so on a particular meaning. The commitment itself is not externally necessitated, and the narrative necessities that follow in the wake of the commitment are thus contingent necessities. When events unfold in ways that challenge the narratives to which we have committed ourselves, we have a responsibility to rethink our commitments. When we are confronted—by other agents or our own unruly experiences—with evidence that our narratives and the commitments they embody are indefensible, constraining, distorting, or otherwise problematic, we again have a responsibility to rethink them. Taking on this responsibility, I believe, is the crux of autonomy. Autonomy, so to speak, is a matter of responsible engagement with (contingent) necessity.

What exactly this means will need much more fleshing out than I can manage here. But I want to emphasize a few points that may help to motivate and clarify the basic idea. First: It is a perfectly harmless (and, in fact, helpful) platitude that autonomy means self-governance. But we needn't think that being self-governed is a matter of being governed by some entity that counts as one's "self." Indeed, work by Lloyd, Jones, and Nelson helps to show why this idea is implausible—to the extent that selves are made up at least in part by trajectory-dependent properties, they don't always have the kind of determinacy required to do the governing. To be self-governing might instead be understood as a matter of occupying the deliberative perspective in a certain way, acknowledging that in the matter of which commitments to accept and retain, there is no higher authority—and no authoritatively "deeper" self—to which we may simply defer. This reading of "self-governance" places more emphasis on the activity of governing than it does on the idea of self, reading the prefix "self-" as marking a reflexive relation rather than as naming a determinate entity that (so to speak) gets to throw its weight around when we decide and act.

Second: governing oneself is plausibly an activity that requires us to commit ourselves in various ways, as well as to take ongoing responsibility for those commitments. We commit ourselves to act when we form intentions, and these commitments are themselves guided by other commitments—to policies, values, desires, narrative frameworks, or what have you. While we cannot and should not always hold our commitments at arm's length, ongoing responsibility for these commitments does require sensitivity to reasons for doubting their adequacy or acceptability. This requires what I've described elsewhere as an attitude of answerability for our action-guiding commitments. When some of our commitments come in narrative form, this attitude translates into a readiness to distance ourselves (as needed) from our own narratives, to recognize their provisional nature, and to entertain alternatives or "counterstories."

Indeed, this picture places the concept of counternarration relatively close to the center of the concept of autonomy. Note, however, that on the view I've been sketching out here, it is not adoption of a *specific* counterstory that constitutes an agent as (now, perhaps for the first time) autonomous, though it is perhaps what gives her life new meaning. Nor is it even precisely the *telling* of the story. Rather, our autonomy is the background self-relation in virtue of which we are disposed to question, challenge, and potentially replace one narrative with another.

Autonomy thus understood does not guarantee success in telling our own stories, especially when social conditions are not favorable. Indeed, it takes a special brand of moral courage to claim a story as one's own against a master narrative that seems to leave no space for it. In telling a counterstory, one trades acceptance of a (apparent) necessity for the gamble that one can create new possibilities, a gamble that may or may not pay off in the freedom to write a sentence in the story of one's life. Nor can one avoid risk by opting for a Spinozistic embrace of the way things are, for the attempt to meaningfully recast oneself within the constraints of one's situation might not succeed, either. Self-governance in the face of such uncertainty cannot amount to self-expression in action. Instead, it requires the ability to selectively distance or alienate ourselves from narratives that we might otherwise be tempted to regard as rigidly self-constituting and is characterized by an attitude of ongoing openness to other narrative possibilities.

It might seem as though we've drifted a long way from the opening story about the girl in *A Book* who decides she must write her own story. But I have, in the end, embraced a kind of connection between autonomy and self-authorship. It is not the straightforward connection with which I began: my view is not that autonomy and self-authorship are the same thing or that one is autonomous just in virtue of being the author of one's own life. Rather, the idea is that the autonomous agent must recognize and accept responsibility for her self-authoring activities—for her role, that is, in the imposition of narrative necessities on her own life. The girl in *A Book* finds an elegant way of doing just that. She learns that no story is authoritative for her in and of itself, in the absence of her acceptance of its interpretive motifs. This might have left her hopelessly uncertain how to proceed. But instead she renders her experience meaningful precisely by incorporating it into a narrative of her own—a narrative, moreover, that builds in awareness of her own "authorial" role in resolving narrative uncertainty.

Of course, if she did not live in a book, her story would have to go on. She would be faced with exactly the same risks and rewards the rest of us face in narrating our lives and, along with those, the same responsibility for revising and "rewriting" her story as necessary. So I conclude on a note of ambiguity. I suspect it is true both that self-narration is a crucial means of making sense of our lives *and* that the fixity it seems to promise nonetheless eludes us. The autobiographical impulse responds to a form of indeterminacy that we cannot entirely overcome. Provisional sense making is the best we can do, and our autonomy might hinge in part on our appreciation of this very fact.

ACKNOWLEDGMENTS

This paper has benefitted from discussions at Lake Tahoe, Northwestern University, UC-Davis, and the University of Vermont. I am grateful to Marina Oshana for her helpful comments, and to the Brady Program in Ethics and Civic Life at Northwestern University for its generous support.

NOTES

1. I do not assume these terms are synonymous, but all three ideas appear in the literature on narrative agency.
2. Here I borrow Iris Marion Young's term "faces" of oppression (Young 2011). Though Young herself does not offer a narrative account of autonomy, she does identify a face of oppression that has to do with symbolic or cultural domination—and it is this face of oppression to which being constrained by a master narrative seems relevant.
3. It is possible, though, that Fischer is right that moral responsibility stands or falls with the kind of freedom he has in mind. I remain neutral on this question in this chapter.
4. To be fair, deciding that your story is the story of someone who becomes an *author* might get you a lot further. See Genevieve Lloyd's fascinating discussion of Sartre's autobiography, *Words*, in Lloyd 2008.
5. See Velleman (1996) and (2009).
6. Sometimes, particularly in circumstances of oppression, one has a particular end socially thrust upon one. But the authority of such a mandate, however difficult it may be to escape, is clearly contestable, and its imposition interferes with the freedom of the agent in the way that a calling or divine mandate intuitively would not.
7. Jones does not say exactly what she means by a practical identity, but given her use of the term, one might reasonably suppose that she has something like Christine Korsgaard's notion in mind. For Korsgaard, a practical identity is "a description under which you value yourself, a description under which you find your life to be worth living and your actions to be worth undertaking" (Korsgaard 1996, 101). Practical identities thus understood give rise to reasons and obligations for the agents who bear them. Jones's two examples, being a political activist and being queer, are consistent with this interpretation. Other examples given by Korsgaard herself include being a daughter, a mother, a friend, a philosopher, a Catholic, and more.
8. As Fischer himself points out, our behavior is subject to interpretation from a multiplicity of perspectives, and one's own perspective is not necessarily privileged relative to that of others (Fischer 2009, 8–9). Fischer's more carefully articulated view is that, when we act freely, we "constrain the plausible stories of our lives" (Fischer 2009, 9) without entirely eliminating defensible alternatives. For this reason, to have a general policy of treating one's own self-narratives as decisive would be a kind of mistake.
9. On the other hand, accepting an otherwise unwelcome event as though it were "meant to be" might sometimes be an instance of mere adaptive preference formation. The question of what distinguishes the adoption of a liberating narrative from the formation of an adaptive preference is one that merits more attention than I can give here. I would, however, argue that it depends on the agent's autonomy with respect to the narratives she adopts. Adaptive preferences are not autonomously held, but a narrative that imparts meaning to accidental events or features of one's circumstances might be. In this chapter, I argue that the autonomous agent must recognize the provisionality of her narrative self-understanding and hold herself answerable for embracing one narrative over alternatives that would cast her choices and actions in a different light. This sort of openness to reinterpretation would also, I think, distinguish her from the agent whose preferences have simply been adapted to her circumstances.
10. Although there is clearly some similarity between Lloyd's and Fischer's conceptions of the connection between freedom and self-narration, there are also

clearly some differences. Fischer's notion of freedom, for example, does not seem to involve the idea of engagement with necessity.

11. David Shoemaker follows in the Frankfurtian tradition, arguing that freedom consists in necessitation by one's cares along with reflective awareness of that necessitation. See Shoemaker 2003.

12. This is where the marriage between modern and ancient ideas can become uncomfortable: competence conditions seem designed to impose control of the content of the self in a way that doesn't necessarily sit comfortably with the idea of authenticity, which, as just described, sometimes seems to involve something more like the embrace of contingent necessities.

13. Again, the earlier story is not part of Nelson's original anecdote; I am hypothetically adding it in order, ultimately, to make a point about the relationship between autobiographical narrative and autonomy.

REFERENCES

Atkins, K. (2008). *Narrative identity and moral identity: A practical perspective.* New York: Routledge.

Atkins, K., & Mackenzie, C. (eds.). (2008). *Practical identity and narrative agency.* New York: Routledge.

Camp, E. (2011). Wordsworth's prelude, poetic autobiography, and narrative constructions of the self. *Nonsite* 3. http://nonsite.org/issues/issue-3/wordsworth%E2%80%99s-prelude-poetic-autobiography-and-narrative-constructions-of-the-self.

Fischer, John Martin. (1999). Responsibility and self-expression. *The Journal of Ethics.* 3 (4), 277–297.

Fischer, John Martin. (2005). Free will, death, and immortality: The role of narrative. *Philosophical Papers* 34 (3), 379–403.

Fischer, John Martin. (2009). Stories and the Meaning of Life. *Philosophic Exchange.* 39 (1), 2–15.

Jones, K. (2008). How to change the past. In K. Atkins & C. Mackenzie (Eds.), *Practical identity and narrative agency* (pp. 269–288). New York: Routledge.

Korsgaard, Christine. (1996). *The sources of normativity.* Cambridge: Cambridge University Press.

Lloyd, G. (2008). Shaping a life: Narrative, time and necessity. In K. Atkins & C. Mackenzie (Eds.), *Practical identity and narrative agency* (pp. 255–268). New York: Routledge.

Mink, Louis. (1970). History and fiction as modes of comprehension. *New Literary History.* 1 (3), 541–558.

Nelson, Hilde Lindemann. (1995). Resistance and Insubordination. *Hypatia.* 10 (2), 23–40.

Nelson, Hilde Lindemann. (2001). *Damaged identities, narrative repair.* Ithaca and London: Cornell University Press.

Shoemaker, David W. (2003). Caring, identification, and agency. *Ethics.* 114 (1), 88–118.

Velleman, J.D. (1996). Self to self. *The Philosophical Review.* 105 (1), 39–76.

Velleman, J.D. (2009). *How we get along.* Cambridge: Cambridge University Press.

Westlund, A. (2011). Narrative necessity and the fixity of meaning in a life. *Narrative Inquiry.* 21 (2), 391–398.

Wolf, Susan. (2010). *Meaning in life and why it matters.* Princeton and Oxford: Princeton University Press.

Young, Iris Marion. (2011). *Justice and the politics of difference.* Princeton and Oxford: Princeton University Press.

Part II

Practical Problems
The Internalization of Oppression
and Questions of Autonomy

6 "Living Constantly at Tiptoe Stance"
Social Scripts, Psychological Freedom, and Autonomy

Natalie Stoljar

INTRODUCTION

In *The Alchemy of Race and Rights*, Patricia Williams tells a story comparing her experience of leasing an apartment with that of a white male colleague when both are newly arrived in New York. The white male colleague does the deal verbally with a handshake. As a black woman, Williams feels that this option is not available to her because of a stereotypical perception of black women that she herself has (partially) internalized. She insists on a formal contract that sets out her and the lessor's obligations and rights:

> It turned out that Peter had handed over a $900 deposit in cash, with no lease, no exchange of keys and no receipt, to strangers with whom he had no ties other than a few moments of pleasant conversation. He said that he didn't need to sign a lease because it imposed too much formality. The handshake and the good vibes were for him indicators of trust more binding than a formal contract . . .
>
> I meanwhile had friends who found me an apartment in a building they owned. In my rush to show good faith and trustworthiness, I signed a detailed lengthily negotiated, finely printed lease establishing me as the ideal arm's-length negotiator . . .
>
> I was raised to be acutely conscious of the likelihood that no matter what degree of professional I am, people will greet and dismiss my Black femaleness as unreliable, untrustworthy, hostile, angry, powerless, irrational, and probably destitute. Futility and despair are very real parts of my response. So it helps me to clarify boundary; to show that I can speak the language of lease is my way of enhancing trust of me in my business affairs.
>
> (Williams 1992, pp. 146–147)

Patricia's case is a variant of Peter's—but where does the difference lie? Patricia and Peter are in the same situation, yet aspects of Patricia's self-conception are constrained in ways that Peter's are not. The negative "social meanings" of black womanness in the United States influence and indeed "script" her self-conception and her sense of the possibilities available to her (Appiah 1994, Oshana 2005, pp. 89–90). It has been suggested that oppressive social scripts undermine agents' autonomy. Marina Oshana argues that racist scripts "encumber a person in a fashion antithetical to autonomy. Being Black in a racist society situates one in a position that narrows the range of one's autonomy" (Oshana 2005, pp. 91–92). Diana Tietjens Meyers claims that "the dominant system of tropes, mythic tales, and pictorial images that encode the various meanings of womanhood and norms applying to women in the United States today . . . suffuses women's voices and undercuts their self-determination" (Meyers 2002, p. 25). If these authors are right, Williams's capacity for and exercise of self-government—her ability to organize her life according to rules that she adopts for herself and to effectively execute her life-plans—is eroded by comparison with that of Peter due to the social script that applies to her.

One might be tempted to reply that Williams's reaction to the racist script is merely a feature of her particular psychology. Perhaps Williams is ambivalent about the norms that apply to her (whereas Peter is not), or perhaps she is especially sensitive to others' perceptions of her or especially cautious (whereas Peter is not). On these purely psychological explanations, Williams's response of inner turmoil to the historical norms of African-American femaleness is unfortunate or unlucky; she is not *morally* worse off due to her own self-conception.[1] This diagnosis, however, does not capture the fact that Williams's self-conception seems to be distorted by the racist script in a morally problematic way.[2] Despite her resistance to the norms articulated in the racist script, it is "internalized" and indeed partially constitutive of her self-conception. A goal of this chapter is to argue that self-conceptions due to oppressive scripts undermine the *psychological freedom* that is necessary for autonomy.[3] In so doing, I aim to show that the importance of psychological freedom conditions and the ways in which they depend on social features of the world have been very much underestimated. For instance, although autonomy theorists pay lip service to psychological freedom conditions, the possible impediments to psychological freedom are understood in a very narrow sense. Either agents' deliberation must be free from some standard list of pathologies such as obsession, depression, or psychosis, or it must be free from coercion by some other agent or agents. I aim to show that, in addition, features of *social* reality can reduce a person's autonomy by undermining her psychological freedom.

Section 1 of the chapter identifies four (types of) necessary conditions of autonomy that have been offered by autonomy theorists: *authenticity* conditions, *external* moral or social conditions, *psychological freedom* conditions, and *competency* conditions. In Section 2, I turn to the literature proposing that authenticity is a necessary condition of autonomy. Drawing on examples from this literature, I argue that Williams's decision to opt for a formal contract reflects her "true" self and hence is authentic. It is not a lack of authenticity that explains how the racist script burdens her autonomy. Section 3 addresses Marina Oshana's social-relational theory. Oshana proposes a requirement of autonomy of "practical control" that can be undermined by certain external social conditions. I claim that Williams and Peter are on a par with respect to the external social-relational conditions offered on Oshana's account. Their practical control over their lives is parallel and, hence, the difference between Williams and Peter is *not* due to external social-relational conditions that undermine practical control. Rather, as I propose in section 4, Williams's autonomy is impaired because the oppressive social script interferes with her will and undermines her *psychological freedom*. I argue that Williams has internalized the script despite not endorsing the oppressive norms embedded in it. Oppressive social scripts are internalized and interfere with psychological freedom in three related ways. First, even if agents do not endorse the script, they *adapt* their decision making and behavior to it; second, they are called on to *take an evaluative stance* to the norms embedded in the script; third, they must *respond to and disavow* the script to see themselves and be seen as equal participants in their daily transactions with others. Agents such as Williams are therefore subject not only to harms of racial stigmatization and negative stereotyping; they are subject also to the deeper harm of autonomy impairment.

1. FOUR NECESSARY CONDITIONS OF AUTONOMY

Four (types of) necessary conditions of autonomy have been proposed in the autonomy literature: *authenticity* conditions, social or moral *external* conditions, *competency* conditions, and *psychological freedom* conditions. Different theorists attempt to develop sufficient conditions for autonomy out of some combination of these necessary conditions. For example, John Christman proposes that authenticity—understood as hypothetical nonalienation—and competency are necessary and sufficient for autonomy. An important controversy is over whether autonomy should be defined using only the internal and psychological notions that seem to be sufficient for authenticity or whether an adequate account of autonomy needs to employ external moral or social conditions as well. I do not here attempt to resolve this debate, to develop sufficient conditions of autonomy, or even to evaluate whether the proffered necessary conditions are in fact necessary.[4] My focus is rather on whether Williams's situation violates one or more necessary conditions. In this section, I briefly sketch the contours of the different necessary conditions.

There has been considerable emphasis since the work of Harry Frankfurt and Gerald Dworkin on analyzing autonomy using some notion of authenticity.[5] Indeed, it has been said that authentic self-constitution is the "core" of the notion of autonomy (Christman &Anderson 2005, p. 3). Authenticity theories are often "identity based;" that is, an action is defined as authentically belonging to the agent when it is "appropriately related to [her] *identity*" (Benson 2005, p. 103). Thus, on authenticity accounts, authentic choices and actions are those issuing from the agent's identity or "true self," and if choices and actions do not issue from the agent's true self or identity—if they are inauthentic—they are not autonomous.[6]

Theories that offer some version of the second set of necessary conditions—external conditions—set aside the identity-based analysis. Instead of focusing on the kind of *self* that is necessary for autonomy, these theories focus on the necessary conditions of self-*rule*. For instance, Oshana claims that constraining external social-relational conditions potentially undermine the "practical control" required for self-rule (Oshana 2006); other proposals are derived from the Kantian idea that effectively ruling oneself requires that the reasons that one applies to oneself as an autonomous agent must correspond in relevant ways to external morality (e.g., Superson 2005).

The third and fourth sets of necessary conditions of autonomy are competency and psychological freedom conditions. John Christman defines competency as the ability to form intentions that are "effective" and as composed of "rationality, self-control, freedom from psychosis and other pathologies, and the like" (Christman 2005, p. 278, 2009, p. 155;). I will here restrict competency to rationality and the ability to form effective intentions and use the term "psychological freedom" to designate freedom from different kinds of interference with the will. Traditionally, psychological freedom has comprised freedom from pathology-related interference with the will, such as obsession or compulsion, *and* freedom from agent-related interference with the will, such as manipulation, coercion, and deception. Psychological freedom requires the "freedom to will otherwise," which both pathology and coercion or manipulation rule out. Persons cannot have freedom of the will when their will could not be otherwise, or, in other words, when their will is "shaped by necessity" (Elster 1992, p. 228). As Frankfurt puts it:

> A person's will is free only if he is free to have the will he wants. This means that, with regard to any of his first order desires, he is free to make that desire his will or to make some other first-order desire his will instead. Whatever his will, then, the will of the person whose will is free could have been otherwise: he could have done otherwise than to constitute his will as he did.
>
> (Frankfurt 1988, p. 24)

In Frankfurt's famous example, neither a willing nor an unwilling addict has freedom to will otherwise—neither has *psychological freedom*—because, due to their addiction, they cannot but desire the drug. The willing addict, however, has a special kind of freedom that the unwilling addict lacks, namely the freedom that is generated by his "identification" with the desire for the drug.[7] As a result of his endorsement of the addiction, the willing addict in effect constitutes himself as an addict and hence makes authentically his own what would otherwise be external to him. Nevertheless, the willing addict is less free than someone who is not driven by addiction because addiction removes his freedom to constitute his will other than as an addict.

2. AUTHENTICITY

The last section identified four types of necessary conditions of autonomy: *authenticity*, *external*, *competency*, and *psychological freedom* conditions. I now turn to an examination of authenticity conditions. By considering three examples of authenticity theories, I show that Williams's decision to act as an arm's-length negotiator counts as authentic, despite the damage to her self-conception due to the social script. Hence the script does not violate the authenticity condition of autonomy.

Consider first the position that authenticity and hence autonomy require active affirmation or endorsement of one's deeply held commitments and concerns. Marilyn Friedman argues that being autonomous requires "self-reflective affirmation" with respect to one's preferences and values. Through a process of critical affirmation (and reaffirmation), preferences and values become a person's *own*: "When someone reflectively reaffirms wants and values that are important to her . . . they become part of the perspective that defines her as the particular person she is. They embody the 'nomos' of her self. . ." (Friedman 2003, p. 6). Meyers proposes that an authentic self emerges when a person actively exercises the "agentic skills" that characterize autonomous people. She writes that "autonomous people exercise a repertoire of skills to engage in self-discovery, self-definition and self-direction, and that the authentic self is the evolving collocation [sic] of attributes that emerges in this ongoing process of reflection, deliberation and action" (Meyers 2005, p. 49). The relevant skills include those of introspection, imagination, communication, and memory (Meyers 2002, p. 20).

On Meyers's account, oppressive social conditions and oppressive socialization can erode autonomy skills or fail to promote the agent's exercise of these skills. For example, gendered "motherhood" scripts prescribe not only that women should adopt certain gendered norms of motherhood but also portray childless women as failures and unable to attain true self-fulfillment. Meyers thinks that acceptance of the ideology recommending motherhood and linking it to flourishing is in effect accepting a script that impedes women's autonomy. Her remedy is that women exercise the skills that constitute autonomy competency to dislodge this script: "patriarchal noise can overwhelm women's voices and choices," but autonomy skills "endow women with the capacity to fashion self-portraits and self-narratives in their own voices and to lead their own lives" (Meyers 2002, p. 32).

It seems, however, that Williams is both acting on concerns and values that are deeply important to her and manifesting a high degree of autonomy competency. In demanding a formal contract, she is acting on a wish that others see her as trustworthy and reliable, and hence her decision is authentic in Friedman's sense. Moreover, it is implausible that Williams does not exhibit autonomy competency; she is skilled in all dimensions of introspection, imagination, communication, memory, and so forth. She is quite aware of the patriarchal and racist noise, yet her high degree of autonomy competency cannot quell it completely because the social script that is applied to her manifests itself in her self-conception whether she likes it or not. Thus, on the views of Friedman and Meyers that require respectively active affirmation of deeply held values and active exercise of autonomy skills, it would be implausible to treat Williams as inauthentic.

John Christman's authenticity condition is weaker. It does not require endorsement or an active exercise of autonomy competency but rather a lack (or counterfactual lack) of what he terms "alienation." Alienation is a "combination of judgment and affective reaction. To be alienated is to feel negative affect, to feel repudiation and resistance. . ." (Christman 2009, p. 144). Christman proposes that an agent is authentic with respect to a particular preference or commitment, if, were she to critically reflect on the historical processes or autobiographical narrative leading to the formation of the preference or commitment, she would not be alienated from it (Christman 2009, pp. 155–156). If one is (or would be) alienated from a preference or commitment after the right kind of self-reflection but does not succeed in repudiating it, one is heteronomous with respect to that preference or commitment.

Williams certainly exhibits the psychological characteristics of alienation: she experiences resistance and negative affect in response to the stereotype of black femaleness as dishonest and untrustworthy, and she is trying to distance herself from it. The alienation is followed by the repudiation of the stereotype and the decision to present herself as an arm's-length negotiator. There are two possible responses within Christman's theory to the presence of such alienation, depending on whether we characterize his test as local or global. If it is the former, the question is whether Williams's local decision to present herself as an arm's-length negotiator is authentic. Since the decision is a successful attempt to resist the stereotype and its goal is to portray herself as an honest and trustworthy professional, she seems locally authentic relative to this decision, despite being alienated from some of the considerations leading up to it. If, however, Christman's test is global, alienation from a characteristic within one's self-conception would render the *agent* rather than merely the decision inauthentic and non-autonomous. As Oshana has pointed out, this latter position would prove too much (Oshana 2005, p. 93). Alienation, namely, feelings of resistance and negative affect as well as a judgment that an offending state should be repudiated, is an all-too-common feature of people's psychological makeup. It is implausible that agent autonomy is cancelled out whenever alienation occurs. We must assume, therefore, that Christman's test is a local test. Considering only the authenticity criterion, it follows that in the lease transaction, Williams is as autonomous as Peter.

3. EXTERNAL SOCIAL CONDITIONS

The key criterion of autonomy discussed in the last section is that of constituting a true or authentic self. An alternative approach focuses on *control* rather than *authenticity*. Oshana claims that "We correctly attribute autonomy to a person when the person has de facto power and authority to direct affairs of elemental importance to her life within a framework of rules (or values, principles, beliefs, pro-attitudes) that she has set for herself" (Oshana 2007, p. 411). Autonomy is not a matter of authentic self-constitution but rather of being free to manage one's life as one sees fit. For Oshana, no matter the degree of subjective self-realization or subjective endorsement of their situation, agents living under constraining external "social-relational" conditions have limited autonomy. According to Oshana, the required social-relational conditions are twofold: first, that agents have options that allow them to develop their capabilities and second, that they have "substantive independence," or "security from arbitrary social control" (Oshana 2006, p. 85). She writes:

> The social background, where this includes social institutions, [must be] such that the person can determine how she shall live in a context of at least minimal social and psychological security. The minimum level of security necessary for autonomy is whatever it takes for an individual to shield herself against (or be shielded against) and to challenge the arbitrary attempts of others to deprive her of . . . de facto and de jure power.
> (Oshana 2006, p. 86)

Consider the example of African-American men who are subject to arbitrary stop-and-search policies. Due to racial profiling, the interference by police in their daily activities is potentially much more significant than it is for their white counterparts. To protect themselves from the prospect of such interference, they might become accustomed to exercising "constant vigilance," by, for example, avoiding areas in which it is unusual to see black drivers (Oshana 2006, p. 88). These men are not necessarily subject to *actual* external constraints. They nevertheless lack autonomy because they are not secure from interference. They are vulnerable to "domination" as a result of the existence of external social constraints that could be applied arbitrarily at any time to constrain their freedom.[8] Thus, on Oshana's account, external social-relational conditions interfere with autonomy when they interfere with agents' security and hence their practical control over daily aspects of their lives.

Note that Oshana's account is global not local. Her theory provides an analysis of the conditions of autonomy conceived as a state of an agent over time rather than that of the conditions under which an agent's particular preferences are autonomous. Agents can lack global autonomy—for example, when they are living under conditions of slavery—but may nevertheless seem to display local autonomy at particular times or in particular restricted domains of their lives (cf. Benson 1991). It seems, however, that Williams exemplifies the converse case. The *condition or state* that Williams inhabits is *not* plausibly one of (global) heteronomy. Like Peter, Williams is a highly educated person who has had the opportunity to develop her capabilities. She also has the same external options as Peter in this particular case; there are no external conditions that would inhibit her from adopting an informal approach to the agreement. Moreover, it seems that her substantive independence is intact. There is no quasi-institutional or external social power being exerted over her that undermines her security from arbitrary interference in her decision making. She and Peter are on a par with respect to the substantive independence condition, and both have sufficient practical control over their lives to meet the threshold of global autonomy. However, it appears that Williams's decision to act as an arm's-length negotiator is prima facie less *locally* autonomous than that of Peter because it is constrained by a racially scripted self-conception. Thus here we have an example of an agent who on Oshana's account is globally autonomous yet who in many aspects of her life does not count as locally autonomous. Although Oshana herself claims that racist scripts "encumber and narrow the range of agents' autonomy" (Oshana 2005, p. 92), it is not clear how this is explained using the resources of her own view.

4. PSYCHOLOGICAL FREEDOM

I argued in the previous section that Oshana's view is underinclusive because it does not provide an account of the apparent impairments of autonomy in agents like Williams who have practical control over their daily routines yet whose wills are often constrained by distorted self-conceptions that are due to oppressive scripts. In this section, I propose that distorted self-conceptions undermine autonomy because they are impairments of psychological freedom. Oppressive social scripts are "internalized" or manifest themselves in the psychologies of members of oppressed groups in a way that is analogous to standard impediments to psychological freedom. Like pathological and agent-related impediments, social scripts interfere with the agent's freedom to will otherwise. I first explain that it is the *interrelation* between the social and the psychological that is left out of Oshana's account and that is responsible for the impairment of psychological freedom in Williams's example. I then develop the argument that oppressive scripts undermine psychological freedom.

Although I have suggested that Oshana's theory is underinclusive, it is more common to argue that it is overinclusive. For instance, Robert Noggle claims that, although Oshana's account seems an apt explanation of certain intuitions, there are others that seem to run counter to it. On her account, constraining external conditions *ipso facto* undermine autonomy. But consider figures such as Rosa Parks, Martin Luther King Jr., or Nelson Mandela. These figures articulated and acted on life-projects that were dedicated to resistance to the oppression to which they were subjected. Noggle suggests that they provide counterexamples to Oshana's view. He claims that their status as resistors indicates that they are engaged in self-rule despite the external impediments to which they were subjected (Noggle 2011).

I do not believe that Noggle's objection is decisive. The intuition that a life of resistance is an autonomous life assumes that when one authentically constitutes oneself as a resistor, this is sufficient for autonomy. However, assuming for the sake of argument that authenticity is a necessary condition of autonomy, there is reason to think that it is not sufficient. Even theorists who propose that authenticity is the core of autonomy introduce additional conditions. For Friedman, self-reflective affirmation is necessary but not sufficient for autonomy; she adds that self-reflection "must be relatively unimpeded by conditions, such as coercion, deception and manipulation" (Friedman 2003, p. 14). Similarly, Christman claims that autonomy can be undermined if the agent's reflection is distorted in some way, for instance, by "constriction, pathology or manipulation" or "being denied minimal education and exposure to alternatives" (Christman 2009, pp. 147, 155). Although it is not fully clear on these theories how these additional conditions are to be spelled out, and in particular whether spelling them out would require the introduction of moral criteria,[9] it is possible that people subject to apartheid or Jim Crow laws would not meet these additional conditions. Thus, even on these standard authenticity theories, the autonomy of agents living under institutions of subordination could be called into question.

Noggle's objection does bring to light a feature of Oshana's theory that may be problematic: on her account, two agents whose psychologies are identical could in principle differ in their status as autonomous agents. This may suggest that Oshana's social-relational conditions would more appropriately be considered conditions of negative freedom, not conditions for autonomy.[10] Although her account offers both psychological and external social-relational conditions of autonomy,[11] it seems to leave out the potential threat to autonomy from the *interrelation* between the social and the psychological that is captured in Williams's description of the social meaning of racist scripts. Martin Luther King Jr. vividly captures this aspect of Jim Crow in his "Letter from Birmingham Jail": ". . . you are harried by day and haunted by night by the fact that you are a Negro, living constantly at tiptoe stance, never quite knowing what to expect next, . . . plagued with inner fears and outer resentments; . . . you are forever fighting a degenerating sense of 'nobodiness. . .'"[12] The examples from Williams and King suggest that it is not external conditions *per se* that impair autonomy. Rather, the pernicious manifestation of oppression in agents' psychologies is incompatible with their enjoying the same degree of autonomy as agents who are not oppressed. Moreover, King's description of the psychological damage that results from living under Jim Crow counters Noggle's intuition that activists who are committed to resistance are autonomous notwithstanding the social conditions to which they are subjected. King's commitment to a life's work of resistance may have rendered him authentic, but he was not thereby autonomous.

The additional conditions mentioned by Friedman and Christman are *psychological freedom conditions*. As we saw in section 2, the standard lists of impediments to psychological freedom include the pathological, such as compulsions and obsessions, and coercion and manipulation due to the activities of other agents. The impediments that arise from oppressive social scripts do not fall neatly into either of these categories. Many agents whose self-conceptions are distorted by oppressive scripts are, like Williams herself, highly self-reflective and psychologically competent. There are no internal, pathological impediments to self-reflection present in these cases. Further, oppressive social scripting is often a form of *structural* oppression: there is no agent or "oppressing group" that intends and is directly responsible for the oppression (Haslanger 2004; Young 1990, pp. 38–39). In the United States, decades after Jim Crow and institutionally authorized segregation were dismantled, African-Americans as a group are still systematically disadvantaged by racist stereotypes and racial segregation that is due to entrenched social practices (Anderson 2010). However, since there is no identifiable agent or group that is responsible for these entrenched practices, the systematic disadvantage cannot be the result of simple coercion. I propose, therefore, that we need a richer conception of the impediments to psychological freedom that focuses precisely on the interrelation between the social and the psychological. Despite King's status as a resistor, and despite Williams's repudiation of the racist norms of black femaleness, in situations in which they confront negative stereotypes and oppressive constraints, their free agency is burdened and their autonomy is diminished. These situations may be local to particular times or domains, or they may apply across time and domain and hence be persisting and systematic constraints that threaten to undermine not only local but global autonomy as well.

Williams's eloquent description of the phenomenology of a black woman in a racist world expresses the interrelation between the third-person script of black womanness and Williams's first-person response to this script. Theorists of oppression have labeled this phenomenon "double consciousness," or "the sense of always looking at one's self through the eyes of others" (Du Bois 1994/1903, p. 2).[13] The first-person perspective of the subordinated is always infused by the third-person ideology of oppression, by the external perspective of the dominant class that leads to the "degenerating sense of nobodiness" described by King. This suggests that agents who are subordinated cannot simply repudiate the dominant social scripts that are applied to them. As Iris Marion Young puts it, "the dominant culture's stereotyped and inferiorized images of the [subordinated] group must be internalized by group members at least to the extent that they are forced to react to behavior of others influenced by those images" (Young 1990, p. 55).

Yet there is a tendency in some literature, including some feminist literature on autonomy, to draw a sharp distinction between third-person ascriptions of identity and the agent's first-person responses to them. For example, Friedman distinguishes between *perspectival* identity, the identity that one embraces and attributes to oneself from the first-person perspective, and *trait-based* identity that is ascribed to agents by third-person social classifications (Friedman 2003, pp. 10–11). In her work on feminist metaphysics, Charlotte Witt adopts a parallel distinction between *persons* and *social individuals* and correspondingly between *voluntarist* and *ascriptivist* accounts of social normativity (Witt 2011, p. 43). Persons can voluntarily accept the norms associated with the social roles they occupy and in virtue of which they are social individuals. In this sense, the norms of social agency are "voluntarist;" people impose these norms on themselves. However, even if people reject the norms associated with a certain role, or indeed, even if they are not conscious of these norms, social normativity can be *ascribed*. For instance, to be a mother, an agent must be "recognized by others as occupying the social position of being a mother, and by virtue of that occupancy, to be placed under the umbrella of a set of maternal norms" (Witt 2011, p. 62). Social normativity is therefore also "ascriptivist;" it "attaches to the social position occupancy itself," and social individuals are "responsive to . . . and evaluable by" the maternal or other norms associated with their social role (Witt 2011, p. 43). But ascribed norms become ethical standards for the *person* and play a role in the agent's self-conception or "practical identity" only if the agent endorses them from a first-person perspective.[14]

Two conclusions may seem to follow from these distinctions: first, that the construction of a self-conception is a purely first-personal, voluntaristic process, which implies that agents can wholly repudiate the third-person conceptions of identity that are applied to them; and second, that a third-person script is not internalized as part of the agent's first-person self-conception unless it is *endorsed*. In what follows, I reject both of these possible conclusions.

Consider first whether there is a sharp distinction between third-person and first-person conceptions of identity that would allow persons autonomously to reject the social classifications and associated meanings that are applied to them. As others have pointed out, there are aspects of self-conception that agents simply find themselves with.[15] These are not the product of voluntary choice or self-reflective endorsement. Moreover, it is unlikely that all these discovered aspects of self-conception can be relinquished or repudiated (Oshana 2005, pp. 89–90). Oshana has suggested that gender and race are what she calls "circumstantial necessities," or inescapable aspects of one's self-conception: "race is very much an inescapable component . . . We cannot escape the racialized norms that define us, and that inform our self-concept, even where we regard these norms as alien. Consciously or not, welcome or not, one's racialized identity contravenes upon most aspects of one's self-conception" (Oshana 2005, p. 90).

Oshana is referring to the epistemological difficulty of divorcing one's sense of self from the racialized and gendered identities that are imposed on one. More strongly, Robert Gooding-Williams argues that having a racialized self-conception at all (having a racialized first-person perspective) *requires* that the agent take up the relevant third-person racial classification (Gooding-Williams 1988). Although one is ascribed a third-person trait-based identity when one is classified by society as black, one becomes a "black person" and has a racialized self-conception as black only when this third-person classification is incorporated into the first-person perspective. Drawing on Ian Hacking's dynamic nominalism, Gooding-Williams suggests that the transition from being classified as black to being a black person occurs when "individuals classified as black . . . begin to act in the world under a description of themselves as racially black . . . [when our] . . . sense of ourselves and of the possibilities existing for us" are a function of these descriptions (Gooding-Williams 1988, p. 23). There is often a moment in the lives of members of subordinated groups when the person encounters the stark social reality of the subordinating classification that applies to her. From that moment on, her self-conception includes a recognition that identifying as black (or as a woman) is not morally neutral but rather requires applying the descriptions and inferiorizing norms that are conventionally associated with the classification to *oneself*. Thus, agents who consider their identities to be racialized (or gendered) cannot entirely repudiate the oppressive social scripts that apply to them because the scripts are partially constitutive of these very self-conceptions.

Racialized and gendered self-conceptions, the first-person perspectives *as black* or *as a woman*, are shaped by the social meanings of race and gender. The intersubjective social scripts are internalized or incorporated into the agent's psychology. These observations raise the second question I want to address, namely whether internalization requires that agents *endorse* these scripts. I argue that it does not; even when the negative aspects of social scripts are repudiated, the script shapes the agent's self-conception. Her sense of herself and of the possibilities open to her, and her plans, preference formation, and life choices, are to some extent a function of the script.

Internalization has been taken to require at least that the contents of the agent's beliefs and desires correspond to the content of the social script. For instance, in her analysis of oppression, Ann E. Cudd contrasts *indirect* and *direct* psychological harms of oppression. Direct harms are due to the intentional activities of an oppressor group, whereas indirect harms are generated within the psychology of the oppressed themselves: they "occur when the beliefs and values of the privileged or oppressor groups are subconsciously accepted by the subordinate and assimilated into their self-concept or value/belief scheme" (Cudd 2006, p. 176). The distorted self-conceptions that we have discussed are candidates for being indirect psychological harms of oppression. However, on Cudd's account, the harm occurs because the content of agents' mental states mirrors the content of the oppressive script. The paradigms of indirect psychological harms of oppression are shame, false consciousness, and deformed desire (Cudd 2006, pp. 176–183). For instance, members of oppressed groups can feel shame purely for the "entirely externally imposed reason that they have less status because of their social group membership" (Cudd 2006, p. 176). For such agents, the content of the mental state, being ashamed, corresponds to the attribution of low status to them. Such agents are ashamed *of* their low status. Similarly, in the examples of false consciousness and deformed desire respectively, agents believe the norms implicit in the ideology of oppression (they believe that they have lower status) and come to have preferences that reinforce their own oppression (they desire their low status). In other words, psychological harms of oppression are internalized and hence indirect when the mental states of the oppressed agent reflect the content of the oppressive script.

Similarly, in the autonomy literature, internalization has been understood to entail that oppressed agents endorse and value the norms embedded in the script. Paul Benson characterizes internalization as a psychological state in which, as a result of oppressive socialization, agents come to value (and believe to be true) the false norms of the oppressive ideology (Benson 1991, pp. 388–389). For example, women who are subjected to traditional feminine socialization come to endorse norms that link appearance to self-worth. This conception of internalization has led to a debate among autonomy theorists over whether the content of what is valued should be included as a condition in the definition of autonomy. For instance, in early work, Benson argued that oppressive socialization undermines the *normative competence* that is necessary for autonomy. On his view, it is not the content of the belief or desire *per se* that impairs autonomy but rather the agent's diminished normative competence. However, normative competence is defined using a distinction between norms that are correct or incorrect relative to some intersubjective normative domain. Agents are normatively competent when they display the competency to deploy norms that are correct relative to some domain but lack competence when they systematically deploy incorrect norms. There are other accounts of autonomy that, like Benson's, employ a notion of internalization as endorsement. These claim, however, that it *is* the content of the agent's beliefs and desires *per se* that undermines autonomy. For instance, Anita Superson argues that deformed desires, or desires for one's own inferior moral status, are incompatible with autonomy because their content is immoral (Superson 2005).

If internalization requires that the agent believe in and value the content of the script, neither Williams nor resistors to oppression such as King would count as having internalized the oppressive scripts that are applied to them. Williams does not endorse the norms of black femaleness. King does not make the moral mistake of thinking that his own moral status and that of other black people is inferior to that of whites. If autonomy is undermined only by the agent's endorsement of the norms of the script, neither Williams nor King has impaired autonomy. I suggest, however, that there is a broader notion of internalization that does not require endorsement. Oppressive social scripts are embedded in agents' psychologies in ways that call for multiple psychological responses—for instance, anticipation, adjustment, accommodation, and evaluation—that are not typically required from agents to whom neutral or "dominant" scripts apply. Agents subject to oppressive scripts are "constantly at tiptoe stance." In the remainder of this section, I argue that oppressive scripts impair psychological freedom in three related areas: first, oppressive social scripts require that agents *adapt* themselves to the script even when they do not endorse it or desire it; second, the scripts demand that agents *respond to the evaluations* of them embedded in the script; and third, agents must respond to the script *to gain equal access to "cooperative interactions"* (Anderson 2010, p. 53).

First, consider the process of adaptation. As Young noticed, oppressive scripts are internalized by members of oppressed groups because "they are forced to react to behavior of others influenced by those images" (Young 1990, p. 55). They expect that others will adopt the script, so they worry about how to avoid it and plan how to react accordingly. For example, as a result of the script, Williams knows that there is a risk that others will see her "unreliable, untrustworthy, hostile, angry, powerless, irrational, and probably destitute." She expects and worries that the people she is dealing with will be influenced by the negative stereotypes that typically are applied to people like her. She forms plans and intentions on the basis of this expectation to try to counteract it. The script is embedded in many aspects of her mental life, and it becomes second nature for her to be constantly aware of the script and make constant efforts to block and circumvent it. Moreover, adaptation can occur even in the absence of conscious awareness of the script. Results from social psychology describing the phenomena of *stereotype threat* and *implicit bias* suggest that agents can be tacitly aware of oppressive social scripts and that this tacit awareness has concrete implications that are manifested in their behavior.[16] People subjected to oppressive scripts, therefore, adapt to them and internalize them despite often correctly believing that the norms of the script are false.

Second, when agents inhabit the social roles to which social scripts apply, they are automatically evaluable under the ascriptivist social normativity associated with the social role (Witt 2011). Someone who occupies the social role of mother is evaluable as a good or bad mother relative to the social norms of motherhood even if she rejects them. Because of the evaluations embedded in oppressive scripts, agents to whom the script applies are called on to take an "adjudicative" or evaluative stance to the script (Oshana 2005, p. 88). Indeed, the demand to take an adjudicative stance may be particularly pressing when agents repudiate the negative evaluations inherent in the script. Being a member of a group that is subject to inferiorizing or arbitrarily constraining norms demands not only that the agent repudiate the application of the norms to the group but also that she justify why the negative evaluations should not be applied in her particular case. In Williams's example, the fact that black women are evaluable under a set of negative stereotypes demands that she show that it is not justified that such evaluations apply *to her*. In addition, when agents subject to oppressive scripts want to diverge from the script, an adjudicative stance is required. Oshana points to the norms of decorum that are associated with being a black woman. She writes that "The African-American academic might be obliged to break away from the decorum expected of a black woman, if this decorum includes, say, eschewing scholarship on the work of colonial and postcolonial men, or foregoing intimate associations with white people" (Oshana 2005, p. 92). The academic here is implicitly called upon to justify her divergence from the norms associated with black femaleness. She is called upon to justify her divergence from the script.

Third, as Elizabeth Anderson has suggested, members of subordinated social groups have to counteract oppressive scripts to gain access as equals to cooperative interactions. She points out that in a racially segregated society, African-Americans live under "a cloud of suspicion in unstructured encounters with strangers":

> One late night in 2007 I was driving in Detroit when I my oil light came on. I pulled into the nearest gas station to investigate the problem when a young black man approached me to offer help. "Don't worry, I'm not here to rob you," he said, holding up his hands, palms flat at face level, gesturing his innocence. . . [N]otwithstanding the fact that I refused to apply the stereotype of the criminally violent black male to him, . . . [t]o gain access to cooperative interactions, he must assume the burden of dispelling this cloud, of protesting and proving his innocence of imagined crimes.
>
> (Anderson 2010, p. 53)

The man is called upon *by the script* (not by Anderson herself) to disavow the stereotype so that he both sees himself and is seen as an equal in the transaction with a white woman. Williams's case is similar: she disavows the script by showing that she can speak the language of lease, the language of a legal equal negotiating at arm's length. In so doing, she permits herself to gain access to the interaction as an equal.

The three aspects of internalization that I have described here, none of which requires that the agent endorse the norms of the script, are endemic to the psychologies of agents to whom oppressive social scripts apply. The internalization of oppressive social scripts significantly interferes with the agent's freedom to will otherwise (relative to agents who are not subject to oppressive scripts) and hence with their psychological freedom and autonomy.

CONCLUSION

I have attempted in this chapter to block the possible suggestion that the difference between Williams and her colleague Peter in their lease-signing transactions is an arbitrary matter of different psychological makeup. The differences between Williams's situation and that of Peter *are* psychological, but they are not *merely* psychological: they are also social, and, more importantly, *moral*. Williams's status as a fully autonomous agent is under threat due to the internalization—in the three senses described—of a social script that in turn undermines her psychological freedom. This is a significant problem for any conception of justice that prioritizes the right to autonomy. Members of oppressed groups suffer not only reputational harm and harm to equality but harm to autonomy as well.

ACKNOWLEDGMENTS

I am grateful to the participants in the Davis Workshop on Self-Government and Social Transformation in March 2012 for helpful comments and to Marina Oshana for her extensive feedback on a previous draft. Devon Kapoor provided valuable research assistance.

NOTES

1. As a member of an oppressed group, Williams may be in a relatively worse moral position due to other factors as well. For instance, she may have restricted equality of opportunity or suffer harm to reputation. Elizabeth Anderson argues that racial stigmatization constitutes public dishonoring and reputational harm (Anderson 2010, p. 55).
2. Susan Babbitt also argues that self-conceptions can be distorted by oppression. For example, she claims that someone whose sense of self is defined by habitual servility will not form preferences or make choices that are in her objective interests. Such an agent would have to undergo a "conversion" in her sense of self to ensure that her preferences correspond with her true interests (Babbitt 1993). To the extent that Babbitt's position implies an account of autonomy, it claims that preferences are autonomous only if their content corresponds to what is truly in the agent's interests. Hence, for Babbitt, distorted self-conceptions violate an external moral condition on autonomy, not a psychological freedom condition.
3. Although here I restrict myself to a discussion of psychological freedom conditions, distorted social scripts may also undermine what have been called "competency conditions," for instance, if they block the agent from forming "effective" intentions. Competency has been defined as the ability to form "effective" intentions (Christman 2009, p. 155).

4. For instance, there is reason to think that authenticity understood as reflective endorsement or nonalienation is *not* necessary for autonomy. In other words, one can be *inauthentic* yet autonomous (See Oshana 2005, 2007; Velleman 2006, pp. 338–389).

5. The "procedural" theories of Harry Frankfurt and Gerald Dworkin have been extremely influential (e.g., Dworkin 1988; Frankfurt 1988). The key idea of these theories is that an agent's choices, preferences, desires, and so forth are autonomous when they are *identified with* or *endorsed* in the right way. This internal, psychological process of identification or endorsement guarantees authenticity. Later theorists who have employed the notion of reflective endorsement (or nonalienation) to explicate authenticity and autonomy include Christman (2009), Ekstrom (2005), Friedman (2003), and Noggle (2005).

6. For a survey and critique of different identity-based theories of autonomy, see Benson (2005, pp. 102–106).

7. For Frankfurt, it is this aspect of freedom—what I have been calling *authenticity*—that is relevant for moral responsibility. I set aside this issue here.

8. Oshana takes the idea of substantive independence as requiring nondomination from Philip Pettit (e.g., Pettit 1997).

9. I argue elsewhere that procedural theorists such as Christman need to introduce moral criteria to explicate some of the additional conditions introduced into the theory, such as those of minimal education and exposure to alternatives (Stoljar 2014).

10. Oshana says that a person has negative freedom "when his choices and activities are minimally impeded by other persons, institutions, or natural obstacles to will and action" (Oshana 2006, p. 150). I take Pettit's notion of republican freedom, namely the conception of freedom relying on nondomination, to be an alternative characterization of negative freedom (e.g., Pettit 1997). Since Oshana's social-relational conditions parallel the conditions required by Pettit's theory of nondomination, her conditions could also be employed to explicate negative freedom conceived as nondomination.

11. Oshana's account includes internal or psychological conditions of autonomy, namely epistemic competence (being self-reflective and self-aware), rationality, procedural independence (freedom from various impediments such as compulsion and addiction), and self-respect (Oshana 2006, pp. 76–83). One can fail to be autonomous if one lacks these internal characteristics to a sufficient degree *or* if one's social situation is incompatible with control, access to options, or substantive independence (Oshana 2006, pp. 83–88).

12. The passage is from Martin Luther King Jr.'s "Letter from Birmingham Jail" (King 1964), quoted in Cudd (2006, p. 177).

13. Young quotes Du Bois on double-consciousness (Young 1990, p. 60), and Oshana discusses the phenomenon of "race consciousness" or one's "awareness of the societal significance of one's race" (Oshana 2005, p. 88). Drawing on the work of Anita Allen, she suggests that, in a racially stratified society, one cannot forget one's race without forgetting oneself (Oshana 2005, p. 88).

14. Witt here relies on Christine Korsgaard's voluntarist idea that rational agents construct their practical identities by endorsing and forming into a unified identity aspects of the social roles that they inhabit. The reasons that apply to agents (the normativity that applies to persons) are delivered by this unified practical identity that the agent constructs (Korsgaard 2009; Witt 2011, p. 43).

15. Christman points out that there are aspects of the socio-historical self that are discovered (e.g., Christman 2009, pp. 124–25). Oshana argues that we cannot "shake ourselves free" of certain of these discovered aspects of the self, such as race and gender (Oshana 2005, pp. 89–90).

16. There is a large literature on the phenomenon of *stereotype threat*, a term first used by Steele & Aronson (1995). See www.reducingstereotypethreat.org for a comprehensive survey of this literature. The research on *implicit bias* originates in Greenwald and Banaji (1995).

REFERENCES

Anderson, E. (2010) *The Imperative of Integration.* Princeton: Princeton University Press.
Appiah, K.A. (1994) "Identity, Authenticity, Survival: Multicultural Societies and Social Reproduction," in A. Gutmann (ed.), *Multiculturalism. Examining the Politics of Recognition.* Princeton: Princeton University Press, p. 149–164.
Babbitt, S.E. (1993) "Feminism and Objective Interests: The Role of Transformation Experiences in Rational Deliberation," in L. Alcoff & E. Potter (eds.), *Feminist Epistemologies.* New York: Routledge, pp. 245–264.
Benson, P. (1991) "Autonomy and Oppressive Socialization," *Social Theory and Practice* 17: 385–408.
Benson, P. (2005) "Taking Ownership: Authority and Voice in Autonomous Agency," in J. Christman & J. Anderson (eds.), *Autonomy and the Challenges to Liberalism. New Essays.* New York, NY: Cambridge University Press, pp. 101–126.
Christman, J. (2005) "Procedural Autonomy and Liberal Legitimacy," in J.S. Taylor (ed.), *Personal Autonomy. News Essays on Personal Autonomy and its Role in Contemporary Moral Philosophy.* New York: Cambridge University Press, pp. 277–298.
Christman, J. (2009) *The Politics of Persons: Individual Autonomy and Socio-historical Selves.* Cambridge: Cambridge University Press.
Christman, J. and J. Anderson (eds.). (2005) *Autonomy and the Challenges of Liberalism: New Essays.* Cambridge: Cambridge University Press.
Cudd, A.E. (2006) *Analyzing Oppression.* Oxford: Oxford University Press.
Dworkin. G. (1988) *The Theory and Practice of Autonomy.* Cambridge: Cambridge University Press.
Du Bois, W.E.B. (1994/1903) *The Souls of Black Folk.* New York, NY, Dover Publications.
Ekstrom, L.W. (2005) "Autonomy and Personal Integration," in J.S. Taylor (ed.), *Personal Autonomy. News Essays on Personal Autonomy and its Role in Contemporary Moral Philosophy.* New York, NY: Cambridge University Press, pp. 143–161.
Elster, J. (1992) "Sour Grapes—Utilitarianism and the Genesis of Wants," in A. Sen & B. Williams (eds.), *Utilitarianism and Beyond.* Cambridge: Cambridge University Press, pp. 219–238.
Friedman, M. (2003). *Autonomy, Gender, Politics.* Oxford: Oxford University Press.
Frankfurt, H. (1988) *The Importance of What We Care About.* New York: Cambridge University Press.
Gooding-Williams, R. (1998) "Race, Multiculturalism and Democracy," *Constellations* 5: 18–41.
Greenwald, A.G., & Banaji, M.R. (1995) "Implicit Social Cognition: Attitudes, Self-Esteem, and Stereotypes," *Psychological Review* 102: 4–27.
Haslanger, S. (2004) "Oppressions, Racial and Other," in M.P. Levine and T. Pataki (eds.), *Racism in Mind.* Ithaca: Cornell University Press, pp. 97–126.
King, M.L. Jr. (1964) *Why We Can't Wait.* New York: Harper and Row.
Korsgaard, C. (2009) *Self-Constitution: Agency, Integrity and Identity.* New York, NY: Oxford University Press.

Meyers, D. T. (2002) *Gender in the Mirror: Cultural Imagery and Women's Agency.* New York: Oxford University Press.

Meyers, D. T. (2005) "Decentralizing Autonomy: Five Faces of Selfhood," in J. Christman & J. Anderson (eds.), *Autonomy and the Challenges to Liberalism. New Essays.* New York, NY: Cambridge University Press, pp. 27–55.

Noggle, R. (2005) "Autonomy and the Paradox of Self-Creation: Infinite Regresses, Finite Selves and the Limits of Authenticity," in J. S. Taylor (ed.), *Personal Autonomy. News Essays on Personal Autonomy and its Role in Contemporary Moral Philosophy.* New York, NY: Cambridge University Press, pp. 87–108.

Noggle, R. (2011) "Review of Marina Oshana, *Personal Autonomy in Society,*" *Journal of Value Inquiry* 45: 233–238.

Oshana, M.A.L. (2005) "Autonomy and Self-Identity," in J. Christman & J. Anderson (eds.), *Autonomy and the Challenges to Liberalism. New Essays.* New York, NY: Cambridge University Press, pp. 77–97.

Oshana, M. (2006) *Personal Autonomy in Society.* Aldershot, UK: Ashgate Publishing.

Oshana, M. (2007) "Autonomy and the Question of Authenticity," *Social Theory and Practice* 33: 411–429.

Pettit, P. (1997) *Republicanism. A Theory of Freedom and Government.* Oxford: Oxford University Press.

Steele, C. M., & Aronson, J. (1995) "Stereotype Threat and the Intellectual Test Performance of African-Americans," *Journal of Personality and Social Psychology* 69: 797–811.

Stoljar, N. (2014) "Autonomy and Adaptive Preference Formation," in A. Veltman and M. Piper (eds.), *Autonomy, Oppression and Gender.* New York: Oxford University Press, pp. 227–252.

Superson, A. (2005) "Deformed Desires and Informed Desire Tests," *Hypatia* 20: 109–126.

Velleman, J. D. (2006) *Self to Self. Selected Essays.* New York: Cambridge University Press.

Williams, P. J. (1992) *The Alchemy of Race and Rights: Diary of a Law Professor.* Cambridge: Harvard University Press.

Witt, C. (2011) *The Metaphysics of Gender.* Oxford: Oxford University Press.

Young, I. M. (1990) *Justice and the Politics of Difference.* Princeton, NJ: Princeton University Press.

7 Stereotype Threat, Social Belonging, and Relational Autonomy

Paul H. Benson

INTRODUCTION

Relational conceptions of autonomy seek to illuminate ways in which the social and interpersonal dimensions of persons' practical commitments, motives, and conduct contribute to their autonomy as agents and so also influence the ethical and political significance of personal autonomy. The term "relational autonomy," as Catriona Mackenzie and Natalie Stoljar observe, "does not refer to a single unified conception of autonomy but is rather an umbrella term, designating a range of related perspectives."[1] Nevertheless, much philosophical study of relational autonomy has concentrated on the particular question of whether personal autonomy includes constitutively or intrinsically social, or relational, elements or whether, on the other hand, persons' social relationships, locations, and attitudes influence their autonomy entirely as a matter of contingent circumstance.[2]

It is no surprise that arguments in support of constitutively relational accounts of autonomy have been primarily conceptual in nature. It may be more surprising, though, that debates over autonomy's constitutively relational components have come to focus largely on the issue of whether personal autonomy intrinsically incorporates substantive, *normative* conditions or whether autonomy can instead be understood entirely in procedural terms, for instance, in light of agents' identification with or reflective acceptance of their preferences, choices, and actions, independent of the content or evaluative character of those attitudes and acts. While substantive conceptions of autonomy may accommodate constitutively relational elements more naturally than can procedural accounts, there is no strictly necessary connection between a conception's intrinsically relational character and its imposing substantive conditions on autonomous agents' attitudes or choices.[3]

In this chapter I consider, in an exploratory fashion, evidence that might be gleaned for some necessarily relational dimensions of autonomous agency considered apart from autonomy's normative content. I am interested in particular in thinking about whether the empirically rich literature in social psychology on stereotype threat and related pressures on agents' sense of social belonging may yield some useful evidence concerning social constituents of autonomy. This literature is intriguing for many reasons: in part because it describes modes of diminished autonomy in motivation and action that have been little studied by philosophers and in part because it appears to afford unusual and well-confirmed insight into powerful ways in which agents' subjective awareness of their social situation and the attitudes that others might hold toward them can impinge psychologically upon what they want to do, how hard they try to achieve it, and whether they succeed in doing so satisfactorily. I do not deny that the literature on stereotype threat is theoretically underdeveloped with respect to some of the broader moral and social implications of invidious stereotyping.[4] Moreover, important questions about the warrant for inferences from controlled, experimental studies of stereotype threat to ordinary contexts of stereotyping call for more investigation.[5]

I begin by surveying some of the predominant findings of psychological studies of stereotype threat and then consider how a familiar sort of *non-relational* theory of personal autonomy would explain stereotype threat's apparent capability to degrade or obstruct autonomous agency. This discussion gives rise to some *prima facie* evidence that points toward certain relational elements of autonomy, evidence which is then revised and clarified through consideration of related research on agents' uncertainty about their social belonging. I propose that this empirical evidence adds weight to a relational conception of autonomy and that the sort of relational constituent it supports coheres well with some independent philosophical arguments for relational conditions of autonomous agency, thereby lending support to those arguments.

In traversing this path, this chapter suggests that we are left with a more psychologically realistic treatment of some proposed features of relational autonomy than has typically been offered, as well as a treatment that largely avoids entering the fray—important though it be—over autonomy's evaluative content and its liberal or illiberal political implications. Lest I be perceived as overpromising, I should emphasize that this chapter investigates *some* evidence from experimental social psychology that favors *some* relational conceptions of autonomy in *some* respects. I do not aim here to demonstrate that autonomous agency is constitutively relational in character, nor do I suggest that empirical evidence concerning stereotype threat would be capable, by itself, of providing such a demonstration. Neither do I seek here to craft in precise terms the relational dimensions that autonomy incorporates. The ensuing discussion explores new ground for theorizing about autonomous agency and suggests some intriguing, albeit tentative, conclusions.

1. STEREOTYPE THREAT

In their landmark study of stereotype threat, Claude Steele and Joshua Aronson describe stereotype threat as a circumstance of "being at risk of confirming, as self-characteristic, a negative stereotype about one's group."[6]

Steele and Aronson explain that, when negative stereotypes about a social group to which one belongs are widely known, "anything one does or any of one's features that conform to it make the stereotype more plausible as a self-characterization in the eyes of others, and perhaps even in one's own eyes."[7] Persons experience such a circumstance "as a self-evaluative threat."[8] Steele and Aronson's early studies explore the effects of this predicament of threat on African-American students' performance on a difficult verbal test.

While classic social scientific studies of the effects of stigmatization and invidious group stereotypes go back more than fifty years to the work of Gordon Allport[9] and Erving Goffman,[10] social psychological studies of the situational threat posed by general knowledge of negative stereotypes about groups to which an agent belongs have been conducted systematically only since Steele and Aronson's 1995 paper. These studies, which now number more than 300,[11] have ranged well beyond negative stereotypes of African-Americans' performance in academic or intellectual testing situations. Research on stereotype threat has documented the significantly debilitating effects of such threat in relation to many kinds of negative stereotype, for a wide variety of social groups, in contexts of human performance far removed from academia.[12] The effects of the predicament on performance have been measured in domains as varied as Latinos in standardized testing, women in math and science, older persons in memorization, whites in athletics, and gay men in childcare, among many others. Even within the domain of academic performance, any individual can be affected by the threat of confirming an applicable stereotype of poor performance. (In noting this, I do not mean to suggest that all such stereotypes have similar moral import or social force.) Moreover, persons' performance of challenging tasks typically improves when they are cued to positive stereotypes of groups with which they identify.[13]

For the sake of developing the arguments I offer about the significance of stereotype threat for relational conceptions of autonomous agency, the following features of the phenomenon hold particular interest. First, the magnitude of the effect of stereotype threat on performance often can be quite large. For example, Gregory Walton and Geoffrey Cohen have performed a series of important studies of academic performance that indicate that stereotype threat can have a prominent role to play in sustaining the so-called racial achievement gap in school and college grades. In one recent study, Walton and Cohen achieved a 90% reduction in the racial achievement gap in their sample's actual classroom performance during the semester following experimental intervention by manipulating variables concerning black students' doubts about belonging in school.[14] In a related study over a three-year period, similar interventions to combat stereotype threat and related group-based doubts about social belonging in college closed the gap between African-American students' grades and grades of their European-American classmates by more than 50%.[15] One of the striking features of research on the efficacy of interventions to combat stereotype threat is that even very brief and modest interventions can have a dramatic effect in improving performance. For instance, Cohen and colleagues report a 40% reduction in African-American seventh graders' achievement gap with European-American classmates as the result of having the students complete a fifteen-minute, in-class writing assignment that enabled the students "to reaffirm their self-integrity."[16]

Second, studies of stereotype threat and related phenomena confirm that subjects' "subjective construal" of the relationship between their likely performance, their ability, their preparation and effort, and known stereotypes implicit in their social situation is an especially important variable that affects the quality of their performance and that persons' subjective attitudes affect performance independently of the character of the discrimination or hostility actually present in their social environment.[17] Accordingly, Walton and Cohen observe that one of the experimental interventions described in their research "robbed adversity of its symbolic meaning for African Americans, untethering their sense of belonging from daily hardship."[18] Similar findings about the significance of agents' subjective attitudes toward their circumstances pervade the literature on stereotype threat.

Third, research indicates that a variety of psychological and other situational factors influence the effect of stereotype threat on motivation and performance. Stereotype threat inhibits performance more powerfully as the person's identification with the stereotyped social group increases or as her personal identification with the importance of the particular performance domain becomes closer. The latter phenomenon led Steele to hypothesize early on that "as [stereotype] threat persists over time, it may have the further effect of pressuring these students to protectively disidentify with achievement in school and related intellectual domains. That is, it may pressure the person to define or redefine the self-concept such that school achievement is neither a basis of self-evaluation nor a personal identity."[19] Brenda Major and colleagues have documented the role of such psychological disengagement as a strategy for coping with stereotype threat.[20] Other situational factors that have been found to influence the effects of stereotype threat on performance include: the salience of the stereotyped group identity to the intended performance; the difficulty of the task; the strength of the person's conviction that the specific task at hand accurately reflects actual competence in the relevant domain; and the extent of open hostility in the agent's environment.

The psychological mechanisms through which stereotype threat affects persons' performance and achievement motivation are believed to include: the production of anxiety; arousal of stress and related physiological conditions known to be correlated with diminished performance; excessive self-consciousness; and a number of means by which agents' cognitive capacities are reduced. Cognitive capacities can be impaired by stereotype threat due to the constriction of attention, the effort required to suppress stereotype-related thoughts and emotions, the demands of excessive monitoring of the performance, and the reduction of working-memory capacity.[21]

Stereotype threat also has been shown to affect performance through self-handicapping strategies that prepare agents to rationalize after the fact what they anticipate will be poor performance. For instance, some studies have shown that persons subject to stereotype threat are inclined to engage in less practice or preparation for difficult tasks or to make less effort in the performance of the task.[22] I already have noted the tendency for those subject to stereotype threat over time to reduce their identification with the stereotyped group in question, to disengage from the performance domain as something they value, or to question the validity of the evaluation of their performance as a measure of a valued trait. These responses can function as deeper extensions of self-handicapping strategies for coping with anxieties about poor performance that could confirm negative stereotypes. For example, "I didn't really try hard to do well" can evolve into "well, academic achievement doesn't really matter to me." In such cases, responses to stereotype threat can become instances of adaptive preference or belief formation.

This overview of some of the primary empirical findings about the character and effects of stereotype threat positions us to consider what some influential philosophical approaches to autonomous agency would say about stereotype threat's implications for personal autonomy. In examining some of these implications, I will suggest that stereotype threat and related features of agents' motivation to augment or preserve their sense of social belonging provide useful, if less-than-conclusive, evidence about the relational character of autonomy.

2. STEREOTYPE THREAT AND NONRELATIONAL CONCEPTIONS OF AUTONOMY

As observed at the outset, "relational autonomy" often functions as a loose, umbrella term that encompasses widely disparate accounts of personal autonomy and engages a variety of distinct philosophical concerns about traditional ways of understanding autonomy. I use the term here to designate those conceptions according to which agential autonomy, or persons' autonomy over their agency, entails requirements concerning agents' interpersonal relationships or other social conditions, where these interpersonal or social requirements are constitutively necessary for autonomy, not merely contributing factors that influence whether the genuine constituents of personal autonomy are present in particular instances. In this usage of "relational autonomy," I concur with John Christman, who writes, "what . . . must be true to make a conception of autonomy *uniquely* 'relational' or 'social' is that among its defining conditions are requirements concerning the interpersonal or social environment of the agent."[23]

I highlight autonomous *agency* here, in contrast with persons' capabilities to lead self-governing lives or to contribute to the legislation of the norms by which they properly may be evaluated, in order to concentrate on persons' local, or episodic, autonomy in the course of arriving at their choices or intentions and performing their actions. Elsewhere, I have employed the notion of persons' capabilities to *take ownership* of their choices and actions to aid in disentangling this concept of autonomy from potentially related notions concerning the global autonomy of persons' lives, the substantive independence of their manner of living, their capacities for such independence, their rights and moral status as autonomous, and so forth.[24] My attention to autonomous agency is important for our discussion, as so many of the effects of stereotype threat concern the quality of persons' efforts and performances and their motivation to attain a certain level of achievement in what they do. Invidious social stereotyping has, of course, many grave implications for other types of autonomy that are worthy of study, too.

When stereotype threat degrades the quality of agents' performance and perhaps also dampens or disrupts agents' motivation or efforts to achieve, persons' autonomous agency has been diminished. This claim may seem curious, as the standard experimental context in which the influence of stereotype threat is displayed involves an agent who has good reasons to want to perform a certain challenging task well and who decides in a routine manner to undertake that task for that reason. In normal circumstances, the mere fact that an agent might fail to perform a valued and difficult task at the level she would like would entail nothing necessarily about any compromise of her autonomous agency. Autonomy affords no guarantee of wholly successful performance. Yet, when the agent's motivation, effort, attention, cognitive capacity, or emotional state is degraded by her awareness of an invidious social stereotype that she might confirm through her conduct, and the quality of her performance is thereby diminished significantly, it is clear that the process through which the agent's action emerges is not such as to realize her autonomy (for reasons elaborated in what follows). With regard to the person's autonomy, the interference of the threat presented by her awareness of the negative stereotype is not categorically different from the interference of a more overt but equally disruptive physical or psychological threat.

Notice that the psychological mechanisms that have been identified in the operation of stereotype threat typically would violate the authenticity conditions routinely advanced in procedural, nonrelational accounts of autonomy. Once again, I turn to John Christman's theory as a recent and representative illustration of such accounts. Persons are autonomous in their choices and actions, according to Christman, when they act on motives whose processes of development they would not resist or disown upon suitable reflection. In order to capture the agent's will authentically, the actual or hypothetical reflection must meet a standard of adequacy. For instance, Christman notes that the reflection

> must be undertaken free from the influence of factors which we know severely restrict free consideration of one's condition and one's options.

> The hypothetical self-endorsing reflection . . . must be such that it is not the product of social and psychological conditions that prevent adequate appraisal of oneself. This includes ability to assess the various aspects of one's being, and the freedom from those factors and conditions that we know independently effectively prevent minimal self-understanding.[25]

Furthermore, nonrelational, procedural accounts of autonomy such as Christman's typically invoke additional competence conditions that must be satisfied in order for persons' reflective nonalienation from the historical development of their motives and conduct to ensure their ownership of their agency. Such competence conditions often include possessing an appropriate degree of self-control and capabilities to think rationally, along with freedom from psychological pathology and from systemic self-deception.[26]

When the awareness that one's poor performance could be perceived as confirming a familiar, negative stereotype about a group to which one belongs results in increased anxiety or stress, constricted attention, excessive self-consciousness, or unduly taxed cognitive capacities, and those effects are sufficiently powerful to impede markedly one's motivation or performance, then the authenticity conditions proposed in Christman's theory also would likely be violated. The perceived threat posed by the stereotype would, in these circumstances, severely restrict free consideration of one's options and thwart adequate self-appraisal or self-understanding. In other words, whatever sort of reflective nonalienation from her conduct an agent might attain in circumstances of operative stereotype threat would not be adequate to confirm the authenticity of her will and conduct. This finding parallels some of the implications that more straightforward forms of social intimidation or threat have for autonomous agency, as intimidation and threat normally impede autonomy by obstructing the authenticity of the agent's actual or hypothetical reflection on her will and intended conduct.

Moreover, some cases of persistent and especially potent stereotype threat also can block fulfillment of some competence conditions for procedural autonomy. Recall that it is not uncommon for persons to cope with stereotype threat unconsciously by weakening their identification with the social group at issue or by disengaging themselves from the arena of performance within which the stereotype could be confirmed. Likewise, some agents in effect handicap themselves before the fact so as to provide themselves with ready-made excuses for eventual performances they fear will be inadequate. Where these phenomena occur and become entrenched over time in the agents' motivation and self-perception, it is likely that agents' powers of self-control, rational thought, or self-understanding would be compromised to the extent that they fail to be competent to attain the sort of reflective nonalienation or acceptance that could confirm their autonomy. In these ways, Christman's procedural account of autonomy, which explicitly eschews constitutively relational requirements, seems *prima facie* to capture relatively well some of the reasons stereotype threat can impede autonomous agency.

However, there seem to be deeper reasons why stereotype threat that is sufficiently intrusive upon effective motivation, effort, and performance to thwart authenticity or competence conditions should be considered an obstruction of autonomous agency. These deeper reasons begin to surface when we consider why the threat of behaving so as to confirm a group stereotype often has these disruptive effects on persons' efforts, expectations, performance, self-identity, or values. These effects would not occur if stereotype threat were not "experienced essentially as a self-evaluative threat," to use, once more, Steele and Aronson's terminology.[27] The agent affected detrimentally by stereotype threat must have certain attitudes toward her membership in particular social groups, in conjunction with certain attitudes toward being characterized by others as the stereotype would dictate, in order to suffer the self-evaluative threat that triggers the anxiety, distraction, overloaded working memory, lowered expectations, and so forth that frustrate the authenticity or competence requirements of nonrelational autonomy.

In this way, two manifestly relational dimensions of the inhibiting influence of stereotype threat on personal autonomy emerge as being necessary for the generation of the psychological mechanisms that degrade persons' motivation and performance in these circumstances. First, the affected agent responds, through anxiety, increased stress, narrowed attention, and so on, to ways in which she feels others are likely to evaluate her in light of the stereotype's social salience. When the relational context of the agent's regarding herself as being under others' critical, evaluative gaze is removed, then most of the psychological force of stereotype threat dissipates.[28] Second, it is necessary for the targeting of this kind of self-evaluative threat that the agent regard herself as being characterized as a member of the specific social group to which the stereotype attaches. Once more, removing or modifying this social dimension of the agent's self-regard undermines substantially the threat's psychological traction on the agent's will and conduct.

The psychological research surveyed earlier on the sorts of experimental intervention that have been found to mitigate or disarm substantially the influence of stereotype threat confirms these claims about relational aspects of agents' attitudes that are embedded in the autonomy-inhibiting operation of stereotype threat. Interventions that successfully mitigate stereotype threat often function by altering the agent's own view of her group membership, thus defeating the salience of the stereotype for the agent's performance, or by revising the agent's sense of how others would be likely to appraise her performance—for instance, as a benign marker of the routine variability in competent agents' success in performing difficult tasks, and so again a means of displacing the salience of the stereotype.

It is noteworthy that the structure of these social dimensions of the functioning of stereotype threat is analogous to the phenomenological structure of shame. Shame is experienced in response to a person's subjective awareness that she could be viewed by others in a light that exposes some profound shortcoming in her value or worth. Like stereotype threat, shame is often (though not necessarily) tied to characteristics linked to some group-based social identity or role. Shame feels to the person like an assault on her self-evaluation, which is why shame normally involves behavioral dispositions to retreat, hide from view, or protect and cover oneself.[29] These structural analogies between the experience of shame and the psychological effects of stereotype threat should not be surprising. Stereotype threat can be thought of as presenting the agent with a serious risk of potential shame, namely, the shame consequent upon being exposed as confirming a hurtful and demeaning stereotype.

Considering stereotype threat from the perspective of some standard, purely procedural conditions of autonomy, then, confirms the impression that stereotype threat can seriously diminish autonomous agency. Yet the very psychological mechanisms that, from such a perspective, explain stereotype threat's obstruction of autonomy also point toward deeper, socially structured dimensions of stereotype threat that are necessary for the triggering of those psychological mechanisms. Perhaps those dimensions reflect necessary constituents of autonomy that concern agents' social self-regard in relation to their perceptions of others' likely attitudes toward them.

Proponents of nonrelational conceptions of autonomy can respond to this suggestion by agreeing that the two relational dimensions I have identified in the operation of stereotype threat are indeed regularly involved in explanations of stereotype threat's obstruction of agents' reflectiveness or autonomy competencies. Such proponents would hold, however, that these social features of stereotype threat do not reveal any conceptually requisite elements of autonomous agency. Rather, agents' subjective attitudes toward their group membership or the likelihood that others will evaluate their actions in a certain light are simply prevalent aspects of the psycho-social circumstances of stereotype threat that regularly happen to trigger psychological obstacles to the authenticity or competency conditions of autonomy. For proponents of nonrelational accounts of autonomy, relational features of the impact of stereotype threat are only regularly predictable factors that contribute to the diminution of autonomy, not evidence of features that belong necessarily to an adequate conception of personal autonomy.[30]

My reliance in this chapter on empirical research in social psychology could be taken to confirm this response. Whatever relational features of stereotype threat might emerge from these studies as being significant for intrusive effects on autonomy would seem to be regarded appropriately as contingent, circumstantial—if regularly present—factors in the etiology of the attitudes and behaviors described in the research. Moreover, the highly variable character of the relational dimensions I have described might be thought to support this manner of understanding them. Persons' attitudinal sensitivities to how others would be likely to appraise their actions are highly variable, as the research on stereotype threat demonstrates. Likewise, persons' sense of their own group membership and its significance for their identity or worth is often subject to change with very minor variations in agents' circumstances. The malleability of these features, both psychologically and socially, could be taken to suggest that they hardly reveal enduring, conceptually requisite elements of autonomous agency.

3. "BELONGING UNCERTAINTY" AND THE RELATIONAL POSITION OF AUTONOMOUS AGENTS

One line of response to the variability in agents' sensitivity to others' likely appraisals of their actions in light of prevailing stereotypes, as well as to the variability in their identifications with particular social groups, would be to emphasize that such variability transpires within a psycho-social human context that does not appear to be wholly contingent or accidental. Human psychology has developed so that ingroup/outgroup identifications and alienations, of one sort or another, grip our cognitive, affective, and volitional dispositions powerfully and consistently. While our sensitivities to particular situations of stereotype threat and our identifications with the social groups that undergird those threats are indeed contingent and malleable, it seems that the psychological constitution of human beings necessarily encompasses an abiding tendency to affiliate with social groups and to be sensitive to others' evaluative judgments of us in light of our group affiliations. It is an all-too-human phenomenon—an inescapably human phenomenon, I am inclined to think—to want to be a member of a distinctive and positively valued ingroup and to construct stereotypes in order to cope with the heterogeneous, complex, potentially threatening, and unforgiving social worlds in which we interact so as to sustain our sense that our social identities are positively affirmed. Summarizing the accounts of stereotyping supplied, for example, in social categorization theory and in self-identity theory, Ann Cudd explains, "stereotypes thus serve not only to group the social world, and then to place oneself in the social order, but also to do so in a way that bolsters the valuation of one's self-identity, insofar as that is possible within the given social realities."[31]

While I concede that the relational dimensions of stereotype threat are, taken by themselves, too variable to afford strong evidence for stable relational constituents of a conception of autonomous agency, there are enduring, deeply entrenched psychological and social mechanisms in human life that render us generally susceptible to stereotype threat and the resultant impingements on our autonomy. Although particular modes of stereotyping and their cognitive, emotional, and social content change over time, it is impossible to conceive of recognizably human life and social interaction in the complete absence of stereotyping and associated aims to maintain positive evaluations of our identities. This structural feature of our humanity points in the direction of some necessarily relational requirements of autonomous agency. Seen in this light, the relational aspects of autonomy regularly engaged by autonomy-inhibiting cases of stereotype threat may function as indicators of deeper, relational constituents that are not merely accidental, contributory influences upon autonomy.

New developments in the literature on stereotype threat are revealing in this regard. Some recent papers by Gregory Walton and Geoffrey Cohen cited earlier present studies of the effects on achievement motivation and academic performance of heightened concerns about social belonging that are regularly experienced by socially stigmatized individuals.[32] These studies focus on the broad-based concern of members of stigmatized groups that "people like [us] do not belong here [e.g., in university or in a particular academic major]."[33] Such sensitization to perceived risks to social belonging can have powerful effects on individuals' motivation to achieve and the quality of their actual performance, "even in the absence of prejudice, fears of confirming the stereotype, or an anticipated intellectual evaluation."[34] Hence, these studies of so-called *belonging uncertainty*[35] examine a more general circumstance than that of stereotype threat. Stigmatized persons are, according to this research, more inclined to construe ordinary adversity or hardship as evidence of lack of belonging than is the case for persons who are not stigmatized in the same contexts. The effects of such belonging uncertainty on motivation and performance, as well as the results of modest experimental interventions that cue the subjects to interpret their circumstances in more benign ways, are similar in magnitude and duration to those found in earlier studies of stereotype threat.[36]

As belonging uncertainty can interfere with the autonomy of persons' motives, efforts, and performance much as stereotype threat can, we see in this research some evidence for a relational feature of autonomy that parallels some of the relational dimensions we noted earlier in cases of stereotype threat. Namely, stigmatized individuals often are sensitized to potential risks to their social belonging or sense of social place, and their attitudes toward whether they belong, in the face of their perceptions of others' anticipated attitudes toward them, seem to be important factors in determining whether their autonomy as agents is impaired. For instance, when Walton and Cohen's experimental subjects manage to avoid regarding mundane challenges as evidence that they do not belong or have no appropriate place in the salient social domain, their motivation to achieve and the quality of their performance both improve significantly. Evidently, their agential autonomy recovers as well (other things being equal). But a central question persists: Why should this research on subjective social belonging and performance tell us anything more about the content of purportedly relational constituents of autonomy than we managed to glean from studies of more traditional types of stereotype threat?

First, the similarity between the structure of the subjective, relational levers of diminished autonomy in cases of belonging uncertainty, on the one hand, and in cases specifically involving stereotype threat, on the other, indicates that agents' sensitivity to self-evaluative threats related to their social position is not confined to performance anxiety concerning the risk of confirming invidious stereotypes. Autonomous agents' regard for some worth-generating features of their social or interpersonal relations, as those agents subjectively experience them, would persist even if many of our current social stereotypes or some features of our general disposition to stereotype were to change significantly.[37]

Second, while the structures of the underlying social bases for the inhibition of autonomous agency in these two kinds of case are similar, and the effects of these phenomena on agents' motivation and performance are quite similar, it is not clear that the particular psychological mechanisms that accompany the effects of stereotype threat, such as increased anxiety, physiological stress, diverted or narrowed attention, or constricted working memory, come into play as primary procedural impairments in cases of belonging uncertainty. Concerns about loss of social belonging may well dampen motivation and impair performance through different proximate triggers than are typically found in performance domains in which the agent experiences stereotype threat. Therefore, accounts of autonomy that ignore the deeper, relational components of these two types of situation and concentrate only on the immediate mechanisms through which belonging uncertainty and stereotype threat influence agents' motivation and conduct will be likely to miss their underlying structural similarity and so misunderstand the common reasons for the suppression of autonomy in both kinds of context.

Third, the reasons for holding that humans' concern for acquiring and protecting some fundamental subjective sense of social belonging is grounded in a ubiquitous and enduring human need would seem to be even more compelling than the claim that the phenomenon of social stereotyping and maintaining positive ingroup identification is an enduring human disposition. The need to achieve and sustain a sense of belonging would appear to be stable even in the midst of social change that would markedly revise current patterns of social categorization and identification.[38] In fact, the very possibility of any practice or pattern of social stigmatization presupposes powerful motivation for social belonging. Walton and Cohen cite in this regard Erving Goffman's statement that "the central feature of the stigmatized individual's situation in life . . . is a question of . . . 'acceptance.'"[39]

Other reasons to pay particular attention to these studies of social belonging and performance draw more heavily upon independent theoretical work on autonomy. I note just two such reasons here. The first is that stereotype threat's effects on autonomy are closely tied to the agent's particular sense of social identity. Recall that disidentification is one strategy that individuals facing stereotype threat may employ to dodge the threat. In contrast, belonging uncertainty can obstruct persons' autonomy even when their identifications are conflicted, unformed, or otherwise unsettled. Whatever group-based identities a person accepts, she will have a strong motivation to sustain her sense that, in the relevant social domains, she belongs, is respected, or has a fitting place. Her fundamental need to belong in this way floats free, to some extent, of the specific identifications she embraces. As I have argued elsewhere, identity-based accounts of autonomy encounter serious philosophical difficulties that are avoided when autonomy is conceived of apart from agents' particular identifications.[40] If such a position is correct, then attention to the relational dimension of autonomy that belonging uncertainty can render vulnerable, where the role of group-based identification does not figure necessarily as it does in stereotype threat, may be more fruitful for philosophical purposes.

A second, theoretically derived reason to attend especially to the relational component of autonomy that is compromised through belonging uncertainty is that this component appears itself to reflect a deep and pervasive feature of intentional agency that has been argued on independent, conceptual grounds to be necessary for autonomous agency. Persons who feel that they have no place or standing to speak or answer for their commitments or conduct in light of potential, external criticisms are persons who lack an elemental sense of social belonging. Even persons whose social belonging is compromised through loneliness, isolation, marginalization, victimization, or misanthropic inclination can retain a minimal sense that they belong if they are able to sustain the disposition to regard themselves as being in a position to speak, or answer, for their actions in response to others' potential criticisms. This basic sense of having a place as a reason-giving agent among other reason-giving agents who may properly hold one to answer for one's conduct has been claimed, on the basis of conceptual argument, to be a necessary condition of autonomy.[41] That is to say, the necessary condition of autonomy that is jeopardized in circumstances of belonging uncertainty may be understood to rest upon a still deeper, more foundational feature of autonomy that is relational—namely, that of agents' regarding themselves as fit potentially to answer to others for their choices and actions.

I am not suggesting that autonomous agents' attitude toward their social belonging consists solely in their regard for their worthiness to answer for their decisions and actions. Clearly, the former attitude encompasses a good deal more than the latter. In particular, social belonging, as interpreted in the studies cited here, encompasses social bases of self-esteem that extend well beyond agents' respect for their own worthiness to speak for their actions. Nevertheless, the demand that autonomous agents regard themselves as belonging in some manner, in the context of their anticipation of others' attitudes toward them, can be seen to be congruent with and to build upon the conceptual requirement that autonomous agents must treat themselves as belonging among the community of persons who hold themselves answerable for their actions. The coherence between the prior philosophical contention that autonomous agents must treat themselves as potential answerers to external criticism of their conduct and the social component of autonomous agency that is obstructed in circumstances of belonging uncertainty lends additional weight to the case that autonomy is constitutively relational, that agents' attitudes toward their worthiness to belong in the social domains within which they act are not merely accidental, contributory factors in their autonomy. In other words, if autonomy is intrinsically relational in virtue of autonomous agents' regard for their own answerability, then we are in a better position to make sense of the empirical findings that belonging uncertainty can disrupt autonomy, for we can see why regard for social place would be deeply important to persons' ability to take ownership of their choices, efforts, and actions.

4. NORMATIVE IMPLICATIONS

I have not entertained here the question of whether the relational constituents of autonomy must incorporate commitments that bear normative substance.[42] As I observed when introducing this chapter, argument over the potential normative content of personal autonomy and the political significance of that purported content has dominated most treatments of autonomy's relational character. I have sought to explore some aspects of autonomy's relational character largely in independence from any normative content it may have. For the most part, the considerations I have presented in evidence for relational autonomy emerge from an effort to take the social psychology of human agency seriously rather than from an effort to uncover substantive, evaluative boundaries on the attitudes, motives, and actions of autonomous agents. In this regard, the relational dimension of autonomy that begins to surface through examination of the literature on stereotype threat and belonging uncertainty does not, by itself, entail any particular conception of how persons ought to live or what they should prefer or choose to do.

This does not mean, however, that, in light of the conclusions sketched here, autonomous agents may hold any attitudes whatsoever toward their social position without jeopardizing their autonomy. Agents who do not regard themselves as worthy of answering for what they do in the face of others' potential criticisms or who do not regard themselves as belonging in this elemental social respect will suffer diminished autonomy. And this means that persons who adopt preferences or attitudes that are incompatible with such self-regard, whether for the sake of adapting to the pressures of oppressive social circumstances, for reasons of psychological malady, or for wholly idiosyncratic reasons, cannot enjoy fully autonomous agency.

ACKNOWLEDGMENTS

I am grateful for valuable discussion of earlier versions of this chapter at a symposium on adaptive preferences at the Central Division Meetings of the American Philosophical Association (February 17, 2012), a symposium on self-government and social transformation at the University California/Davis (March 1–2, 2012), and a conference, "Defensible in Theory,

Workable in Practice," organized by the Essex Autonomy Project at the Institute of Philosophy, University of London (March 15–16, 2013). I also am indebted to Marina Oshana's insightful comments on the penultimate version of this chapter.

NOTES

1. Mackenzie and Stoljar (2000: 4).
2. The claim that autonomy conceptually encompasses relational content was suggested early on in the contemporary literature by Jennifer Nedelsky in the context of feminist legal theory. See Nedelsky (1989: 7–36).
3. Andrea C. Westlund offers important arguments for this claim (2009: 26–49).
4. Blum (2012).
5. See Aronson and Dee (2012: 264–79).
6. Steele and Aronson (1995: 797).
7. Ibid. Also see Steele (1997: 613–29).
8. Steele and Aronson (1995: 797).
9. Allport (1954).
10. Goffman (1963).
11. Aronson and Dee (2012: 265).
12. For a useful review of the literature, see Aronson and McGlone (2009:153–78). It is worth noting that stereotype threat takes multiple forms depending upon who is the target of the threat and whose judgment is regarded as the threat's source. For more discussion, see Shapiro (2012: 71–88).
13. See McGlone and Aronson (2006: 486–93). Also see Shih and colleagues (2012: 141–56).
14. Walton and Cohen (2007: 94).
15. Walton and Cohen (2011: 1448). See also Cohen and colleagues (2006: 1307–10); and Cohen and colleagues (2009: 400–3). The latter study emphasizes the damaging recursive effects of stereotype threat and the long-term benefits of early intervention.
16. Cohen and colleagues (2006: 1307).
17. Walton and Cohen (2011: 1448). This is not at all to deny, however, that such attitudes normally originate in features of persons' social circumstances.
18. Walton and Cohen (2011: 1449).
19. Steele and Aronson (1995: 797). Cf. Steele (1992: 68–77).
20. Major and colleagues (1998: 34–50).
21. While research confirms that all of these factors may be at play in the phenomenon, study is ongoing to identify more precise explanations for the balance and relationships among these factors and the conditions that trigger them. For recent discussion of the psychological processes triggered by stereotype threat, see Schmader and Beilock (2012: 34–50).
22. See Stone (2002: 1667–78). Also see Jeff Schimel and colleagues (2004: 75–99).
23. Christman (2004: 147). See also Westlund's (2009: 27) helpful way of framing Christman's account of what it means for a conception of autonomy to be distinctively relational.
24. Benson (2005: 101–26).
25. Christman (2004: 154).
26. Christman (2004: 155). For more on Christman's development of these authenticity and competence conditions, see Christman (2009: 142–56). Also cf. the account of autonomy competencies presented in Meyers (1989). I set aside

here the issue of whether such conditions can be justified adequately in purely procedural conceptions of autonomy.

27. Steele and Aronson (1995: 797).
28. Note that, while being liable to be the target of others' critical evaluations is a normal feature of human social life, in circumstances of stereotype threat, the agent's attention is directed toward the presumed likelihood of others' negative evaluations of the person, as those criticisms are embodied in some widely known social stereotype. There is an important difference, then, between the ways in which we routinely are liable to others' critical appraisals and the way in which this occurs through stereotype threat. Nonetheless, the issue of whether stereotype threat should be regarded as merely "a specific instance of a more general threat—that of being judged and treated negatively by others" is one that deserves further examination. See Steele (2012: 298).
29. For discussion of the character of shame and ways in which shame can diminish autonomous agency, see Benson (1994: 650–68).
30. Hence, John Christman writes, "to mark out such [relational or social] accounts from others in the literature, social conditions of some sort must be named as conceptually necessary requirements of autonomy rather than, say, contributory factors." See Christman (2004: 147–8).
31. Cudd (2006: 73). Cudd goes on to explain that incentives of both a material and psychological nature are also significant factors in shaping the maintenance of social stereotypes and their change over time. See Cudd (2006, ch. 3).
32. See Walton and Cohen (2007, 2011). Also see Walton and Carr (2012).
33. Walton and Cohen (2007: 83).
34. Walton and Cohen (2007: 86).
35. Walton and Cohen (2007: 82).
36. Walton and Cohen's recent studies also found substantial improvements in self-reported health and subjective happiness over a three-year period when interventions were designed to modify first-year, African-American college students' subjective interpretations of intermittent difficulties they were facing as evidence that they did not belong in college. See Walton and Cohen (2011).
37. There are many reasons this would be the case, having to do with the character of human sociality and the structure of our sense of our own worth. I explore some of these reasons in what follows.
38. For psychological study of the fundamental character of the human disposition to seek social belonging, see Baumeister and Leary (1995) and MacDonald and Leary (2005).
39. Walton and Cohen (2011: 1447).
40. See Benson (1994, 2005).
41. See Westlund (2009); Benson (1994, 1995, 2014).
42. For recent interchanges on this question, see the discussions in *Symposia on Gender, Race and Philosophy* 7 (2011) http://web.mit.edu/sgrp/2011/no1/SGRPvol7no12011.pdf of Westlund (2009), and of Catriona Mackenzie and Jacqui Poltera (2010).

REFERENCES

Allport, Gordon W. (1954) *The Nature of Prejudice*. Reading, MA: Addison-Wesley.
Aronson, Joshua, and Thomas Dee (2012) "Stereotype threat in the real world," in M. Inzlicht and T. Schmader (eds.), *Stereotype Threat: Theory, Process, and Application*. New York, NY: Oxford University Press, pp. 264–79.

Aronson, Joshua, and Matthew S. McGlone (2009) "Stereotype and social identity threat," in Todd D. Nelson (ed), *Handbook of Prejudice, Stereotyping, and Discrimination*. New York: Psychology Press, pp. 153–78.

Baumeister, Roy F., and Mark R. Leary (1995) "The need to belong: Desire for interpersonal attachments as a fundamental human motivation," *Psychological Bulletin* 117: 497–529.

Benson, Paul (1994) "Free agency and self-worth," *Journal of Philosophy* 91: 650–68.

Benson, Paul (2005) "Taking ownership: Authority and voice in autonomous agency," in John Christman and Joel Anderson (eds), *Autonomy and the Challenges to Liberalism: New Essays*. New York: Cambridge University Press, pp. 101–26.

Benson, Paul (2014) "Feminist commitments and relational autonomy," in Andrea Veltman and Mark Piper (eds), *Autonomy, Oppression and Gender*. New York: Oxford University Press, pp. 87–113.

Blum, Lawrence (2012) "The too minimal moral and civic dimension of the 'stereotype threat' paradigm." American Philosophical Association, Central Division Meetings, Symposium II-F, February 16, 2012.

Christman, John (2004) "Relational autonomy, liberal individualism, and the social constitution of selves," *Philosophical Studies* 117: 143–64.

Christman, John (2009) *The Politics of Persons: Individual Autonomy and Sociohistorical Selves*. Cambridge: Cambridge University Press.

Cohen, Geoffrey L., Julio Garcia, Nancy Apfel, and Allison Master (2006) "Reducing the racial achievement gap: A social-psychological intervention," *Science* 313: 1307–10.

Cohen, Geoffrey L., Julio Garcia, Valerie Purdie-Vaughns, Nancy Apfel, and Patricia Brzustoski (2009) "Recursive processes in self-affirmation: Intervening to close the minority achievement gap," *Science* 324: 400–3.

Cudd, Ann E. (2006) *Analyzing Oppression*. New York: Oxford University Press.

Goffman, Erving (1963) *Stigma: Notes on the Management of Spoiled Identity*. Englewood Cliffs, NJ: Prentice-Hall.

Inzlicht, Michael, and Toni Schmader, eds. (2012) *Stereotype Threat: Theory, Process, and Application*. New York: Oxford University Press.

MacDonald, Geoff, and Mark R. Leary (2005) "Why does social exclusion hurt? The relationship between social and physical pain," *Psychological Bulletin* 131: 202–23.

Mackenzie, Catriona, and Jacqui Poltera (2010) "Narrative integration, fragmented selves, and autonomy," *Hypatia* 25: 31–54.

Mackenzie, Catriona, and Natalie Stoljar (2000) "Autonomy refigured," in C. Mackenzie and N. Stoljar (eds), *Relational Autonomy: Feminist Perspectives on Autonomy, Agency, and the Social Self*. New York: Oxford University Press, pp. 3–31.

Major, Brenda, Steven Spencer, Toni Schmader, Connie Wolfe, and Jennifer Crocker (1998) "Coping with negative stereotypes about intellectual performance: The role of psychological disengagement," *Personality and Social Psychology Bulletin* 24: 34–50.

McGlone, Matthew S., and Joshua Aronson (2006) "Social identity salience and stereotype threat," *Journal of Applied Developmental Psychology* 27: 486–93.

Meyers, Diana T. (1989) *Self, Society, and Personal Choice*. New York: Columbia University Press.

Nedelsky, Jennifer (1989) "Reconceiving autonomy: Sources, thoughts and possibilities," *Yale Journal of Law and Feminism* 1: 7–36.

Schimel, Jeff, Jamie Arndt, Katherine M. Banko, and Alison Cook (2004) "Not all self-affirmations were created equal: The cognitive and social benefits of affirming the intrinsic (vs. extrinsic) self," *Social Cognition* 22: 75–99.

Schmader, Toni, and Sian Beilock (2012) "An integration of processes that underlie stereotype threat," in M. Inzlicht & T. Schmader (eds.), *Stereotype Threat: Theory, Process, and Application.* New York, NY: Oxford University Press, pp. 34–50.

Shapiro, Jenessa R. (2012) "Types of threats: From stereotype threat to stereotype threats," in M. Inzlicht & T. Schmader (eds.), *Stereotype Threat: Theory, Process, and Application.* New York, NY: Oxford University Press, pp. 71–88.

Shih, Margaret J., Todd L. Pittinsky, and Geoffrey C. Ho (2012) "Stereotype boost: Positive outcomes from the activation of positive stereotypes," in M. Inzlicht & T. Schmader (eds.), *Stereotype Threat: Theory, Process, and Application.* New York, NY: Oxford University Press, pp. 141–56.

Steele, Claude M. (1992) "Race and the schooling of black Americans," *The Atlantic Monthly* 269: 68–77.

Steele, Claude M. (1997) "A threat in the air: How stereotypes shape intellectual identity and performance," *American Psychologist* 52: 613–29.

Steele, Claude M. (2012) "Extending and applying stereotype threat research: A brief essay," in M. Inzlicht & T. Schmader (eds.), *Stereotype Threat: Theory, Process, and Application.* New York, NY: Oxford University Press, pp. 297–303.

Steele, Claude M., and Joshua Aronson (1995) "Stereotype threat and the intellectual test performance of African Americans," *Journal of Personality and Social Psychology* 69: 797–811.

Stone, Jeff (2002) "Battling doubt by avoiding practice: The effect of stereotype threat on self-handicapping in white athletes," *Personality and Social Psychology Bulletin* 28: 1667–78.

Symposia on Gender, Race and Philosophy. Winter 2011. Vol. 7, no. 1. Available online at <http://sgrp.typepad.com/sgrp/winter-2011-symposium-mackenzie-poltera-and-westlund-on-autonomy.html>.

Walton, Gregory M., and Priyanka B. Carr (2012) "Social belonging and the motivation and intellectual achievement of negatively stereotyped students," in M. Inzlicht & T. Schmader (eds.), *Stereotype Threat: Theory, Process, and Application.* New York, NY: Oxford University Press, pp. 89–106.

Walton, Gregory M., and Geoffrey L. Cohen (2007) "A question of belonging: Race, social fit, and achievement," *Journal of Personality and Social Psychology* 92: 82–96.

Walton, Gregory M., and Geoffrey L. Cohen (2011) "A brief social-belonging intervention improves academic and health outcomes of minority students," *Science* 331: 1447–51.

Westlund, Andrea C. (2009) "Rethinking relational autonomy," *Hypatia* 24: 26–49.

8 Adaptations to Oppression
Preference, Autonomy, and Resistance

Ann E. Cudd

1. INTRODUCTION: PREFERENCES AND THEIR PLACE IN MORAL AND POLITICAL PHILOSOPHY

Why do we care about what people prefer? There are at least three categories of *prima facie* reasons. Liberals care about people getting what they want because they choose it. Preference is seen as connected to liberty. Utilitarians care about people's preferences because preference is seen as related to utility. Getting what we want seems to make us happy. More broadly, welfarist consequentialist theories tie preference to well-being because it is generally thought to raise persons' well-being to get what they prefer. Each of these connections depends on a tight connection between something and preference satisfaction: freedom or autonomy and preference satisfaction for the liberal, utility and preference satisfaction for the classical utilitarian, well-being and preference satisfaction for the (welfarist) consequentialist. The connection is defeasible, of course. For each of these theories, preferences for immoral ends are not necessarily worthy of being satisfied. In addition to the morality of the ends, there may be perfectionist worries or worries about harms to self or others.

Connections between preferences and what the theory takes to be morally significant may thus be broken under some circumstances. First, there are epistemic problems that sever the connection between what state of affairs an agent thinks she prefers and what actually comes from satisfying that preference. The agent may have incomplete information about the full description of the state or how the state will be experienced once it is achieved. Or there may be unexpected changes in the agent's circumstances, such that by the time the preference is satisfied, it is no longer desirable to the agent. Second, there can be character problems such as weakness of will that compromise the link between the preference and the morally significant things, where an agent prefers something in the short run but not as a part of an overall plan for life. Third, there are potential moral problems, both self-regarding and other-regarding, with preferences. Preferences can be for states that allow the agent less freedom in the future, which is clearly problematic if satisfying the preferences puts the agent in a situation in which she cannot satisfy her future preferences. Or they can be for states in which the agent sacrifices her dignity or self-respect. Finally, preferences are morally problematic if their satisfaction harms others.[1]

In this latter context, I want to examine adaptive preferences and in particular those adaptive preferences that form in reaction to oppressive social conditions. Feminists have explored how adaptive preferences, sometimes pejoratively termed "deformed desires" in the context of oppression,[2] reinforce the conditions that reduce freedom for themselves and others in their oppressed social group.[3] Some recent preference theorists have attempted to show that adaptive preferences are not problematic for the agent who has them or for society.[4] Such a view would reduce the imperative to change oppressive conditions whenever the oppressed have become resigned or adapted to living in unjust conditions of lack of freedom and opportunity. In this chapter, I will defend the view that adaptive preferences that are caused by oppressive circumstances are problematic for morality and justice. Deformed desires are problematic not only because they sever the connection between autonomy and preference, as feminists have noted, but also, and more importantly, because they harm others. As a result, we can derive an obligation to resist such preferences and a *prima facie* reason to intervene to change the preferences that reinforce oppression.

2. DEFINING ADAPTIVE PREFERENCES

Defining adaptive preferences is inevitably a partly normative project; adaptive preference is a moralized concept because it picks out preferences that have been formed in a way that makes those preferences suspect. Adaptive preferences are preferences that adapt or adjust to the agent's feasible set of possible states of affairs but do so in a way that we would find somehow psychologically or morally problematic. We will know that we have a good definition when we pick out a kind that can be clearly distinguished from other kinds of preferences but also that identifies a psychological, moral, or political problem with those preferences.

Jon Elster first identified adaptive preferences in the context of discussing freedom and autonomy.[5] Preferences that we are caused to have but do not intentionally choose to form because our freedom has been constrained are, he reasoned, non-autonomous. For Elster, the paradigmatic example of adaptive preference formation is the story of the fox who, when he found that he could not reach the grapes that he wanted, changed his preference, declaring the grapes to be sour. In Elster's view, the characteristics of adaptive preferences that make them non-autonomous changes in preference are (1) the change is in response to a (perceived) constriction of the set of states of affairs that the agent could feasibly bring about and (2) the change happens not as a result of intentional planning of one's character but rather by an "essentially" unconscious process that happens "behind the back" of the agent. In Elster's view, the nature of the process of change is really more important than the constriction of the feasible set; as long as one intentionally chooses to change one's preferences, then the change does not compromise freedom. So if the fox were to say to himself, "The grapes are out of my reach, so I am going to cultivate a taste for berries that I can reach and convince myself that I like them better than grapes," then Elster would not classify such a change as an "adaptive preference" change in the sense that he claims compromises autonomy.

Elster offers a test of adaptive preferences that allows us to tell the difference between those that come about by an irrational process and those that are permanent, planned character changes. If the preference change would reverse were the feasible set to be enlarged again to include the state that is now dispreferred, then the change is a problematic adaptive preference. But if the preference change would remain intact after the feasible set had been enlarged to include the dispreferred state, then the change would be considered a rational character-planning process. For example, once I realized that I did not have the physical gifts to become a star athlete, I became more interested in philosophy and came to realize that intellectual activities gave me deep and long-lasting pleasure, as opposed to the fleeting pleasures of athletic grace and glory. If I now were endowed with those physical gifts, I would not choose to devote my life to athletic pursuits but would still prefer the life of the mind. This is a change that involved learning and cultivation of the talents that I found I had, but it is a permanent change in my preferences and so a rational, nonadaptive one. If society is arranged to encourage such character planning, say by inviting only the gifted athletes to sports camps but making sure that everyone has the chance to study philosophy, it is not freedom denying.

While Elster's preference reversal test is a good one for preference changes that are motivated by restrictions of one's feasible set that result from either natural obstacles or social ones that come from just social conditions, it does not fit when the change results from oppressive social conditions. Suppose, for example, that the story about my preference change really is that women were not permitted to be athletes because that pursuit was considered to be immodest for women, and so the preference change I described happened. Now apply the preference reversal test, and suppose that my preferences still do not reverse, not because of the attractions of philosophy so much as my internalized sense that as a woman, I should not be an athlete. I would now say that this preference change was coerced, and that is morally problematic. That is, if permanent character changes are made in response to oppressive social conditions, it does not matter that the changes are permanent. In fact, it seems somewhat worse to me if they are permanent! The oppressive social conditions have warped my sense of the good, making me into someone other than who I might otherwise be. I am less likely to protest or resist the oppressive conditions if I am satisfied with them, and others are unlikely to do so on my behalf. Such preferences create a sense of inevitability and even satisfaction with an unjust status quo. Furthermore, why should we only be concerned about *changes* in preferences? If the process by which preferences are induced in persons are coercive and unjust, which amounts to an adaptation to oppression, then the preferences are also morally problematic. Thus, I claim that Elster is not correct to say that adaptive preferences have to be changes made by unconscious causal processes in order to be suspect from the perspective of freedom.

Elster argues that adaptive preferences arise from internal, unconscious processes. This differs from manipulation by others, which is to him a clear case of external coercion, or character planning by the self, because he thought that the latter type of process had to be autonomy enhancing or at least autonomy preserving for the person. As he writes, "I am not arguing that character planning *ipso facto* makes for autonomy, but surely it could never detract from it."[6] Elster is concerned about autonomy, but in my view, he fails to see how autonomy can be compromised by oppressive social conditions through the rational responses of victims to their conditions, that is, through what he would term character planning.

Feminist concerns about adaptive preferences suggest a different way of drawing distinctions than Elster does. The problematic preferences for feminists are preferences of the oppressed that are morally problematic for the oppressed. These are the adaptive preferences that are preferences caused by oppressive conditions and are for states that reinforce those conditions. Let's call these "preferences that are adaptations to and for oppression," or PAOs for short. Even so, it is a contentious matter to show how just how adaptive preferences are morally problematic for the oppressed.

Several theorists have pointed out that adaptive preferences cannot be morally problematic simply because they are formed by an unconscious process, since most of our desires come about through unconscious processes that we find unobjectionable, such as the normal process of learning in early life.[7] Another proposal for why PAOs are morally suspect is because they are not the agents' authentic preferences, and so they compromise the agency or autonomy of the ones who have them.[8] Let us first take the proposal that they compromise agency. On the standard account of agency, this is to say that the oppressed are not fully rational agents, or not really voluntarily acting when they choose to satisfy adaptive preferences. But to portray the people in this way is to portray them as mere "dupes."[9] While there may well be those who have been duped by oppressive circumstances, the examples that some feminists have offered have been criticized by others who have shown that most adult women living under oppressive circumstances are in fact better described as making the best of their situation by choosing within the social norms that they take as given. As Uma Narayan puts it, they are better described as "bargaining with patriarchy," making voluntary, preference-maximizing choices within their constraints. Examining a particular example of Sufi Pirzada women, she argues that they are even keenly aware of the injustice of the patriarchal nature of these social constraints and choose to work within them because that is their best option (objectively considered, arguably). They take such injustice as one of the fixed features of the environment that they must choose within. If the oppressed can be so characterized, they are better seen as acting rationally, shrewdly, with full agency, and not as mere dupes.

I agree that PAOs should not be characterized as problematic because they necessarily compromise agency. What about autonomy? I want to argue that PAOs are typically non-autonomous preferences, but not (or at least not only) because of the nature of the preferences or the way that they have been formed. It is beyond the scope of this chapter to fully develop a theory of autonomy and defend it, but it is crucial for me to indicate the type of theory that I support. I find the most plausible theory to be a substantive, relational theory, which requires that agents have adequate social freedoms as well as the internal capacities and skills to make use of them. By adequate social freedoms, I mean that basic material needs are satisfied and that there is the basis for each person to live a dignified life as a moral equal with others. Among other things, this requires that one not face categorical exclusion or discrimination based on arbitrary, ascribed social group status. Autonomy requires that one rationally plan one's life and live according to a moral code that one can see reasons for. Social circumstances can be so constraining that they rule this out, if one has to act in ways that one would, absent those circumstances, consider immoral in order to survive. Somewhat less constraining options that make it difficult to resist wrongdoing are not autonomy-supporting social conditions. For example, an environment where one is punished for not obeying some oppressive social norm makes it difficult to choose not to contribute to oppression. Thus, on this view, persons' autonomy can be compromised by their social circumstances. Autonomy is thus both a social and an individual achievement.

Serene Khader criticizes the view that adaptive preferences represent autonomy deficits in the agent who has such preferences. She first argues that adaptive preferences are not procedural autonomy deficits. Since this is not my view either, I will pass over this part of her argument. Khader then argues that adaptive preferences are not substantive autonomy deficits. While she provides good reasons to reject some versions of substantive autonomy, the view that substantive autonomy is thwarted by accepting oppressive social norms withstands her critique. The primary reason she rejects that view is that such a view of autonomy would encourage people to abandon their existing systems of value, and this is illiberal and condescending. By recommending that a person abandon her values, they seem to blame the victim for her plight. Khader's critique applies to my view because I argue that oppressive societies compromise autonomy. First, societies that fail to provide social freedom because they are oppressive would clearly fail to support autonomy. Second, as mentioned previously, oppressive societies may, through incentive or coercion, motivate persons to act in ways that contributes to oppression, and so fail to support autonomous action.

Hence, my view entails that oppressive societies need reorientation to support autonomy, which may amount to abandoning existing systems of value.

Khader's critique of adaptive preferences as autonomy deficits seems to me to be misguided. She claims that because it is not legitimate to recommend that people abandon (aspects of) their cultures, it cannot be the case that adaptive preferences are non-autonomous. First, the argument at best begs the question of whether it is legitimate or effective or good to recommend that people abandon aspects of their cultures. One might easily disagree and hold that it is in fact good for people to abandon aspects of their culture that are oppressive, and therefore it is good to recommend that they do so. Second, the conclusion of the argument is a non sequitur. The claim that some particular preferences are autonomous is a claim about what autonomy is and where particular preferences come from. The claim could be true even if it is false that people should interfere with other cultures.

However, that said, I do agree with Khader that non-autonomy should not be seen as *definitional* for PAOs. A useful definition of PAOs should point to their cause and indicate why they are morally problematic in every case. I would agree with Khader's observation that it is possible for people to have adaptive preferences and still be autonomous in some sense for some decisions, despite their oppressive circumstances.[10] I propose that we define the class of adaptive preferences that she and I are interested in, namely PAOs, as those preferences that are caused by adaptation (whether planned or unplanned, conscious or unconscious) to oppressive circumstances that restrict the feasible set of options for the oppressed group. This definition indicates the cause of the preferences (adaptation to oppression) and why they are problematic. Furthermore, the definition points to the social circumstances as the root cause, not the individuals who have the preferences, and so it avoids victim blaming.

Ann Levey argues that adaptive preferences (where she, too, is interested primarily in PAOs) sometimes result from an expansion of the feasible set, and this would seem to contradict my definition.[11] She cites studies of women in North America showing that they enjoy domestic work and argues that this preference has developed because of enhanced opportunities for women (as compared with men) to do that kind of work. Thus, it could be expansion of the feasible options that cause the PAOs. I agree that some new opportunities arise as a result of oppressive social norms, but there are also restrictions of the feasible set in this case that are relevant. I believe that my definition still captures what is going on with the example better than her analysis does. It is not the expanded opportunities but rather the fact that those opportunities look better than the other ones in the feasible set, a set that lacks opportunities that men have, that makes them attractive and causes the adaptation. Such expansions of options are not real expansions of freedom, but rather booby prizes, like women being the beneficiary of the door-opening ritual as a part of their being considered inferior to and thus in need of the protection and assistance of men. The feasible set is still restricted in crucial ways—it lacks opportunities that would give women equal social power with men. These are arbitrary restrictions that are the result of oppression.

Another worry about the definition is that it might be question begging if oppression is defined in terms of circumstances that give rise to adaptive preferences. Elizabeth Barnes objects to the use of "adaptive preference" to describe disabled people who come to prefer their disability to a life without it.[12] She argues that there is no way to prove that a disabled life is less desirable than a life without disability without begging the question by assuming that a disabled life cannot be as desirable as a nondisabled life. But my definition of adaptive preference, which relies on oppressive circumstances, does not fall victim to this objection as long as we can define oppression separately from the fact that there are objectionable preferences involved. Since oppression involves many social distortions and states that are clearly dispreferred by the oppressed, it can be recognized separately from the alleged presence of adaptive preferences.[13] Barnes would agree; she offers a criterion she calls "social warrant" for identifying adaptive preferences, according to which, "we are only warranted in diagnosing adaptive preference behavior in situations that represent some form of social distortion."[14] Oppressive social norms cans be seen to present social distortions by offering persons unjust differential rewards or punishments for complying with the norms depending on ascribed group status. Thus, this definition of PAOs, an important subset of adaptive preferences for social and political philosophy, is not question begging.

3. WHY SHOULD WE NOT SATISFY OR HELP PEOPLE TO SATISFY PAOS?

Some recent theorists have argued that adaptive preferences are acceptable preferences, and it is therefore best for society to help people get what they prefer. It will be worth examining why they think that adaptive preferences can be defended before I present my argument against them in the case of PAOs.

Harriet Baber argues that the adaptiveness of preferences is not morally important (a "red herring") because either they are authentic preferences after all, or if they are not, then such preferences should be satisfied because the person is better off if they are.[15] Again, I think that Baber is primarily concerned with the subset of adaptive preferences that I call PAOs, and so her view, at least in part, opposes mine. Some apparent preferences are inauthentic, she admits, because they are caused by brainwashing or a lack of information about alternatives. But such preferences should not be considered the actual preferences of such persons, since actual preferences require good information and sufficient time and ability to rationally consider what one really prefers. These cases are not like that, so in Baber's view they should not be termed preferences at all.

Another possibility for mere apparent adaptive preferences occurs when persons are making the best of their circumstances. But in this kind of case the questionable preference for x has to be construed as preference for x over y in presence of condition z, not for x over y in all conditions. For example, the woman who chooses not to go out of her home because she fears for her physical safety is preferring not to go out over going out in a situation where going out may well result in her being beaten. And this is not the same thing as preferring not going out over going out in a situation where she will be safe. So again, we cannot assume that the person actually has that preference, and hence not real adaptive preferences.

Setting aside these cases in which the apparently adaptive preferences turn out to be not the agent's actual preferences, Baber argues that adaptive preferences, including PAOs, that are an agent's real preferences ought to be respected. She examines the case of Srey Mom, a prostitute who had been sold to a brothel as a child by her rural Cambodian parents. After Nicolas Kristof purchases her in order to return her to freedom in her hometown, she returns to the brothel, apparently preferring life as a prostitute to that in her rural home. It may be that these are her real, authentic preferences (i.e., those for which she has good information and sufficient time and ability to rationally consider) and that they are the result of adaptation to circumstances in which girls are often sold by their parents. In that case, Baber claims it is better that her preferences be respected, since it improves her welfare to get what she authentically wants. Baber admits that it is an empirical question whether this is a case of authentic preference rather than a preference for being a prostitute over living in her home village under the circumstances of oppression, when she would prefer living in the village without those circumstances. But let us suppose that it is the relatively low standard of living and not female oppression that Srey Mom has reacted to in choosing to live as a prostitute in the city; even with the oppression of women, if there were as many consumer goods available in her home village, she would choose to live there rather than be a prostitute. It is still a PAO on my definition because the female oppression has caused these preferences in the sense that they caused her to be sold into prostitution. This would be a case where, according to Baber, adaptive preferences should be respected because the agent has shown these to be her actual preferences, and it raises her welfare by satisfying them. For Baber, the social circumstances in which preferences arise are not relevant; a preference is problematically adaptive only if it is insufficiently informed or if the agent has failed to rationally consider it.

Baber offers one more case where she thinks adaptive preferences should be respected. Sometimes persons will express preferences for a state of affairs that appears adaptive to oppression out of a sense of commitment. According to Amartya Sen, this is not a preference at all; acting out of commitment is at times counterpreferential.[16] Whether or not this makes sense (and I cast doubt on that elsewhere),[17] it is clear that this is how many women who embrace the conditions of their oppression interpret their situation. For example, right-wing Christian women, who express a preference for obeying their husbands when, absent his command, they would otherwise prefer a different action, explain their apparent preference as a religious commitment to wifely obedience. The commitment might be best understood as a belief and hence a case of false consciousness. But such a case fits my definition of adaptive preference if we see this as preferring the commitment and what it entails and this commitment was caused by the conditions of their oppression. Baber holds that these adaptive preferences should be respected, presumably because they reflect actual commitments of rational agents.

Donald Bruckner agrees that adaptive preferences ought to be respected if they are a person's authentic preferences.[18] He does not restrict the causes of adaptive preferences to oppressive circumstances, but he does include adaptive preferences that have been caused by oppression as among those that should be seen in a favorable light. He writes, "in making the case in favor of adaptive preferences, I mean to be arguing in favor of their pursuit, in favor of their being normative for the agent who holds them."[19] He offers a test for when we should favor pursuing the satisfaction of adaptive preferences: if the agent endorses the preference upon reflection, then regardless of the origin of the preference, it carries positive normative weight. One of Bruckner's cases is that of Yvonne, who is forced by her mother to help with traditional female chores and comes to prefer those activities over the traditional male activities that she does not get to experience as a child. Although he never puts it this way, I assume that Bruckner includes this example precisely because it is an example of internalized oppression and so something of a hard case for his claim that such preferences have positive normative weight. On his account, as long as she reflectively endorses her preferences for traditional female over male activities, then these preferences are normatively valuable not only for Yvonne but also as inputs into social decision making.

We now have three cases in which adaptive preferences that are caused by oppression (what I call PAOs) are argued to be acceptable preferences, so that other things being equal, we ought to pursue or support the pursuit of their satisfaction.

1. "Actual" preferences that are caused by oppressive circumstances, where the agent is making the best of a bad situation;
2. Preferences for states that express a commitment to an oppressive ideology;
3. Preferences that are caused by internalizing oppression, but on reflection and with full information about the oppressive condition, the agent endorses the preference.

In my view, PAOs ought to be resisted and perhaps even changed if doing so does not sacrifice something of even greater moral significance. These cases pose challenges to my view and require me to argue that there is some-thing wrong with the preferences such that they should not be granted the normative presumption argued for by these preference theorists.

Let's consider four problems with PAOs that can tell against giving them normative presumption. First, long-run gains to resisting PAOs may outweigh the short-run gains from their satisfaction. Consider Lisa, who, because of an oppressive stereotype about women as domestic caregivers, adapts her preferences to preferring the domestic work of raising her chil-dren and supporting her husband but then is bereft when her children grow up, her family moves on, and she is left with no fulfilling activities. She, or some examples of her type, surely fit Baber's criteria of agents who have actual preferences for unpaid domestic work, and yet they later come to regret that they did not find outside work that would enable them to find a life beyond their children's childhood.[20]

The second problem that may arise with PAOs is that they reinforce the social circumstances that gave rise to them for the individual, further restricting her feasible set. Take the case of Lisa, a nonprofit grant writer who quits her job when the first kid is born because her husband, Larry, has a higher-paying job, and they both prefer one parent to stay home with the children. Let's stipulate that the gendered wage gap as a manifestation of women's oppression is the root cause of the wage gap between Larry and Lisa.[21] Because he earns more, all things considered, she prefers being a stay-at-home mom. But this causes her human capital to deteriorate over time, which means that in the future, the wage gap between them—the cause of her preference — becomes wider. This compromises her bargaining situation with Larry and makes her vulnerable to many bad outcomes in both home and future work opportunities. Her adaptive preference to be a stay-at-home mom is clearly not good for her in the long run, at least not materially. It does not come out of a theoretical commitment to an oppressive ideology, but she has arguably made the best of a bad situation, and she might, given the situation she faces, reflectively endorse it. So we might use her future loss of human capital as an argument to try to persuade her about what she ought, rationally, to do with her life. But we probably don't want to prevent her from having these adaptive preferences or insist that she change them just because acting on them forecloses certain options that would have made her better off. After all, people form preferences for and engage in all kinds of activities that foreclose better options in their future, which a liberal soci-ety ought to allow and respect.

A third problem is that in some cases, the PAOs may be immediately self-defeating. Examples of this type may seem hard to find, but I submit they are not. Take, for example, the abused wife who has the kinds of pref-erences that Lisa has, but also has an abusive spouse. By playing the role of the domestic wife, she makes it almost impossible to escape abuse, since she is economically dependent on her spouse and more attached to their children, whom she cares for. For agents who may end up in this situation, their adaptive preferences are not good for them, even on their own terms, since by satisfying them, they end up immediately worse off. That is, by satisfying her preference to be a stay-at-home mom, Lisa becomes the victim of abuse. At the same time that they satisfy their preferences, they wind up in what almost anyone would say is a dispreferred state. These preferences might be making the best of a bad situation, but the situation is so horrible that it cannot be endorsed. They might also come out of a commitment to some religious view about the nature of men and women, but even so, it would be implausible to assert that they should therefore be respected. Could such preferences be reflectively endorsed by Lisa? The difficulties that prosecutors and law enforcement officers have in getting abused women to prosecute their husbands suggests that they sometimes are reflectively endorsed; abused women often choose to return to their spouses for a variety of reasons even after they have had a chance to consider other options. So we have a counterexample to the arguments for respecting adaptive preferences on the grounds that it raises welfare. However, this is a limited class of cases. I wish to make the stronger claim that no adaptive preferences caused by oppressive circumstances should carry normative presumption.

The fourth and most general reason to reject PAOs is that they almost inevitably reinforce the social structures that oppress the group as a whole, and hence they run a high and unacceptable risk of harming others. Social norms work by motivating many individual actions that in turn create the motivations to follow them. Lisa's situation is replicated many times in society, since women are raised to be mothers, and they are likely to have lower expected wages, due to a variety of oppressive circumstances. But all the Lisas who prefer to be stay-at-home moms reinforce the norms of women as unpaid domestic workers, contribute to the conditions for implicit bias and stereotype threat against women, and lower the expected wage for women with otherwise equal qualifications to those of men. They recreate for their children the stereotypes of women as mothers and men as breadwinners and construct gender as a relevant vector of discrimination in the workplace, education, childrearing, and so forth. Thus, Lisa participates in a social norm that harms others. Not resisting these adaptive preferences harms others of her social group. Hence, these adaptive preferences ought to be given negative normative weight.

One might object that one person's participating in a social norm that is harmful for others is too insignificant to actually harm others and could be overridden morally by a significant value to the person who does participate.[22] In response, I distinguish between material values and the identity-value that accrues to an individual participating in a social norm. Identity-value is the increase in well-being from embracing a particular identity, even if it is disvalued by society. I grant that there may be significant material benefits for the person so acting that override the material losses to others. Similarly, one's psychological well-being can be enhanced by acting according to a social norm. But identity-value can be embraced in different ways, including by identifying with others in one's social group by collectively resisting an oppressive social norm. Protest and other forms of collective resistance can create positive identity-value for a disvalued group. At the same time, being forced into a disvalued identity through the force of a pervasive, oppressive social norm is highly negative.[23] Thus, at least where resistance or protest is possible, one cannot count the identity-value created by acting in accordance with an oppressive social norm as normatively positive.

Another objection to my analysis of the harms of PAOs is that none of these problems result from the adaptiveness of the preferences but rather from something else (imprudence, self-defeatingness, or immorality). I have two responses to this. First, my aim is to show that there is some reason to oppose adaptive preferences that have adapted to oppressive circumstances, not necessarily to show that their adaptiveness is the problem in itself. But second, I believe that the fourth problem is a problem with the fact that PAOs are *adaptive to oppression*. The fact that PAOs almost inevitably reinforce social structures that oppress groups as a whole and hence risk harming others offers the strongest argument against granting adaptive preferences normative presumption. While I grant that the first three kinds of problems can arise from preferences that are not adaptive or that are not adaptive to oppression, the fourth is a kind of problem with PAOs that is important to consider for moral and political reasons. Although the first three problems for adaptive preferences do not apply in each case, I will argue in the next section that the fourth type of problem always applies. I will conclude that this gives us good reasons to oppose, resist, and change the adaptive preferences if we can do so without sacrificing something of even greater moral value.

4. ADAPTATIONS TO OPPRESSION REINFORCE OPPRESSION

In other work, I have argued that oppression lasts for generations when and because it co-opts the oppressed to acting in ways that further their oppression.[24] This is not to say that the oppressed bring oppression on themselves, since they are not in the first instance responsible for the oppressive social structures. Oppression begins with forceful subjugation, and it is the dominator, not the subjugated, who bears full responsibility for this beginning. But once oppression has begun, norms that keep the oppressed and the privileged in their social roles arise and are reinforced. These roles create stereotypes that make people believe that the oppressed and the privileged are different. They enforce boundaries around social groups and exaggerate differences between groups, which are then used as rationales for, even justifications of, differential treatment. The differences divide the two groups into those who are to be denied or offered opportunities, status, and other social goods.

Once there are bounded social groups, the boundaries are policed by both ingroup and outgroup members. Norms motivate behavior by assigning social penalties for transgressing group boundaries but also by rewarding those who are exemplary members of the group to which they are seen as belonging, even when it is the oppressed group. The stereotype of the dumb blonde may be bad for women generally, but it does not stop individual women from wanting to live up to the stereotype for the small rewards of male attention if one can be a really good example. Think of the Dallas Cowboy Cheerleaders or the waitresses at Hooters. They may fully recognize that the stereotype is harmful to other women and to themselves sometimes, but by playing up their conformity to the stereotype in a given situation, they receive the locally greater rewards of more money and attention than other women receive. In this sense, they are making the best of the oppressive social norms that they find.

Not all conformity to stereotypes is done with intent *to benefit at others' expense*. Members of oppressed groups often believe that the differences between social groups are natural and inevitable, and they may even come to see those differences as good and to be preserved. The right-wing women who are sincerely committed to fundamentalist Christian ideology, which prescribes different lives for men and women and commands wifely obedience, exemplify this phenomenon. Acting from such commitments is of course intentional, although the intent is not to benefit at others' expense but rather from the belief that the oppressive social norms are good ones to uphold. Thus, the oppressed can be co-opted either through their conscious bargaining or through being kept in thrall by ideology, in Narayan's words, either "bargaining with patriarchy" or being "dupes of patriarchy."[25]

It will be objected that we should not hold individuals responsible for reinforcing social norms when their individual actions are not causally necessary for the maintenance of the norms.[26] That is, many of us have to act in ways that reinforce the norms in order for those norms to continue; any one of us acting alone would not create or even maintain a social norm in the absence of many others' actions. I agree that no individual's action is causally necessary in most cases; social norms are essentially products of collective actions. However, individuals still bear moral responsibility for collective actions that they participate in intending to conform to the norm. My argument is that by acting according to oppressive social norms, with the intention to conform, we are *complicit with* the maintenance of an oppressive social norm, and for this we are blameworthy.

Christopher Kutz defends what he calls the "Complicity Principle: I am accountable for what others do when I intentionally participate in the wrong they do or the harm they cause."[27] In the case of oppressive social norms, the harm or the wrong is oppression. Although the individual actor does not himself cause the wrong in the counterfactual sense that, had he not so conformed, the social norm would still have continued, this principle offers a weaker claim. The claim is that one is complicit with oppression because if no one conforms, the social norm would no longer exist, and for that complicity one is accountable. It is weaker in two ways: the strength of the causal connection and the degree of responsibility. The causal connection between complicit behavior and the harm is twofold. First, one is in a position to be that last person necessary for the harm to occur. Suppose maintaining the social norm requires n persons to continue to behave according to it. Then by being complicit one is in the position to be that nth person that still behaves according to the norm. Second, if one behaves according to a social norm, one encourages others by one's behavior to continue, making it more difficult for others who observe one's behavior to resist behaving according to the social norm. Even if one is not causally responsible for the maintenance of an oppressive social norm, behaving according to it is causally relevant. This causal relevance is sufficient for responsibility, albeit reduced responsibility for the maintenance of the social norm.

PAOs inevitably reinforce oppression because they are seen as reasons to reinforce it. It is not only liberal or consequentialist philosophers who believe that people should get what they prefer, after all. Most members of oppressed groups come to identify with and proclaim their preferences to live according to the stereotypical preferences and prescribed social norms of their groups. That fact seems to give us reason to respect their preferences. One might even object that it is cruel and demanding to require that adaptive preferences be given up by the oppressed, especially when they seem to be self-sacrificing preferences. But that is just what I think morality demands: that the oppressed resist social norms that are motivated by PAOs.

5. RESISTANCE, REPROACH, AND INTERVENTION

If I am right that acting on PAOs almost inevitably harms others and typically harms the one who has the preferences, then it ought to be resisted. To be clear, I am arguing that all of us, including the oppressed, have the obligation to resist oppressive social norms in some way. This is because we have only two options: either we reinforce the oppressive norm by not resisting it, or we resist it. Since PAOs uphold oppressive social norms, acting in accord with them is wrongdoing. Hence, they have to be resisted. Resistance can take the form of protesting a norm, acting counternormatively, supporting someone who is flouting a norm, quietly refusing to go along with a norm, or avoiding situations where the norm applies, among others. Both the positive effects on changing the norm and the dangers and penalties for resisting have to be taken into account, of course, in deciding what one should do in any particular circumstance.

One problem with oppression and the adaptive preferences that it causes is that those preferences are often not noticed. This may seem to mitigate the obligation we have to resist PAOs. As I have said, oppressive norms last for generations because they become part of the fabric of social norms. The norms define persons in their discriminatory and excluded roles so that life within these norms appears normal and inevitable. It is difficult to see how life might be otherwise, and almost no one is eager to live an abnormal life flouting oppressive social norms, since such behavior makes them outcasts.

For example, gay people until very recently had every reason to prefer to remain in the closet, but the existence of the closet made gayness unusual, fearful, even disgusting. These emotions of fear and disgust reinforced the oppression of gay people, made it likely that they would be treated violently, and made the closet that much more preferable to coming out. But the paucity of out gay people in society reinforced the attitude towards homosexuality that it was something strange or queer. That created a difficult epistemic situation for people to see gayness as a normal way of being. In such a situation, it may seem that people should not be held responsible for changing their attitudes and accepting gayness. But I want to resist this conclusion and hold us responsible to resist. As Cheshire Calhoun has argued, holding people responsible for resisting oppressive norms is justified even in situations in which the oppressive social norm appears to be reasonable and, well, normative.[28] For in these situations, not resisting is acting in a way that harms others, which is wrongdoing.[29]

To say that PAOs ought to be resisted is one thing; it is quite another to say how society should intervene to change adaptive preferences. I agree with Calhoun's view that in interpersonal situations, reproach is the best approach. But different methods of delivering a reproach are possible, and some are more likely to achieve a good result. What is a good result? It is twofold: first, that the person with adaptive preferences is brought to reconsider them and attempt to change them or at least not to act on them, and second, that this is done with the least harm possible to the oppressed person who is now being asked to change her preferences. For it must be remembered that she is a victim of oppression and has a difficult duty to bear.

The onus is not only on the oppressed to change their preferences; society more generally should create the conditions in which preference change can readily occur. It will be objected that responding to PAOs may create unfreedom that is unacceptable. If a society removes the unearned privileges from a currently privileged social group in order to benefit an oppressed group, then that restricts the freedom of the former group. For example, regulations of employment or lending practices that open employers or lenders to liability for racially disparate outcomes restrict freedom. Such measures may require that those employers and lenders make significant efforts to educate and advertise to oppressed groups in order to change their preferences for types of employment or housing opportunities. But by definition, the employers' and lenders' freedoms from scrutiny are unearned privileges. There is no moral requirement to preserve *unearned* privileges. So removing them does not violate justice if it is in the service of remedying oppression.

6. CONCLUSION

This paper has explored one aspect of the claim that it is better for people to get what they prefer, focusing on the specific cases of adaptive preferences that are formed under and are preferences for behaving in accord with oppressive social norms. I examined several arguments that defend such preferences as autonomous, authentic, or otherwise giving us reasons to give them positive normative weight personally and socially. I argued that such preferences are often harmful to the one who has them, but more importantly, that they are always harmful to others, namely to the members of social groups oppressed by those norms. Acting in accordance with preferences that are adaptive to oppression thus makes one complicit with the immorality of oppression. Finally, I argued that this fact generates an obligation to resist one's own such preferences and to design social institutions that will help one to change those preferences.

My argument has implications for the autonomy of those who hold PAOs as well. Oppressive social norms inhibit autonomy for the oppressed by taking away their freedom to do and to be. That much is clear from the very definition of oppression. But oppressive social norms also seep into the motivational set of the oppressed in the form of PAOs, which means that they come to prefer or want harm to others. Preferences for states that harm others are not substantively autonomous. Thus, I have argued that PAOs jeopardize one's personal autonomy (as a substantivist relational phenomenon) even where the connection between preference and authentic choice is preserved. PAOs are problematic for autonomy regardless of whether the PAO is deemed authentic or conducive to welfare enhancement and thus of some positive normative weight. Preferences for behaving in accord with oppressive social norms are harmful to self and others and cannot be the motivation for autonomous action.

ACKNOWLEDGMENTS

This chapter has benefitted from discussions in presentations at the University of Kansas Department of Philosophy Colloquium, the 2012 Central Division APA, the University of Pennsylvania Institute for Law and Philosophy, the University of Northern Michigan Philosophy Department, and the University of Connecticut. I am especially grateful for helpful comments on earlier versions of this paper from Dale Dorsey, Derrick Darby, Tom Tuozzo, Jack Bricke, Richard DeGeorge, Cristian Dimitriu, Donald Bruckner, Claire Finklestein, Serene Khader, Sarah Jones, Marina Oshana, Zac Cogley, and Carol Hay.

NOTES

1. I use the term "problematic" to signal a *prima facie* worry rather than the *pro tanto* judgment that satisfaction of such preferences is categorically "proscribed." All in, the utilitarian may argue that preferences that harm others should still be satisfied, of course.
2. Anita Superson, "Deformed Desires and Informed Desires Tests," *Hypatia*, 20 (2005): 109–126. I am using the term "deformed desires" in her sense to signify only those adaptive preferences that are caused by oppression.

Ann E. Cudd

Among those who argue this are Martha Nussbaum, *Women and Human Development*, Oxford, 2001; Ann E. Cudd, *Analyzing Oppression*, Oxford, 2006; Sandrine Berges, "Why Women Hug Their Chains: Wollstonecraft and Adaptive Preferences," *Utilitas*, 23 (2011): 72–87; Ann Levey, "Liberalism, Adaptive Preferences, and Gender Equality," *Hypatia*, 20 (2005): 127–143; and Serene Khader, *Adaptive Preferences and Women's Empowerment*, Oxford, 2011.
4. Donald Bruckner, "In Defense of Adaptive Preferences," *Philosophical Studies*, 142 (2009): 307–324.
5. Jon Elster, *Sour Grapes*, Cambridge, 1983, 117.
6. Elster, op. cit., 138.
7. Lisa Fuller, "Knowing Their Own Good: Preferences & Liberty in Global Ethics," in Thom Brooks, ed., *New Waves in Ethics*, Basingstoke, UK: Palgrave MacMillan, 2011; Nussbaum, 2001; Levey, 2005; Khader, 2011.
8. Those who hold some version of this view include Superson, Nussbaum, and Levey.
9. Uma Narayan, 2002. "Minds of Their Own: Choices, Autonomy, Cultural Practices, and Other Women." In Louise M. Antony and Charlotte E. Witt, eds., *A Mind of One's Own: Feminist Essays on Reason and Objectivity* (2nd ed.). Boulder, CO: Westview Press, 2002, 418–432.
10. Khader, 2011, ch. 3.
11. Levey, 2005.
12. Elizabeth Barnes, "Disability and Adaptive Preference," *Philosophical Perspectives*, 23, Ethics (2009): 1–22.
13. I provide an analysis of oppression separate from the definition of PAOs in *Analyzing Oppression*, Oxford, 2006.
14. Barnes, 2009, 13.
15. Harriet Baber, "Adaptive Preference," *Social Theory and Practice*, 33, No. 1 (January 2007): 105–126.
16. For a recent statement of his view on commitment as a counterpreferential motivation, see Amartya Sen, "Why Exactly is Commitment Important for Rationality?" *Economics and Philosophy*, 21 (2005): 5–14.
17. Ann E. Cudd, "Commitment as Motivation: Sen's Theory of Agency and the Explanation of Behavior," *Economics and Philosophy*, 30 (2014): 35–56.
18. Bruckner, 2009.
19. Bruckner, 2009, 312.
20. Of course, not all examples of this type have these regrets. Furthermore, even if later they come to have these regrets, the same could be said for nonadaptive preferences for other risky outcomes. Sometimes we reject those preferences, such as when they are *akratic*, but sometimes we do not. If the preferences come out of a commitment to a higher principle, then we would not reject them. The reflective endorsement test rejects *akratic* preferences, but not these. So if I want to claim that in all cases these adaptive preferences ought to be rejected, then I need to find another argument.
21. In "Oppression by Choice," *Journal of Social Philosophy*, 25 (1994): 22–44, I initially presented the Larry-Lisa example as an example in which the gendered wage gap is a manifestation and cause of the oppression of women.
22. I am grateful to Serene Khader for pressing this objection.
23. Nyla Branscombe, Saulo Fernández, Angel Gómez, Tracy Cronin, "Moving Toward or Away from a Group Identity: Different Strategies for Coping with Pervasive Discrimination." In Jolanda Jetten, Catherine Haslam and S. Alexander Haslam, eds., *The Social Cure: Identity, Health and Well-being*, New York: Psychology Press, 2012, ch. 7. Their research indicates that embracing identity through resistance to oppression raises well-being for disvalued groups.

24. Cudd, 2006.
25. Narayan, 2002.
26. Daniel Silvermint, in "Resistance and Well-Being," *Journal of Political Philosophy* (2012): 1–21, 5, offers this reason for why nonresisting cannot be seen as causing oppression. The claim he rejects is perhaps a stronger claim than the one considered here, that conforming causes oppression, but is essentially the same objection as the one considered here.
27. Christopher Kutz, *Complicity: Ethics and Law for a Collective Age*, New York: Cambridge University Press, 2000, 122.
28. Cheshire Calhoun, "Responsibility and Reproach." *Ethics*, 99 (1989): 389–406.
29. One might also argue that living with PAOs is a harm to oneself since it compromises one's own autonomy. While I agree that undermining one's own autonomy is a way of harming oneself, I am not convinced that we have an obligation not to do so. Such an argument is made by Carol Hay, *Kantianism, Liberalism, and Feminism: Resisting Oppression*, New York: Oxford University Press, 2013.

REFERENCES

Baber, Harriet. "Adaptive Preference." *Social Theory and Practice*, 33, No. 1 (January 2007): 105–126.

Barnes, Elizabeth. "Disability and Adaptive Preference." *Philosophical Perspectives*, 23, Ethics, (2009): 1–22.

Berges, Sandrine. "Why Women Hug Their Chains: Wollstonecraft and Adaptive Preferences." *Utilitas*, 23 (2011): 72–87.

Branscombe, Nyla, Fernández, Saulo, Gómez, Angel, Cronin, Tracy. "Moving Toward or Away from a Group Identity: Different Strategies for Coping with Pervasive Discrimination." In Jolanda Jetten, Catherine Haslam and S. Alexander Haslam, eds., *The Social Cure: Identity, Health and Well-being*. London: Psychology Press, 2012.

Bruckner, Donald. "In Defense of Adaptive Preferences." *Philosophical Studies*, 142 (2009): 307–324.

Calhoun, Cheshire. "Responsibility and Reproach." *Ethics*, 99 (1989): 389–406.

Cudd, Ann E. *Analyzing Oppression*. Oxford: Oxford University Press, 2006.

Elster, Jon. *Sour Grapes: Studies in the Subversion of Rationality*. Cambridge: Cambridge University Press, 1983.

Fuller, Lisa. "Knowing Their Own Good: Preferences & Liberty in Global Ethics." In Thom Brooks, ed., *New Waves in Ethics*. New York: Palgrave MacMillan, 2011.

Hay, Carol. *Kantianism, Liberalism, and Feminism: Resisting Oppression*. New York: Oxford University Press, 2013.

Khader, Serene. *Adaptive Preferences and Women's Empowerment*. Oxford: Oxford University Press, 2011.

Kutz, Christopher. *Complicity: Ethics and Law for a Collective Age*. New York: Cambridge University Press, 2000.

Levey, Ann. "Liberalism, Adaptive Preferences, and Gender Equality." *Hypatia*, 20 (2005): 127–143.

Narayan, Uma. "Minds of Their Own: Choices, Autonomy, Cultural Practices, and Other Women." In Louise M. Antony and Charlotte E. Witt, eds., *A Mind of One's Own: Feminist Essays on Reason and Objectivity* (2nd ed.). Boulder, CO: Westview Press, 2002.

Nussbaum, Martha. *Women and Human Development: The Capabilities Approach.* Cambridge: Cambridge University Press, 2001.

Silvermint, Daniel. "Resistance and Well-Being." *Journal of Political Philosophy,* 21: 4 (2012): 405–425.

Superson, Anita. "Deformed Desires and Informed Desires Tests." *Hypatia,* 20 (2005): 109–126.

9 Autonomy Under Oppression
Tensions, Trade-Offs, and Resistance

Suzy Killmister

1. INTRODUCTION

It is a commonplace in philosophical discussions of oppression to assume that it compromises personal autonomy.[1] Indeed, this is often taken to be one of oppression's most distinctive and insidious harms. My aim in this chapter is to explore precisely *how* oppression compromises personal autonomy and what individuals might be able to do to insulate themselves from these effects. The focus of my discussion will be on the distinctive harms of double binds. Double binds occur when an agent is faced with a decision, either side of which subjects her to some form of sanction or frustration. In this respect, they are analogous to moral dilemmas. A classic example of a double bind is the situation faced by many women in contemporary Western societies with respect to career and family: given the absence of adequate child-care options, many women must still choose between fulfilling their career goals and raising a family.[2] I argue that double binds such as these compromise personal autonomy: by their very nature, such double binds prevent individuals from realizing some or other goal or value. Moreover, given the inescapability of choice, these double binds force individuals to actively frustrate one of their goals or values, which, as I will go on to show, necessarily constitutes a reduction in the agent's autonomy.

At this point a curious problem emerges: if, as I will go on to argue, autonomy is compromised because of mutually unrealizable goals and values, then it looks like personal autonomy could flourish under oppression if the agent successfully undertook a project of self-modification. In other words, if the agent molded her values and goals to fit the demands of the oppressive society, then the conflict that threatened her autonomy would be avoided.[3] I will concede that insofar as this process is viable, some individuals may be better able to protect their autonomy by capitulating to oppression than by resisting it. However, I suggest that the extent of modification required to both avoid double binds and preserve autonomy is psychologically implausible. For the most part, such modifications will fall short, and when they do, they merely relocate the reduction in autonomy from one dimension of autonomy to another (what these dimensions are will be outlined shortly).

Moreover, even if an agent *could* sufficiently modify her goals and values in the face of oppression, to do so would be to preserve autonomy at the cost of integrity. In the face of oppression, then, agents are thus commonly forced to either make trade-offs *within* autonomy or make trade-offs *between* autonomy and another core personal value. Agents under oppression are thus faced with a particularly tragic dilemma.

Before I begin, a few words are in order about the theory of autonomy I am relying on in what follows. This theory takes the idea of self-governance as a starting point of analysis, where to be self-governed means governing oneself in accordance with one's reasons and commitments.[4] Importantly, on my view, self-governance is both outward looking and reflexive, encompassing both the effective realization of the agent's plans and goals in the world and the effective authority of the agent's judgments over her own psychological profile. The reflexive aspect of self-governance, which I will be calling Self-Definition, is achieved insofar as the agent judges her motivational attitudes to be reasonable.[5] Self-Definition is typically disrupted in cases of phobia, whereby the agent experiences a motivational attitude, fear, that she judges to be unreasonable. The outward-looking aspect of self-governance can be broken down into two distinct dimensions, which I will call External Self-Realization (measuring the extent to which the agent's actions correspond to her intentions) and Internal Self-Realization (measuring the extent to which the agent's intentions express what she takes herself to have reason to do). The former is what is disrupted in standard cases of physical interference, insofar as the agent intends to do x but is forced to do y; the latter is what is disrupted in standard cases of weakness of the will, insofar as the agent intends to do other than what she judges best.

On this view, then, autonomy has three distinct dimensions. All three dimensions of autonomy—Self-Definition, External Self-Realization, and Internal Self-Realization—are independent variables, and each comes in fine-grained degrees.[6] Each of these dimensions is necessary to fully capture the scope of self-governance, in that reductions in any indicate a reduction in the agent's overall autonomy. If the agent's actions fail to accord with her intentions (low External Self-Realization), then she is like the captain of a ship that is permanently moored to a dock. Though she can issue directives, insofar as these fail to direct where the boat goes, it is misleading to say she is controlling the ship. If the agent's intentions fail to accord with what she takes herself to have reason to do (low Internal Self-Realization), then she is like a captain seduced by the Sirens. Insofar as her directives are successful, they actually undermine the extent to which the boat follows her chosen path. Finally, if the agent's psychological profile falls short of standards that she herself recognizes (low Self-Definition), she is like a captain who recognizes the futility of the obsession that compels her. While the boat may follow her chosen path, it is a path that she disavows and thus cannot be an unequivocal expression of self-governance.

I will begin in Section 2 by noting the ways in which oppression commonly compromises each of these three dimensions of autonomy. While all three dimensions suffer under autonomy, the primary focus here will be on Internal Self-Realization, as it is with respect to this dimension that double binds play their most important role. I will then turn in Section 3 to consider the possibility that an agent may be able to increase her autonomy through capitulation to oppressive forces by deliberately cultivating her motivational attitudes to cohere with oppressive norms. I argue that in most cases, such tactics merely protect Internal Self-Realization at the expense of Self-Definition. In other words, they simply shift the harm from one dimension of autonomy to another. However, while I suggest that the success of such adaptations is in practice deeply implausible, I concede that it is not conceptually impossible. In Section 4, I explore the implications of this in terms of a tension between protecting one's autonomy and preserving one's integrity.

2. HOW OPPRESSION COMPROMISES AUTONOMY

2.1. Self-Definition

A commonly recognized effect of oppression concerns the self-understanding of oppressed citizens. Take the oppressive practices of heteronormativity as an example: part of the practice of heteronormativity is the construction of a social standard that deems homosexual desire deviant. Putting this in the terms of the theory of autonomy I am working with, heteronormativity threatens to reduce the Self-Definition of gay citizens.

On my account, an agent is Self-Defined to the extent that she is not subject to motivational attitudes that she rejects as unreasonable. Consider two agents, each of whom experiences fear of nonvenomous spiders. On my account, the agent who considers that fear to be reasonable would be more Self-Defined than the agent who considers that fear to be unreasonable. This is so irrespective of the objective reasonableness of the fear. The reason Self-Definition, thus defined, is a necessary dimension of personal autonomy is that the persistence of attitudes that the agent judges to be unreasonable indicates a gap between how she believes she should be and how she is. Insofar as we are subject to motivational attitudes that we take to be unreasonable, we exhibit a psychological profile that is criticizable by our own lights. Unless and until we manage to rid ourselves of such attitudes, then, we are failing to shape ourselves in accordance with how we judge we should be—we are failing to instantiate the reflexive aspect of self-governance.

As it stands, this still does not tell us enough to determine the effects of oppression on Self-Definition. For that, more needs to be said about what it means to take a motivational attitude to be unreasonable. I am using "unreasonableness" as an umbrella term to cover any standard the agent might appeal to in explaining why she finds the experience of a particular attitude to be problematic. For instance, an agent may find herself frightened of a puppy and be baffled by her own response. In explaining her bafflement, she might point to such things as the puppy being obviously unthreatening. Such a response would suggest that this agent takes something like fittingness to be a relevant standard for assessing the reasonableness of fears (at least in some contexts).[7] By contrast, another agent may find herself sexually attracted to a particular individual but deem that attraction to be morally inappropriate (perhaps because that individual is her best friend's partner). What is important to stress here is that the idea of reasonableness is subjective in two distinct senses. First, the standard by which an attitude is judged (i.e., fittingness or moral appropriateness) is up to the agent herself. If an agent doesn't take moral inappropriateness to compromise motivational attitudes, then it doesn't affect her Self-Definition if she experiences a motivational attitude that she takes to be morally inappropriate. Second, whether or not the motivational attitude meets whatever standard the agent takes to be relevant is also up to the agent. So even if, objectively, fear of a puppy should be considered unfitting, if the agent herself considers the fear fitting (and hence reasonable), then her fear of the puppy makes her no less Self-Defined.

To return to the example of sexual oppression, if an agent in a deeply homophobic society comes to believe that her homosexual desires are deviant, as she is relentlessly socialized to do, then she will very likely be led to reject them as unreasonable. Her society offers her a moral standard by which to judge her desires, and if she internalizes that standard as appropriate, then the judgment of unreasonableness follows as a matter of course. For such an agent, to experience homosexual desires will conflict with how she takes herself to have reason to be and will thus constitute a reduction in her autonomy.

2.2. External Self-Realization

A second way in which oppression typically compromises autonomy is through frustration of External Self-Realization. According to External Self-Realization, if an agent intends to *A* but in fact *B*s, she is failing to fully govern herself. One of the paradigmatic ways in which External Self-Realization can be frustrated is through an external agent's intervention in the realization of an intention. For instance, if you have formed an intention to eat a cookie, but I physically prevent you from eating it (perhaps reasoning that you can't *really* want it), then I have frustrated your External Self-Realization. By substituting my will for yours, I have constrained your relation to yourself in the same way as the captain moored to the dock has a constrained relation to her ship: your ability to issue directives to yourself may remain untouched, but insofar as those directives are blocked from receiving uptake in action, they cannot fully secure your self-governance.

Under conditions of severe oppression, an agent simply may not have the option to convert her intention into the corresponding action. For instance, take a Palestinian youth in the Occupied Territories. Her intention to visit a friend in Israel is subject to the approval of the checkpoint guard; if he refuses her access, her intention cannot be realized and her External Self-Realization is thus frustrated. Or consider a woman in an abusive relationship. Though she may repeatedly form an intention to leave, her fear of the consequences of following through on that intention, for both herself and her children, may prevent her from translating that intention into action.[8]

2.3. Internal Self-Realization

A third way in which oppression commonly compromises autonomy, and the primary focus of this chapter, is through the creation of double binds. Double binds, I suggest, inevitably reduce an agent's Internal Self-Realization through the presence of reasons that cannot be fulfilled. The greater the extent to which those unrealizable reasons reflect core values or commitments of the agent, the greater the extent to which the agent's autonomy is reduced. As such, the greater the extent to which a double bind creates a dilemma between two or more of the agent's core values or commitments, the greater the extent to which that double bind reduces the agent's autonomy.

As noted, Internal Self-Realization measures the extent to which the agent's intentions map onto the reasons she takes herself to have. Akrasia would be a paradigmatic case of reduced Internal Self-Realization: the agent judges that she has most reason to A, but she nonetheless forms the intention to ~A. Insofar as the agent's intention comes apart from her practical judgment, she is failing to realize her commitments—she is failing to fully govern herself.

The crucial question for Internal Self-Realization is what it means for an agent to take something to be a reason for action. While I do not think that reasons for action necessarily reduce to motivational attitudes, for simplicity's sake I will consider desires as paradigmatic candidates for reasons for action in what follows. On a simple model, weighing reasons would simply amount to weighing up one's desires; the stronger my desire for x, the more reason I have to pursue x.[9] Building on Scanlon, however, I suggest that not all desires are necessarily taken up as reasons for action in an agent's deliberation; they may instead be "bracketed" as reasons.[10] Even when they *are* taken up as reasons for action, moreover, their strength as a reason may not necessarily correspond to their motivational strength. For an example of the latter case, we can consider an agent deliberating about whether to continue watching TV or instead to go to the gym. Whether her ensuing intention to continue watching TV exhibits high or low Internal Self-Realization depends not on whether her desire to watch TV is stronger than her desire to go to the gym but instead whether the agent takes her desire to watch TV to provide her with greater reason than her desire to go to the gym.

Bracketing is a more complex phenomenon, but the following example illustrates the point. Imagine experiencing a sudden desire to eat a Big Mac despite not being remotely hungry or even particularly enjoying the taste of Big Macs. You know, moreover, that the only explanation for your sudden desire is that you have just seen a billboard advertising a Big Mac. In such a case, you may take your desire for a Big Mac to provide you with *no* reason whatsoever to stop at MacDonald's. It is not that this desire is outweighed—perhaps by concerns for your health—but rather that the desire is denied *any* weight in your consideration of what to do.

If an agent acts solely on the basis of a desire that she has bracketed, then by her own lights she is acting without reason. This would involve a serious reduction of Internal Self-Realization. Less damaging but still problematic are cases in which an agent forms an intention to fulfill an unbracketed desire that she takes to be outweighed by other reasons. While the intention is suboptimal as an expression of the agent's will, it at least finds some traction in her calculus of reasons. Finally, and perhaps less intuitively, if an agent forms an intention that corresponds with what she takes herself to have most reason to do, she will still experience a reduction in Internal Self-Realization insofar as that intention fails to realize outweighed but unbracketed desires. For example, if on the earlier example I take myself to have more reason to watch TV and thus form that intention, the fact that my reasons for going to the gym remain unrealized reduces my Internal Self-Realization. As noted, typically an agent's core values and commitments will constitute stronger reasons than mere inclinations, meaning that to assess the degree of harm to Internal Self-Realization of an unfulfilled reason, it will be helpful to know whether that reason was tracking a value or commitment, on the one hand, or simply an endorsed whim, on the other.[11]

Double binds, by their very nature, limit the possibility for an agent to realize all the reasons that she takes herself to have. To consider a mundane example, take a woman in contemporary U.S. society deciding whether to shave her legs. On the one hand, she takes herself to have strong reasons not to: she considers it an oppressive patriarchal norm; not to do so would set a good example to younger generations; shaving one's legs takes time and money better spent on other activities. On the other hand, she recognizes strong reasons to capitulate: precisely because it's a patriarchal norm, she will be subject to varying degrees of social discipline if she presents herself *au natural*; moreover, having been socialized into Western beauty norms, she knows she will struggle with a visceral aversion to the way she looks unshaven. The structure of this dilemma is common enough. One of the key characteristics of oppression is that it creates disincentives for members of the oppressed group, which give them reasons not to do that which the societal norms deem inappropriate for agents like them.[12] Examples abound: women trying to balance a career with the desire to have a family; gay people deciding whether to come out to friends and family in the face of homophobia; people of color hoping to pursue a career in academia despite institutional racism. Whatever path the agent takes under such double binds, she will be falling short of doing all that she takes herself to have reason to do; some of her reasons will go unrealized in her action, and some of those reasons may well reflect core values or commitments. So if our original agent decides to shave her legs, she will be thwarting her commitment to making a stand against patriarchy; if she decides *not* to, she will be thwarting her value of experiencing a positive self-image. While in neither of these scenarios is she thereby *non*-autonomous, the requirement to "bargain with patriarchy"[13] reduces her autonomy by restricting the extent to which her intentions can realize all of her reasons for action.

In situations of double binds, I am suggesting, the agent is less autonomous than she would be if she experienced *no* countervailing reasons, because even outweighed reasons remain reasons for action; insofar as her action frustrates *any* of her reasons for action, she is less autonomous than she might otherwise be.[14] This claim may strike some as counterintuitive and so requires further comment. When our reasons for action conflict, I believe that it is a mistake to too strongly identify the self with the "winning" side. If I am torn between protecting my career and caring for my children, *both* of these motivations speak for me because both reflect a core value. Whichever decision I make, some important part of me is frustrated, and so that choice does less to realize my self than it might otherwise, such as if there were a path available that allowed both values to be fulfilled simultaneously.[15] If there were a way for these values to both be fulfilled, my action could more fully capture what I took myself to have reason to do and thus could more closely express my will. An action that fulfilled everything I took myself to have reason to do would be closer to the ideal of self-governance, whereby what I do and who I am fully reflects my reasons and commitments.

It may be objected that there are obvious counterexamples to this claim. For instance, take two agents each deciding whether to order tea or coffee at a restaurant. Both prefer coffee, but one dislikes tea while the other likes it. Surely we do not want to have to say that the agent who likes tea but prefers coffee has her autonomy reduced by her conflicting desires. However, this kind of conflict is importantly disanalogous to double binds. In these standard choices, the reason we have for either option is in fact the same reason: in this case, to drink a tasty beverage. Once I have settled on which tasty beverage I prefer, that reason is fulfilled, and I no longer have a reason to drink tea.[16] This is manifestly not the case in all exclusive choices, particularly when the agent's core motivational attitudes are at stake. To make this especially vivid, consider an agent confronting a particularly tragic dilemma, such as Sophie in the eponymous book *Sophie's Choice*.[17] When the concentration camp guard confronts Sophie with the tragic decision of which child to sacrifice, he thereby reduces her autonomy, because he makes it impossible for her to act in accordance with what she takes herself to have profound reason to do. Her desire to protect her daughter does not cease to be a reason for her just because, in that instant, she has a stronger desire to protect her son. Or, to put it slightly differently, her reason to protect her daughter is not *the same* reason as her reason to protect her son; doing the latter does not fulfil the former. The same holds for the vast proportion of coercive threats: even though the agent does what she most wants to do, given the threat situation, the defeated desires continue to function as reasons, and their frustration thus reduces the agent's autonomy. Precisely what is wrong with coercive threats is that they use some of the agent's motivational attitudes against herself—they rely on the strength of the desire to survive, avoid pain, and so on, to frustrate other of the agent's goals. If we suppose that the failure to fulfill conflicting reasons does not reduce autonomy, we lose the ability to explain why coercive threats reduce autonomy. Once the autonomy-reducing nature of coercive threats is understood, however, we can see that the very same dynamic is in play in double binds.[18]

3. SELF-MODIFICATION TO PRESERVE AUTONOMY

So much for the ways in which autonomy is commonly reduced under conditions of oppression. I want to turn now to consider the possibility that—for at least for some agents, some of the time—capitulating to oppression can augment autonomy. The motivation for this suggestion is simple: if the problem with double binds is that they leave some of the agent's values or goals unfulfilled, then the problem would dissolve were the agent to bring her values and goals into alignment with the oppressive norms. To put it slightly differently, an agent whose motivational attitudes, values, and goals wholeheartedly reflected the norms and expectations of society would not face double binds. What we see here is essentially a Stoicist move: it doesn't matter if society only gives me limited space to move, provided I can shrink myself to fit the space that I am given. This is what Isaiah Berlin has famously characterized as a "retreat to the inner citadel."[19] Since on the theory that I have put forward autonomy is constituted by satisfaction with, and realization of, our motivational attitudes and commitments, it is at least conceptually possible that autonomy could be augmented by the kind of "retreat to the inner citadel" that so concerns Berlin. I might become more autonomous by capitulating to oppression.

While conceptually possible, I will argue that such a move is nonetheless implausible. There are two reasons for such implausibility. First, only some kinds of double binds can be resolved through aligning one's attitudes with oppressive norms. Second, even where aligning one's motivational attitudes with oppressive norms *does* dissolve the conflict inherent in double binds, it commonly does so merely by pushing the problem onto another dimension of autonomy. An agent making this move is thus making a trade-off: she is augmenting one aspect of her autonomy at the price of another.

The first problem with the claim that autonomy could be protected through the cultivation of different motivational attitudes is that not all double binds are of the form presented in the leg-shaving example. In that case, the bind was primarily caused by a clash between the agent's values and the oppressive norms. If the agent aligned her values with the oppressive norms, her behavior would presumably receive no sanction, and thus she would not face any impediment to the realization of those values. Compare this to the kind of double bind that interests Marilyn Frye, whereby *whatever* the agent does, she is subject to sanction and censure; double binds of this type "expose one to penalty, loss or contempt whether one works outside the home or not, is on welfare or not, bears children or not."[20] For a woman in a deeply patriarchal society, cultivating motivational attitudes that favor working in the home or bearing children won't necessarily help, because even if the agent succeeds in realizing those now internalized values, she will nonetheless be confronted with social contempt in view of the low esteem placed on what are seen as traditional women's roles. Nor could she escape censure by cultivating motivational attitudes for working outside the home or remaining childless: such roles would also induce social contempt in virtue of the violation of proscribed gender roles. Assuming she places some value on self-respect, any way she acts will frustrate that value.[21]

Let's return now to the kind of double bind that may initially look like it could be resolved through the cultivation of different motivational attitudes, such as the woman deciding whether to comport with oppressive standards of beauty. In contrast to Frye's examples, we may suppose that in such cases, the woman would face no censure or sanction for comporting with those standards; it is not the case that, *whatever* the agent does, she is subject to sanction and censure. Instead, all that stands in her way are her own desires and values, which provide her reasons for not comporting with the oppressive standards. There are at least two avenues such an agent might pursue, were her only concern to augment her autonomy. On the one hand, she could try to erase the desires and values that provided the reasons not to comport with the oppressive standards. Conversely, she could tolerate the desires and values while rejecting them as reason giving. To explain this latter move: since reductions of Internal Self-Realization only occur when the agent fails to realize *unbracketed* desires, the agent's Internal Self-Realization would be unaffected by failure to realize desires that she did not take to be reason giving.

While the latter strategy may appear more psychologically plausible, I want to suggest that it is nonetheless deeply problematic. The problem is that this strategy merely displaces the problem from Internal Self-Realization to Self-Definition, and this is because to reject the relevant desires in this case as reason giving, as opposed to simply taking them to be outweighed, involves taking them to be false.[22] It is important to be clear that this is not necessarily the case for all bracketed desires. As Scanlon explains, desires are commonly bracketed when we engage in moral reasoning; an agent may well bracket a self-interested desire when it conflicts with moral requirements, without rejecting that desire in other contexts. However, in those kinds of cases, we have a ready story for why the desire in question is only conditionally reason giving, and this story necessarily invokes the role of morality in deliberation. By contrast, what story could we possibly tell ourselves about why our desire to resist oppression should be bracketed, as opposed to merely being outweighed? Because such a desire is already in the moral domain, I suggest, it can only plausibly be bracketed by being deemed irrelevant to the situation. We would have to assume that the relevant beauty norms were not oppressive, or that such oppression does not call for personal resistance. Such an assumption, however, would be exceptionally difficult to reconcile with the judgment that the desires to resist those norms were reasonable. In other words, assuming that a norm is not oppressive would typically be accompanied by the judgment that a desire to resist that norm is, *ceteris paribus*, unreasonable. Any emotional resistance to oppressive beauty norms would thus come to be seen as misguided; the agent would be subject to motivational attitudes that she deemed unreasonable. What this means, then, is that typically an agent can only manipulate her motivational attitudes to protect her Internal Self-Realization at the cost of reducing her Self-Definition.

This leaves the possibility that the agent could simply rid herself of her resisting desires. If this were possible, there would be no motivational attitudes that the agent deemed unreasonable, and hence no reductions in Self-Definition. Likewise, there would be no reason-giving desires that failed to be realized in her intentions and actions, and hence no reduction in either Internal or External Self-Realization. Such an agent would augment her autonomy through careful manipulation of her motivational attitudes, weeding out those in conflict with either social norms or other of her attitudes. She would augment her autonomy by, in Berlin's phrase, retreating to the inner citadel.

I am accepting for the purposes of this chapter that such projects of self-modification are possible. If adaptive preferences are a real phenomenon, as I am assuming they are, then desires are malleable, particularly in the face of social pressure. Since the self-modification we are imagining is toward a self that coheres with social demands, it can piggyback on the multitude of socialization practices that are already urging her in that direction.

At this point, a simple objection may suggest itself, namely that motivational attitudes induced in such a way are by definition non-autonomous. Surely, we might think, there's a difference between an agent who has cultivated motivational attitudes under conditions of freedom and one who has cultivated such motivational attitudes in response to oppressive conditions?[23] Unfortunately, this simple objection does not go through. To appeal to the fact that certain kinds of socialization are qualitatively different in that they are *oppressive* is simply to push the problem back a step. What is it about oppressive socialization that is supposed to compromise autonomy? If the answer is simply "that it is oppressive," it looks worryingly ad hoc. What's needed is an explanation as to how, by virtue of their origins, oppressive norms are necessarily heteronomous in a way that other norms into which we're socialized are not. Yet if there is nothing within the agent's psychology that resists these norms, then it is hard to see where the accusation of heteronomy is supposed to gain traction.

It may be objected that lack of resistance is insufficient, since that lack is due to precisely the forces that we are worried about as autonomy undermining. Yet attempting to accommodate this worry seems to inevitably cast the net too wide. For instance, if we try to explain what's wrong with oppressive norms in terms of whether the agent would approve of the new norms in advance of the modification, we seem to rule out cases of radical transformations. When an agent undergoes a religious conversion or some other kind of transformative epiphany, it is commonly true both that the agent's earlier self would not approve of the result of the transformation and that she would not approve of its means. Just as for the oppressed agent, the religious convert's lack of resistance to her new motivational attitudes is explicable entirely in terms of a transformative process that she neither chose nor preemptively endorsed. Unless we want to say that in all such cases the posttransformation agent is heteronomous, we need to concede that antecedently disapproving of the later motivational attitudes is insufficient to label those attitudes non-autonomous.

There is a grain of truth, though, in the worry that a wholesale retreat to the inner citadel can undermine autonomy. To see why this is so, it will be useful to revisit and extend Berlin's political analogy. If a government under siege were to cede *all* of its territory, retreating to an underground bunker but continuing to send unheeded orders into the outside world, we would rightly mock any claims of self-governance. There is simply no realm left to govern. The same phenomenon can occur at the individual level. My resistance to following the standard line on adaptive preferences lies in a concern to index autonomy to the agent's self, and in particular to her reflectively endorsed motivational attitudes and commitments. Even if that self is impoverished, in that it is composed of a limited, socially sanctioned set of values, the agent can still be self-governing, since she has the self she wants to have, and that self is effectively governing her actions. She is acting in accordance with her commitments. However, there is a point at which impoverishment of the self turns into self-effacement; and without a minimal self, there can be no-self-governance.[24]

To be self-governing, the agent must be able to acknowledge at least some of the motivational attitudes she experiences as her own and, more importantly, she must be able to accept at least some of them as reason giving. Otherwise, the self loses all capacity to govern—there is nothing there from which a direction might issue. Consider Paul Benson's example of the gaslighted woman: an agent becomes convinced of her own insanity, such that she no longer trusts herself to competently self-govern.[25] In such cases, arguably, the agent becomes fully estranged from her motivational attitudes, such that they are no longer even candidates as reasons for action.[26] Such extreme cases amount to a kind of erasure of the self. It is like a government trying to rule in the absence of a realm. While such an outcome remains a possibility under conditions of severe oppression, it is important not to overstate the case: in most cases, oppression is insufficient to bring about such complete erasure of the self, and insofar as there remains a self, we cannot assume that the agent is incapable of self-governance. There is, however, an additional reason to suspect that the project of modifying one's motivational attitudes might not be as conducive to autonomy as this response might suggest. To see why, though, requires a clarification of the conditions of autonomy.

As I have sketched Self-Definition and Internal Self-Realization, I have been concerned only with the actual judgment of the agent concerning the reasonableness and reason-giving force of her motivational attitudes (which we might think of as two varieties of endorsement). However, as the extensive literature on this issue attests, actual endorsement—however it is construed—leaves the door open to cases in which that endorsement is secured via various modes of manipulation.[27] If the only reason I take my fear of puppies to be reasonable is because I have been interfered with by a nefarious brain surgeon or brainwashed by a cult leader, it would seem strange to say that I am nonetheless autonomous. Similarly, if I take myself to have most reason to drink the contents of the glass because, and only because, I have been hypnotized to think the glass contains water, when in fact it contains petrol, it would seem strange to say that in drinking the contents of the glass, I am acting autonomously. Clearly, a modification is called for.

The required modification takes the agent's endorsement to be necessary but not sufficient to secure autonomy; full autonomy requires both endorsement—in both the "reasonableness" and "reasons for action" senses outlined—and an additional condition, which I will call the "consistency condition." This consistency condition builds on the work of John Christman, though in terms that stray quite far from his theory.[28] For Christman, what matters is whether the agent would revoke her endorsement for (or, in his terms, feel alienated from) her desire were she to know of its history. I see no reason to stop with the introduction of this particular realm of facts, however. We could similarly ask, and for the same reasons, whether the agent would revoke her endorsement of a desire were she to know pertinent facts about its object—for instance, that the person she is attracted to is in fact her best friend's partner.

This raises the difficult question of which facts to introduce. The danger is that, in requiring endorsement to survive the introduction of relevant facts, autonomy will collapse into orthonomy. Why should it matter that an agent acts on the basis of a misguided norm if that norm is what she is truly committed to? What is needed is a way to ensure that the facts that are introduced are relevant to the agent's autonomy and not merely to the objective correctness of her action or attitude.[29] Moreover, putting the modification in terms of counterfactual endorsement introduces all the problems that typically attend counterfactuals and is thus best avoided.[30]

To get around these problems, I propose the consistency condition. It matters for an agent's autonomy whether her endorsement is consistent with the vast web of epistemic and practical commitments that she otherwise holds, because failure to uphold any of these epistemic or practical commitments is a failure to act in accordance with one's own rules—it is a failure of self-governance.[31] So in the hypnotism case, I take myself to have a reason to drink the contents of the glass; but I also have a practical commitment to acting in light of how the world actually is. This makes the content of the glass relevant to my determination of my reasons for action and hence a fact that needs to be taken into consideration. As such, we need to ask whether I am currently disposed to take myself to have a reason to drink the contents of the glass, given that it is petrol. If the answer is no, then my intention to drink the contents of the glass does not realize what I am committed to taking myself to have reason to do and so that fulfilling that intention does not raise my Internal Self-Realization. A similar story can be told about the puppy case. I take my fear to be reasonable; but I also have a background commitment to fear being sensitive to fittingness (at least in these kinds of cases) and to nondangerous things being unfitting (again, in cases relevantly similar to the one at hand). Since there is an inconsistency between my judgment that my fear is reasonable and what I am committed to accepting as reasonable, that fear reduces my level of Self-Definition.

What this means in practice is that it would be insufficient for an agent to strip away the motivational attitudes that directly conflict with oppressive norms; to augment her autonomy, she would also have to strip away all of the epistemic and practical commitments that were inconsistent with her endorsement of her new motivational set. Our agent confronted with patriarchal beauty norms would thus have to come to desire to uphold those norms *and* rid herself of any commitment that conflicted with endorsing those desires. This would require a wholesale reconfiguration of her orientation to the world, potentially involving rooting out any commitments she might have to justice, equality, and truth.

Just as attempts to rescue Internal Self-Realization by changing what we take ourselves to have reason to do tend to simply relocate the problem to Self-Definition, so too attempts to rescue Self-Definition by changing our motivational attitudes tend to simply relocate the problem to the consistency condition. The agent concerned for her autonomy will thus be reduced to simply making trade-offs within the different dimensions of autonomy. Nonetheless, it would be too strong to say that wholesale modifications are actually impossible. As I will argue in the final section, however, while such far-fetched modifications may be able to augment autonomy, they do so at the cost of another trade-off; not between dimensions of autonomy this time, but between autonomy and integrity.

4. AUTONOMY VERSUS INTEGRITY

The concept of integrity is no less contested than the concept of autonomy, and I do not intend to enter into the debate over competing understandings of what integrity is here.[32] What I will do instead is present a particular desirable character trait that could plausibly be captured by the term "integrity", and argue that this character trait is incompatible with the kind of modifications that could augment autonomy under oppression. If readers prefer to give this trait a different name, nothing is lost from the argument. Similarly, if readers prefer to think of this trait as an internal component of autonomy, the thrust of the argument remains the same; rather than seeing the final trade-off as one between autonomy and the distinct value of integrity, this revision would reframe this final trade-off as once more between distinct aspects of autonomy itself.

The character trait I have in mind is composed of the motivation and the fortitude to uphold one's core values and commitments in the face of unjust pressure to relinquish those values and commitments. Paradigmatic examples of people with integrity, on this definition, would include Rosa Parks, Edward Snowden, and Malala Yousafzai. Each of these people has stood firm on their commitment to racial equality, government transparency, or the right to education despite the risk of great personal cost.

This idea of standing firm has two components. The most obvious way in which one can fail to stand firm is to fail to *act* on the basis of one's values and commitments in the face of unjust pressure. In such cases, the agent ignores the practical demands of her values and commitments, thus displaying lack of integrity. The second component is more pertinent to the focus of this chapter. To uphold one's core values and commitments also requires refusing to *abandon* or *modify* them in the face of unjust pressure. The potential fault line here is not between the commitment and the action it demands, but between the commitment and the dispositions of character required to retain it.

Having integrity, on this view, is compatible with a wide range of modifications an agent may choose to make to herself or that may happen beneath the level of her conscious awareness. A person could abandon a relationship, a career, or even a moral commitment, and it would not necessarily reflect a lack of integrity. What matters is what is motivating the person to abandon her commitment. If it is a case of recognizing a shift in one's values or reassessing one's priorities, then one's integrity may well remain intact through the modification. What is incompatible with maintaining integrity is to modify oneself (or allow oneself to be modified) because of unjust pressure.

If one's motivation to abandon a commitment is that doing so will make it easier to live in an unjust society, the modification may be understandable, but it involves a loss of integrity.

To be clear, the kind of integrity-damaging modification I am imagining is compatible, at least conceptually, with fully maintaining one's autonomy. On the account sketched earlier, autonomy requires that one judges one's motivational attitudes to be reasonable, and that one forms and enacts intentions that reflect what one takes oneself to have reason to do. If one were to successfully modify one's motivational attitudes in order to make it easier to live in an unjust society, along with the web of epistemic and practical commitments with which these attitudes and their cultivation must cohere, then one's autonomy would remain intact.[33]

The upshot of this is that the kinds of modifications that seek to preserve autonomy under oppression necessarily undermine integrity, and this is so whether or not those modifications are successful. The modifications are undertaken as a response to the pressure created by oppressive circumstances, and as such, they are incompatible with maintaining one's integrity. Agents under oppression thus face yet another tragic choice: if they aim at preserving their autonomy, they must accept the loss of their integrity.

5. CONCLUSION

I have argued that oppression compromises autonomy through the generation of double binds. Under double binds, agents are unable to fully realize their goals, values, and commitments and are thus less than fully autonomous. While such agents retain some control over their own autonomy, this control largely amounts to the power to undergo trade-offs. Agents can choose to protect their External Self-Realization by only developing intentions that are possible to realize, but this reduces their Internal Self-Realization; they can undergo a process of modifying what they take themselves to have reason to do in order to protect their Internal Self-Realization, but then problems emerge for their Self-Definition; they can try to strip away all of the motivational attitudes that conflict with the oppressive norms, but this merely pushes the problem onto the consistency requirement. Finally, they could attempt to undergo a wholesale reorientation of their epistemic and practical commitment, but to do so would be to abandon their integrity. Oppression thus presents the oppressed with a particularly egregious type of tragic dilemma: whatever they do, something of value must be sacrificed.

Marilyn Frye has described oppression as like a cage. Focusing on any single bar makes it seem like it should be possible to escape, but this promise disintegrates once the cage is viewed in its entirety. For an agent concerned with protecting her autonomy under oppression, there are many bars that appear circumventable. Circumventing any one, however, merely runs her headlong into a neighboring bar. Agents under oppression may well have the freedom to choose which aspect of their autonomy to sacrifice or whether to protect their autonomy at the price of their integrity, and this is better than no freedom at all. But it is still just the freedom of the caged bird to choose which bar impedes her flight.

ACKNOWLEDGMENTS

Many thanks to Marina Oshana and Natalie Stoljar for helpful comments on earlier drafts and to the audience at the Workshop on the Duty to Resist One's Own Oppression, University of Connecticut, 2014, where this chapter was first presented.

NOTES

1. See, e.g., Susan Babbitt, *Impossible Dreams: Rationality, Integrity, and Moral Imagination* (Boulder: Westview Press, 1996); Sandra Bartky, *Femininity and Domination: Studies in the Phenomenology of Oppression* (New York: Routledge, 1990); Paul Benson, "Autonomy and Oppressive Socialization," *Social Theory and Practice* 17 (1991), 385–408; Ann Cudd, *Analyzing Oppression* (Oxford: Oxford University Press, 2006); Natalie Stoljar, "Autonomy and the Feminist Intuition," in *Relational Autonomy: Feminist Perspectives on Autonomy, Agency, and the Social Self*, ed. Catriona Mackenzie and Natalie Stoljar (New York: Oxford University Press, 2000); Anita Superson, "Deformed Desires and Informed Desire Tests," *Hypatia* 20 (2005), 109–126.
2. See Cudd, *Analyzing Oppression.*
3. This claim goes against the grain of much of the literature on oppression, whereby adapting one's desires to align with oppressive norms is considered necessarily autonomy undermining. For a variety of arguments supporting the standard view, see, e.g., Cudd, *Analyzing Oppression*; Jon Elster, *Sour Grapes: Studies in the Subversion of Rationality* (Cambridge; Cambridge University Press, 1985); Martha Nussbaum, *Women and Human Development: The Capabilities Approach* (Cambridge: Cambridge, 2001); Superson, "Deformed Desires and Informed Desire Tests"; Natalie Stoljar, "Autonomy and Adaptive Preference Formation," in *Autonomy, Oppression and Gender*, ed. Andrea Veltman and Mark Piper (New York: Oxford University Press, 2014), 227–252.
4. I take these reasons and commitments to constitute the relevant notion of "self" being appealed to in the idea of "self-governance" in that they form the standpoint with the authority to speak for the agent (though I take no stance here on broader metaphysical questions of the self, such as identity over time). This theory thus follows in the tradition of the procedural theories of autonomy first developed by Harry Frankfurt and Gerald Dworkin and has much in common with Michael Bratman's theory of self-governance. See Harry Frankfurt, *The Importance of What We Care About* (Cambridge: Cambridge University Press, 1988); Gerald Dworkin, *The Theory and Practice of Autonomy* (Cambridge: Cambridge University Press, 1988); Michael Bratman, *Structures of Agency: Essays* (Oxford: Oxford University Press, 2007). For a discussion of how and why my theory diverges from these, see Suzy Killmister, "The Woody Allen Puzzle: How 'Authentic Alienation' Complicates Autonomy," *Noûs* (10.1111/nous.12069). The theory is developed in more detail in Suzy Killmister, *Taking Autonomy's Measure* (MS).

5. As will become clear, my condition of Self-Definition differs significantly from Diana Meyers's condition of the same name. For Meyers, self-definition involves bringing a set of agency skills to bear on questions such as "What sort of person am I?" and "What really matters to me?" See Diana Meyers, *Self, Society, and Personal Choice* (New York: Columbia University Press, 1989); *Gender in the Mirror: Cultural Imagery and Women's Agency* (New York: Oxford University Press, 2002).

6. To be a maximally autonomous agent, on this theory, each dimension would need to be fully realized. I am assuming that such a feat is beyond the abilities of all human persons. As such, this theory is not intended to directly set a threshold for what counts as "autonomous" but instead to provide a schema for analyzing the various ways in which autonomy can be compromised.

7. For a discussion of fittingness, see, e.g., Justin D'Arms and Daniel Jacobson, "The Moralistic Fallacy: On the 'Appropriateness' of Emotions," *Philosophy and Phenomenological Research* 61 (2000), 65–90; Wlodek Rabinowicz and Toni Rønnow-Rasmussen, "The Strike of the Demon: On Fitting Pro-Attitudes and Value," *Ethics* 114 (2004), 391–423.

8. I should stress that frustration of External Self-Realization may not be sufficient for an all-things-considered judgment of non-autonomy: an agent's level of autonomy is a factor of all three dimensions. It is part of my broader approach that different applications of autonomy (i.e., as part of moral responsibility or as a basis for valid consent) will privilege different dimensions, so that the same agent may be judged autonomous in one respect but not in another.

9. Cf. George Ainslie, *Breakdown of Will* (Cambridge: Cambridge University Press, 2001).

10. See T. M. Scanlon, *What We Owe to Each Other* (Cambridge, MA: Harvard University Press, 1998), 50–55. On the related phenomenon of silencing, see John McDowell, "Virtue and Reason." *The Monist* 62 (1979), 331–350; Jeffrey Seidman, "Two Sides of 'Silencing.'" *The Philosophical Quarterly* 55 (2005), 68–77.

11. The extent to which Internal Self-Realization is reduced is a product of the strength of the reason that is unrealized, where for most agents this will in turn be a product of that reason's relationship to their core values and commitments: the more central a value or commitment is to the agent, the greater the extent to which its failure to be realized reduces the agent's autonomy. On my account, then, even trivial frustrations will technically reduce an agent's Internal Self-Realization, but for virtually any purpose for which we're concerned with the level of an agent's autonomy, these reductions will prove inconsequential.

12. See, e.g., Cudd, *Analyzing Oppression*; Marilyn Frye, *The Politics of Reality: Essays in Feminist Theory* (Trumansberg, NY: The Crossing Press, 1983).

13. Cf. Uma Narayan, "Minds of Their Own: Choices, Autonomy, Cultural Practices and Other Women," in *A Mind of One's Own: Feminist Essays on Reason and Objectivity*, ed. Louise Antony and Charlotte Witt (Boulder, CO: Westview Press, 2002).

14. Cf. Joseph Raz's discussion of unfortunate conflicts, "whatever the agents do there will be an unsatisfied reason left behind." *From Normativity to Responsibility* (Oxford: Oxford University Press, 2011), 181.

15. As this example may suggest, oppression is not the only way in which such tragic conflicts can arise. Sartre's example of the young man choosing between fighting for his country and staying with his ailing mother has precisely the same shape and so, on my view, will be equally damaging to his autonomy as cases that arise through oppression. What's distinctive about oppression is not *that* it affects autonomy but that it does so in ways that disproportionately target disadvantaged groups, and is politically imposed rather than inevitable.

16. Cf. Raz, *From Normativity to Responsibility*.

17. William Styron, *Sophie's Choice* (New York: Random House, 1976).

18. This is not to suggest that all double binds reduce autonomy to the same extent. What matters for measuring Internal Self-Realization is the weight we give to the reasons that we fail to realize. On this measure, the extent to which Sophie's autonomy is reduced by the double bind she faces is exponentially greater than the extent to which the leg shaver's autonomy is reduced be her double bind.

19. Isaiah Berlin, *Four Essays on Liberty* (London: Oxford University Press, 1969), 135–136.

20. Frye, *The Politics of Reality*, 3.

21. This final assumption could be challenged: if such an agent were to cultivate a desire to be treated with contempt, then adopting traditional gender roles could bring about the full realization of her goals and values. This suggests that another trade-off may be on the horizon, this time between autonomy and self-respect. Space does not allow for exploration of this possibility here, but cf. John Rawls' claim that the social bases of self-respect are a primary good, *A Theory of Justice* (Oxford: Oxford University Press, 1999).

22. For a more detailed discussion of the relationship between treating an attitude as reasonable and treating it as a reason for action, see Killmister, "The Woody Allen Puzzle."

23. See, e.g., David Zimmerman, "Sour Grapes, Self-Abnegation, and Character Building: Non-Responsibility and Responsibility for Self-Induced Preferences," *The Monist* 86 (2003), 220–241. Zimmerman draws a distinction between character building and resigned self-abnegation: in both cases, the agent consciously alters her preference structure, but because the latter is merely a response to oppressive circumstances, according to Zimmerman, it cannot increase the agent's freedom.

24. Cf. Babbitt, *Impossible Dreams*, who makes a similar argument with respect to Thomas Hill's deferential wife.

25. Paul Benson 1994, "Free Agency and Self Worth," *The Journal of Philosophy* 91 (1994), 650–668. It should be noted that Benson does not present the example in terms of self-erasure.

26. This suggests that a minimal degree of self-trust is necessary for Internal Self-Realization. Arguably, it is also necessary for Self-Definition, insofar as the agent needs some degree of self-trust to generate judgments of reasonableness, and for External Self-Realization, insofar as the agent needs some degree of self-trust to generate the confidence to convert her intention into action. This requirement for self-trust should be distinguished from Andrea Westlund's requirement that the agent have a disposition to answer for herself. For a critique of Westlund's view, see Suzy Killmister, "Autonomy and the Problem of Socialization," *Social Theory and Practice* 39 (2013), 95–119.

27. For a particularly convincing objection of this form, see Al Mele, *Autonomous Agents: From Self-Control to Autonomy* (New York: Oxford University Press, 1995), 145–147.

28. John Christman, "Autonomy and Personal History," *Canadian Journal of Philosophy* 21 (1991), 1–24; *The Politics of Persons: Individual Autonomy and Socio-Historical Selves* (Cambridge: Cambridge University Press, 2009).

29. Cf. Connie Rosati, "Agency and the Open Question Argument," *Ethics* 113 (2003), 490–527.

30. I have in mind in particular the problems of finking and masking. See C. B. Martin, "Dispositions and Conditionals," *Philosophical Quarterly* 44 (1994), 1–8.

31. I take it that commitments don't have to be consciously held; they can be revealed through our deliberative and practical histories.

32. For an overview of the debate, see Damian Cox, Marguerite La Caze, and Michael Levine, "Integrity," *The Stanford Encyclopedia of Philosophy*

(Fall 2013 Edition), ed. Edward N. Zalta. Accessed June 13, 2014. http://plato.
stanford.edu/archives/fall2013/entries/integrity/.

33. More accurately, we might say that one would end up with a higher level of
autonomy. Presumably one's autonomy would take a hit during the process of
cultivation, before the conflicting commitments had been weeded out.

REFERENCES

Ainslie, George. *Breakdown of Will.* Cambridge: Cambridge University Press, 2001.

Babbitt, Susan. *Impossible Dreams: Rationality, Integrity, and Moral Imagination.*
Boulder, CO: Westview Press, 1996.

Bartky, Sandra. *Femininity and Domination: Studies in the Phenomenology of
Oppression.* New York: Routledge, 1990.

Benson, Paul. "Autonomy and Oppressive Socialization." *Social Theory and Practice* 17 (1991), 385–408.

Benson, Paul. "Free Agency and Self Worth." *The Journal of Philosophy* 91 (1994),
650–668.

Berlin, Isaiah. *Four Essays on Liberty.* London: Oxford University Press, 1969.

Bratman, Michael. *Structures of Agency: Essays.* Oxford: Oxford University Press,
2007.

Christman, John. "Autonomy and Personal History." *Canadian Journal of Philosophy* 21 (1991), 1–24.

Christman, John. *The Politics of Persons: Individual Autonomy and Socio-Historical
Selves.* Cambridge: Cambridge University Press, 2009.

Cudd, Ann E. *Analyzing Oppression.* Oxford: Oxford University Press, 2006.

D'Arms, Justin and Jacobson, Daniel. "The Moralistic Fallacy: On the 'Appropriateness' of Emotions." *Philosophy and Phenomenological Research* 61 (2000), 65–90.

Dworkin, Gerald. *The Theory and Practice of Autonomy.* Cambridge: Cambridge
University Press, 1988.

Elster, Jon. *Sour Grapes: Studies in the Subversion of Rationality.* Cambridge: Cambridge University Press, 1983.

Frankfurt, Harry. *The Importance of What We Care About.* Cambridge: Cambridge
University Press, 1988.

Frye, Marilyn. *The Politics of Reality: Essays in Feminist Theory.* Trumansberg, NY:
The Crossing Press, 1983.

Killmister, Suzy. "Autonomy and the Problem of Socialization." *Social Theory and
Practice* 39 (2013), pp. 95–119.

Martin, C. B. "Dispositions and Conditionals." *Philosophical Quarterly* 44 (1994),
pp. 1–8.

McDowell, John. "Virtue and Reason." *The Monist* 62 (1979), pp. 331–350.

Mele, Al. *Autonomous Agents: From Self-Control to Autonomy.* New York: Oxford
University Press, 1995.

Narayan, Uma. "Minds of Their Own: Choices, Autonomy, Cultural Practices, and
Other Women." In *A Mind of One's Own: Feminist Essays on Reason and Objectivity,* ed. Louise M. Antony and Charlotte E. Witt, Westview Press, 2nd edition,
2002, pp. 418–432.

Nussbaum, Martha. *Women and Human Development: The Capabilities Approach.*
Cambridge: Cambridge University Press, 2001.

Rabinowicz, Wlodek and Rønnow-Rasmussen, Toni. "The Strike of the Demon: On
Fitting Pro-Attitudes and Value." *Ethics* 114 (2004), pp. 391–423.

Rawls, John. *A Theory of Justice.* Oxford: Oxford University Press, 1999.

Raz, Joseph. *From Normativity to Responsibility*. Oxford: Oxford University Press, 2011.

Rosati, Connie. "Agency and the Open Question Argument." *Ethics* 113 (2003), 490–527.

Scanlon, T. M. *What We Owe to Each Other*. Cambridge, MA: Harvard University Press, 1998.

Seidman, Jeffrey. "Two Sides of 'Silencing.'" *The Philosophical Quarterly* 55 (2005), 68–77.

Stoljar, Natalie. "Autonomy and the Feminist Intuition." In *Relational Autonomy: Feminist Perspectives on Autonomy, Agency, and the Social Self*, ed. Catriona Mackenzie and Natalie Stoljar. New York: Oxford University Press, 2000, pp. 94–111.

Stoljar, Natalie. "Autonomy and Adaptive Preference Formation." In *Autonomy, Oppression and Gender*, ed. Andrea Veltman and Mark Piper. New York: Oxford University Press, 2014, pp. 227–252.

Styron, William. *Sophie's Choice*. New York: Random House, 1976.

Superson, Anita. "Deformed Desires and Informed Desire Tests." *Hypatia* 20 (2005), 109–26.

Zimmerman, David. "Sour Grapes, Self-Abnegation, and Character Building: Non-Responsibility and Responsibility for Self-Induced Preferences." *The Monist* 86 (2003), 220–241.

10 Honky-Tonk Women

Prostitution and the Right to Bodily Autonomy

Anita M. Superson

I. INTRODUCTION

How do persons identify themselves sexually? The question that interests me is what it means to identify oneself as a sexual agent at all, or what conditions must be met in order for a person to identify herself sexually. I am particularly interested in how (heterosexual) women[1] can identify themselves as sexual agents under patriarchy, given various constraints—external, internal, and social—that threaten their control over their own sexual identity. To explore this question, I take up the case of the prostitute. This is because some people believe that the prostitute is the paradigm case of a woman who completely controls her sexual identity, making free and autonomous choices about when and with whom she has sex. The prostitute dismantles sexist stereotypes about women's passivity and submission in sex, and so may serve, strangely enough, as a model for other (heterosexual) women to emulate.

Feminists, who are concerned with whether women legitimately exercise their autonomy, are divided about whether the prostitute controls her own sexual identity. Some believe that prostitution is degrading, non-autonomous, sexual slavery, while others, like Martha Nussbaum, believe that it need not threaten women's autonomy any more than other paid work for which we use our bodies and that it can even be enjoyable.[2] The deeper, underlying issue that I am most interested in is the right to bodily autonomy. Feminists in the first group might believe that the prostitute does not exercise her right to bodily autonomy, while those in the second group might believe that she does exercise this right, sometimes describing it as a "right to do *with* our bodies what we choose."[3] I want to say more about the right to bodily autonomy, particularly in connection with sexual identity; in fact, I want to defend the view that having the right to bodily autonomy is a necessary condition for one's being able to control one's sexual identity, and that internal, external, and social constraints interfere with a person's right to bodily autonomy and thus her control of her sexual identity. But before I elaborate on the right to bodily autonomy, I will examine the issue of prostitution in connection with bodily autonomy and control of one's sexual identity. I focus on Nussbaum's view about prostitution partly because her liberal sentiments, which I share, challenged me more than any other view to say, without resorting to conservative or puritanical views about sex, exactly what is bad about selling oneself in sex, and partly because I find her work on prostitution at odds in places with her work on two other issues, namely, deformed desires and objectification in sex. Nussbaum's paper[4] focuses on the legality of prostitution, but I am concerned with the moral issues of controlling sexual identity and exercising the right to bodily autonomy. Nussbaum implies that the prostitute does or can do both. Following Nussbaum, I focus on the stereotypical prostitute who sells her sexual services to a man rather than the "sex worker" who performs other kinds of sexual services.

2. NUSSBAUM ON PROSTITUTION

According to Nussbaum, the main reason prostitution is stigmatized is connected to gender hierarchy: the prostitute as a sexually active woman is seen as a threat to the notion that men are to control women, especially when it comes to sex. Prostitutes are seen as "bad women," different from "good women" who are focused on sex only within monogamous marriage and for purposes of reproduction.[5] Stigmatizing prostitution, like stigmatizing veiling and female genital mutilation (FGM),[6] is a way of controlling women's sexuality.

The first part of Nussbaum's paper attempts to diffuse the stigmatization of prostitution by comparing it to six other kinds of "bodily service," or jobs or professions in which a person uses her body in ways that many of us do not find morally objectionable but which in some respects are not much different from the ways the prostitute uses her body in her trade. These range from the factory worker who doesn't have much control over her work to the nightclub singer who uses her voice to provide pleasure to the customer whose pleasure is primary, the philosophy professor who takes money for ideas that are intimate and definitive of selfhood, and to the (thankfully fictitious) colonoscopy artist who allows herself to be probed without anesthesia in an intimate invasion of her bodily space for purposes of medical education.[7] The further down the list we go, the closer the "bodily service" is to prostitution, challenging us to say why prostitution deserves its stigma. Despite the commonalities in these uses of one's body, I think prostitution differs in a morally significant way from the others, for reasons having to do with the nature of prostitutional sex in particular.

We might infer from Nussbaum's view that we are effectually controlling women's sexuality when we insist on banning prostitution but not these other bodily services and that *not* banning prostitution enables women to control their sexuality in the sense that they are free to choose whether to engage in prostitution and the sex acts involved therein. Furthermore, given the analogies to other ways of using one's body, we might also infer that not banning prostitution would mean that women exercise their right to bodily autonomy as much in prostitution as in the other "bodily services." Indeed, these views are consistent with the fundamental tenets of liberalism with which Nussbaum and I agree, namely, that "[In the liberal tradition, the treatment of persons at the hands of society and politics] must respect and promote the liberty of choice, and it must respect and promote the equal worth of persons as choosers,"[8] whose worth lies with planning a life in accordance with their own evaluation of their own ends. Nussbaum admits that liberals differ as to what promotes or undermines respect for persons, but since she favors the legalization of prostitution, she must believe that allowing prostitution appropriately respects women's choices. I will argue against both the view that the prostitute has control over her sexuality even when prostitution is legal and the view that the prostitute exercises her right to bodily autonomy.

The second half of Nussbaum's paper consists of various liberal arguments against arguments for criminalizing prostitution. Basically, having liberty, being autonomous, and being able to consent are the criteria that speak against criminalizing prostitution and seem to be necessary conditions for a person's having control over how she identifies herself sexually. In what follows, I propose a view of sexual identification in order to see whether the prostitute really does meet these conditions.

3. CONSTRAINTS ON SEXUAL IDENTIFICATION AND THE RIGHT TO BODILY AUTONOMY

I understand a person's sexual identity to be a matter of what kind of sexual being she is—whether or not she engages in sex, when, with whom, and under what conditions. At least three constraints stand in the way of a person's being able to control her own sexual identity. First are external constraints, including physical coercion (e.g., forced genital mutilation) and the unavailability of effective, reliable, safe birth control, protection from sexually transmitted diseases, and abortion services. External constraints limit one's *liberty* to define oneself sexually.[9]

Second are internal constraints, or factors that can interfere with a person's *autonomously* choosing to define herself sexually, such as deformed desires that a person acquires when she internalizes the norms of patriarchy. Nussbaum notes in "American Women" that women's desires can be deformed through unequal education, indoctrination into sexist beliefs about women's capabilities, psychological manipulation, lack of information or false information, lack of reflection, lack of options, and the "sour grapes" phenomenon, according to which the fox's conviction that he is prevented from eating grapes that are out of his reach causes him to believe that grapes are sour and so to prefer not to eat them.[10] Women who live in a patriarchal culture that teaches women to look to men for protection, security, and strength rather than to cultivate an ability to protect themselves and be independent and strong are more likely to want as their mates men who can offer protection and a sense of security and who appear strong. This can affect women's being self-directing about their sexuality when they have to forgo the satisfaction of some of their sexual desires and put the man's sexual desires ahead of their own in exchange for these benefits or have to exhibit the corresponding "feminine" traits of weakness and passivity even in sex, allowing men to control the terms of sex.

Third are social constraints, by which I mean stereotypes that are ascribed to a person by a dominant social group in virtue of the person's membership in a subordinate social group.[11] These can take the form of internal constraints, or they can underlie external constraints, but they warrant a separate category. Cynthia Willett argues that the stereotypes imposed on an oppressed group partly identify its members, and this identity often flies in the face of the identity that each member of an oppressed group carves out for herself independent of these stereotypes; in order to be an authentic self and to have freedom, oppressed persons have to square these two identities.[12] The group, men in virtue of its dominant status, imposes stereotypes on the group, women in ways that constrain women's sexual identity. Let us flesh out the patriarchal model of good sex, according to which the man is dominant, aggressive, perhaps even violent, and the woman is passive and submissive.[13] These traits are instantiated in the following way. Men are expected to initiate and control relationships and sex with women, and women are expected to be passive and wait for men to make the first move. Men are expected to have complete and exclusive sexual access to the woman they are with while they are allowed to roam free, and women are expected to be chaste and monogamous in exchange for protection from men. There is a "whore/virgin" divide applied to women—the bad women who buck these norms and try to take on the male role, and the good women who live out these norms to the fullest extent. On this model of "good sex," women's desires fall out of the picture: women lack full control over their own sexual identity because it is defined for them and imposed on them in the form of stereotypes they are expected to fulfill no matter how they want to sexually define themselves. The practices of rape, date rape, sexual harassment, female genital mutilation, and woman battering[14] are means through which men keep women "in line" sexually and impose the concomitant stereotypes on them.[15]

These three constraints on sexual self-definition interfere with a person's right to bodily autonomy, or right to bodily self-determination, and this explains why these constraints prohibit a person's being able to control her own sexual identity. I follow Judith Thomson, who defines the right to bodily autonomy as follows: " . . . if a human being has any just, prior claim to anything at all, he has a just, prior claim to his own body . . . the woman has a right to decide what happens *in* and *to* her body."[16] Thomson thinks of this right much like a right to self-defense, or a right to defend one's body against things happening in and to it,[17] which she grounds in the fact that a person *owns* her own body, making claims about it prior to other claims.[18] Her view is narrower than the view that the right to bodily autonomy consists in a right to do what one wants *with* one's body, as some of the feminists mentioned earlier seem to believe underlies prostitution. I think Thomson is correct, because the right certainly doesn't cash out as a right to use our bodies, for instance, to kill another person. We have the *freedom* to do things with our bodies—for example, we should be free to express ourselves sexually and free to go out in public without being objectified by oglers, but we have a *right* to determine what happens in and to our bodies. Most philosophers assume we have a right to bodily autonomy and assume in addition that this right is so fundamental it does not need defense.

Thomson elsewhere defends this right in a way that is interestingly similar to Hobbes's defense centuries earlier. Briefly, in the Hobbesian State of Nature, each of us has as his or her strongest desire a desire for self-preservation. We each have a right, best understood as a privilege since morality is absent in the State of Nature, to everything, including use of another's body. We form a contract of morality by "laying down," or giving up, some of our rights when others do so as well, thereby incurring corresponding obligations. But Hobbes believes we are not rational to give up rights that sacrifice the satisfaction of the desire for self-preservation. So a rational person can never give up his right to self-defense, which presumably includes protecting one's body from another's use of it. Hobbes's reason is that all voluntary acts must have as their object some good to the person, and were you to give up your right to self-defense, including your right to protect your own body, you could not be understood as if you meant it, since you would open yourself up to another's killing you. This can never be good for you; indeed, there would be no "you" left—you are, that is, for Hobbes, fundamentally your body.[19] The right to self-defense or to bodily autonomy puts us in the "moral game" in the sense that without it, entering bargaining schemes aimed at maximizing the satisfaction of our other desires is rendered pointless.

Thomson argues that certain rights, including one of our most fundamental rights, which is a right against bodily intrusion, are grounded in two related features of persons, namely, that we have what she calls "inherently individual interests," including interests in bodily integrity and life, and the fact that we are subject to the moral law, that is, that we are creatures for whom morality is possible. Thomson rejects the Hobbesian State of Nature on the Kantian grounds that "the capacity to conform your conduct to the moral law is a necessary and sufficient condition for the moral law to apply to you."[20] In order to have the capacity to conform her conduct to the moral law, that is, to understand morality and to follow it, a person needs to have inherently individual interests.[21] For Thomson, morality ought to allow us to cherish such interests. And if a person lacks such interests, Thomson questions whether she understands morality. Thomson's point, I believe, is that morality is often opposed to self-interest, and only if a person understands that she ought to perform some action when performing it is not necessarily in her interest can she understand what it is to make a moral sacrifice. A person's individual interests are ones that matter to her in such a way that not satisfying them as morality requires is sacrificial. Thomson goes on to reject ethical egoism for the reason that it requires that we act in ways best promoting our own interest even to the behest of respecting others' rights, and she rejects act utilitarianism because it requires an agent to sacrifice her rights even to her own bodily integrity for the sake of the general welfare. For Thomson, as for Hobbes, having certain interests is essential for being in the "moral game."[22]

Since the act of sex is essentially a bodily activity, identifying oneself sexually necessarily involves the right to bodily autonomy. A person cannot determine what happens in and to her body, sexually speaking, and cannot exercise her right to bodily autonomy unless she is not restricted by external, internal, and social constraints. Or, better, since these constraints exist under patriarchy, the more we remove such constraints, the more likely a person can exercise her right to bodily autonomy. A right to bodily autonomy is prior to, or a condition for, being able to identify oneself sexually, and one cannot fully exercise the right to bodily autonomy unless one is free from the aforementioned constraints. So, for example, exercising a right to bodily autonomy is compromised when abortion is unavailable and women are forced to bear unwanted fetuses, when a woman is completely under the sway of a deformed desire to have sex with men on their terms, and when the group, men, imposes the identity of sex object on the group, women, and this is at odds with the sexual identity a woman sees herself as having.

4. PROSTITUTION, THE RIGHT TO BODILY AUTONOMY, AND CONTROL OF SEXUALITY

Let's examine whether the prostitute is free from the constraints outlined and exercises her right to bodily autonomy and in doing so controls her sexual identity. It is reasonable to believe that many or most women who become prostitutes do so because of external constraints on their liberty: they lack money, are coerced into sexual services at a young age and cannot escape, they lack the education and the skills to do something else, or they have been treated with such disrespect that they do not see themselves doing anything else.[23] Nussbaum acknowledges some of these constraints but believes there are women who have plenty of choices who voluntarily choose prostitution, and as long as there are sufficient safeguards against abuse and disease, which the legalization of prostitution may make possible, their choices are morally unproblematic.[24] For the sake of argument, I grant the possibility that there are women whose prostitution is not the result of external constraints impeding their control over their sexual identity. So let's narrow our focus to women who engage in prostitution but not due to external constraints.

Surprisingly, Nussbaum does not acknowledge in her article on prostitution that prostitutes have internal constraints in the form of deformed desires. It is not unreasonable to think that many prostitutes are under the sway of deformed desires, despite the fact that some of them insist they really want to be prostitutes and are happy in their business. In a culture like ours that puts a premium on women's beauty while divorcing beauty from intellectual capacity and links beauty to sexual desirability, a lot of women come to want to be mere sex objects for men's pleasure.[25] Having deformed desires can stand in the way of one's autonomy because, as Sandra Bartky argues, their satisfaction benefits the system of domination and the privileged persons in it rather than those who have the deformed desires.[26] Satisfying deformed desires does not seem to be an indication of an agent's *self*-determination, which autonomy requires, but rather the agent's subordination to the system and its ends.[27] The more deformed desires an agent has in her desire set, the greater the likelihood they will not be counteracted by nondeformed desires; the more likely an agent is under the sway of her deformed desires, the less likely she will be self-determining. In a culture in which many women have had to exchange sex for goods or even for survival and are seen primarily in terms of their sexual desirability, the claims of those prostitutes who say they are happy doing what they do are suspect. But again, for the sake of argument, I will grant the possibility that a woman's choice to prostitute herself stems purely from nondeformed desires, in which case she seems to control her sexual identity. If so, the second constraint might be avoided.

The third constraint, social constraints in the form of stereotypes imposed on all women by the dominant group, men, will be harder to dismiss for any particular woman who is a prostitute. Such stereotypes stand in the way of the prostitute's controlling her sexual identity. For example, the stereotype of women as passive and acquiescent is at odds with a particular woman's being aggressive and assertive about her sexual desires. Here the stereotype, not the person, sets out the person's sexual identity for her. Since the stereotype applies to all members of the group, women, it cannot be overthrown by any particular member of the group. So it seems that we cannot exempt the prostitute from the third constraint in the way Nussbaum exempts the prostitute from the first two constraints by imagining a woman who autonomously chooses prostitution because she has no external or internal constraints on her choice. Nevertheless, Nussbaum believes that the prostitute's behavior might actually overthrow sexist stereotypes. She claims that the prostitute is stigmatized because she is seen as a threat to male control of women. This is because on the face of it, the prostitute challenges head on the sexual identity that men impose on women under patriarchy, acting directly against the expectation that women should be passive, subordinate, chaste, and monogamous, while herself exhibiting the stereotypical male traits of dominance, aggression, and control in sex. This view of the prostitute should win the applause of feminists, who favor eradicating sexist stereotypes: it seems that in challenging these sexist stereotypes, the prostitute exercises her right to bodily autonomy, taking into her own hands her bodily self-determination and thereby controlling her sexual identity.

But on closer inspection, I believe that the prostitute actually perpetuates another sexist stereotype that the group men impose on the group women namely, that of sex object. Sexual objectification, according to Sandra Bartky, occurs when a person's sexual parts or sexual functions are separated from the rest of her personality and reduced to the status of mere instruments or else regarded as if they are capable of representing her. As Rae Langton states, objectification treats a person as identical with her body or her body parts.[28] To see how prostitution perpetuates the stereotype of sex object, we need to examine what goes on in prostitutional sex. In selling her sexual services, the prostitute allows for the possibility that her client will aim to satisfy only his sexual desires in the encounter; indeed, one explanation for why men seek the sexual services of prostitutes is that they can freely focus on satisfying only their sexual desires without the emotional commitment and the obligation and burdens of satisfying the sexual desires of a sexual partner who expects and is entitled to reciprocation.[29] The client can have sex solely on his own terms—this is what he pays for. The prostitute lets her client use her body sexually in a way that suspends the satisfaction of her own sexual desires. She lets him objectify her—or at least attempt to objectify her (I am going to say more in just a bit about whether she actually *becomes* an object)—in the sense that her sexual desires and interests do not count at all. In the encounter, only her desire to make money from sex is respected, but this is not a sexual desire. This kind of objectification seems to be a *bad* kind of objectification, according to Nussbaum.[30] It involves at least some, if not all, of the following features Nussbaum lists that make objectification morally problematic: instrumentality (treating the object as a tool of one's purposes), denial of autonomy (treating the object as lacking in self-determination), inertness (treating the object as lacking in agency), fungibility (treating the object as interchangeable with objects of the same type), ownership (treating the object as something that is owned by another and can be bought or sold), and denial of subjectivity (treating the object as something whose experiences and feelings need not be taken into account).

Nussbaum does not believe that *all* sexual objectification is bad. She appeals to D.H. Lawrence, an early 20th-century English novelist who believed that the power of sexuality was most authentically experienced when the partners willingly surrendered their autonomy and subjectivity and allowed themselves to be object-like. Lawrence describes the character Brangwen, whose blood surges up in him in sex and blinds his intellect and destroys him, and whose wife in the same moment appears to him as a thing-like presence who summons him to surrender his personhood.[31]

Furthermore, Lawrence's view of objectification is connected with a reduction of persons to their bodily parts as well as an attribution of a kind of independent agency to these bodily parts.[32] Nussbaum cites a scene from *Lady Chatterley*, in which the partners basically personify their sexual bodily parts and identify themselves and each other with them. She disagrees with Kant that such scenes describe a reduction of a person to her or his bodily parts and says instead that this intense focus of attention on one's bodily parts is an addition, not a subtraction, and the objectification is actually liberating. The kind of objection Lawrence describes, which Nussbaum believes goes on in some of our own sexual experiences and not just in novels, is not bad because it is "symmetrical and mutual" and takes place "in a context of mutual respect and rough social equality." The surrender of autonomy and subjectivity is "a kind of victorious achievement in the prison house of English respectability."[33] The willingness to allow another person to be this close involves enormous trust. Finally, the identification of a person with her or his bodily parts is not dehumanizing but rather "can coexist with an intense regard for the person's individuality," and even the naming of the other's genitals can indicate that they are not fungible but have their own character and are parts of a person.[34] Thus, for Nussbaum, the *context* cancels out the badness of objectification: a context of mutual respect, trust, and regard for individuality makes objectification harmless.

However, this ideal context is simply not the context in which at least most prostitutional sex occurs. I want to defend the view that the prostitute conforms to the conservative and sexist stereotype that women should not have pleasurable sex—that is, sex that aims to satisfy their own desires—and conforms to the sexist stereotype that heterosexual sex should aim only at men's pleasure. Thus, instead of carving out her own sexual identity, the prostitute adopts a sexual identity that the group, men, impose on the group, women, that women are primarily sex objects to be used at men's discretion. This flies in the face of her exercising her right to bodily autonomy, of determining what happens in and to her body sexually, and thus of controlling her sexual identity. What's more, in feeding the stereotype of sex object, the prostitute fosters the sexist division between "loose" and "good" women or between women whom men can use sexually on their own terms and women whom men must respect sexually. In doing so, the practice of prostitution constrains all women's control of their sexual identity because they have to try to identify themselves sexually against a context in which women are stereotyped as mere sex objects.

An objector might claim that it is possible for a prostitute to have her own sexual desires satisfied in prostitution, as is the case with the dominatrix who advertises her sexual talents and whose prostituting is reflective of her sexual desires.[35] I admit this possibility: if this woman's desires are not deformed and are truly reflected in her prostitution, then she is not objectified in a bad way. But, in the typical case, if the prostitute's sexual desires are, in fact, satisfied in her prostituting, this is only happenstance, and she has no grounds for complaint if her desires are *not* satisfied.

5. PROSTITUTION AND OBJECTIFICATION

Is the prostitute really objectified, that is, turned into an object, in prostitutional sex, and if so, is this kind of objectification bad?

5.1. Kant on Objectification: An Inconsistency

The notion of objectification stems from Kant. Barbara Herman notes that Kant believes that *all* sex, not just prostitutional sex, is objectifying.[36] If Kant is right, no one can have hope of fully exercising their right to bodily autonomy in sex and of identifying themselves sexually. For Kant, sexual interest in another is not interest in the other as a person but in the eroticized body or sexual bodily parts, which compels regard of the person as an object. Even stronger, Kant believes that when a person becomes the object of appetite for another, the person actually *becomes a thing*:

> Taken by itself [sexual love] is a degradation of human nature: for as soon as a person becomes an Object of appetite for another, all motives of moral relationship cease to function, because as an Object of appetite for another a person becomes a thing and can be treated and used as such by every one.[37]

I understand the problem with sex for Kant to be that in sex, a person turns the partner into a thing or object by not respecting the rationality of their partner, focusing only on their body. This is bad objectification, because it renders null the person's rationality and subjectivity. Since Kant thought that *all* sex was objectifying in a bad way, and so morally wrong, he is faced with the problem of ending the human species unless we act immorally! Herman explains that Kant's solution to the problem that all sex is objectifying is marriage. Kant believes that in satisfying sexual desires, one party surrenders use of a part of her or his body for the purposes of pleasure, giving the other a "right of disposal," which Herman understands to be a right of free use over that part. But since a human being is a unity, on Kant's view, the right is gained over the whole person, allowing the other free use of the whole person of the partner. But since Kant also believes that persons are not things, this treatment would be unacceptable. Marriage is supposed to explain how sex within its confines does not turn us into things after all, or to the extent that it does, it does so in an unproblematic way. In marriage, A lets B use A, but at the same time B lets A use B. Each grants the other partner equal reciprocal rights and surrenders the whole of their person to the other with a complete right of disposal over it.[38] Since the "using" is mutual, no one loses anything—each wins herself or himself back.[39]

Herman rightly objects that Kant's solution never gets off the ground because the self is not the kind of thing over which there can be rights of disposal in the first place—we cannot have a right of disposal over anyone, so it makes no sense for us to have reciprocal rights of disposal.[40] Kant's view about objectification in these passages is at odds with his more general view that a person *never* loses her or his status as a person, an entity with dignity who is never to be treated merely as a means to an end.[41] That is, Kant is inconsistent. On the one hand, he believes that we objectify another person in sex. On the other hand, he believes that we can never reduce a person's status as a person. For he says that if a person acts in non–self-respecting ways, ways that treat her own humanity as a mere means to an end, say, by defiling, abasing, dishonoring, or rejecting her own humanity, she still retains her status as a person.[42] Furthermore, if a person acts immorally toward another person, we must not treat him as worthless or incapable of improvement but must respect him as an end in itself in virtue of his capacity for rationality and not treat him merely as a means to an end.[43] And if a person is treated by another in a way that attempts to lower the person's value, the person does not lose humanity or value as an end in itself. Jean Hampton explains this last point in terms of the rapist, who tries to lower the intrinsic value of his victim by objectifying her in making her less than human, an instrument to be used at the rapist's discretion, but actually does not, because her value as a person is not the kind of thing that can be lowered.[44] Indeed, for Hampton, the rapist attempts to lower the value of all women, representing himself as superior in value to women, who are inferior objects. This is because rape sends the message that "Your kind isn't the equal in worth of my kind" . . . and that "As a woman, you are the kind of human being who is subject to the mastery of people of my kind," confirming that women are "for" men; to be used, dominated, treated as objects.[45] Hampton explains that there is merely the appearance of degradation, which she calls "diminishment" of one's value.

Given his views about our worth as persons, then, Kant should say the same about objectification in sex: no one can become an object in sex so long as she or he remains the kind of being that has the capacity for rationality. One person *cannot* make another a mere thing, in sex or otherwise. This is an empowering view for women. If it is right, then no one, not even the prostitute, can be reduced to an object. If she is not an object, then she might be more in control of her sexual identity, and have more bodily autonomy, than I originally believed.

5.2. Anderson and Estes: A Remedy for Kant's Inconsistency

But this is too quick. Clelia Anderson and Yolanda Estes offer a plausible Kantian analysis that gets Kant out of his inconsistent views about a person's worth as a person as explained previously, but shows there is still a problematic sense of objectification inherent in prostitutional sex even though it does not involve the prostitute's actually becoming an object.[46] Anderson and

Estes claim that the prostitute "accommodates men's desires for women who cease to exist when they are no longer wanted."[47] Prostitution allows men to have sex without the responsibility and burdens of dealing with a woman with subjectivity, that is, with desires and other features that persons have that inanimate objects lack. Yet the prostitute has to pretend to her client that she is a woman with subjectivity, for he "wants his woman-thing, body, mind, and soul," a willing slave. Thus the prostitute "veils her selfhood."[48] This analysis suggests that Anderson and Estes endorse Kant's view that a person never loses her humanity or subjectivity—the prostitute (as all others) doesn't lose it in sex but hides it from her client. Anderson and Estes go on to explain that the client expects the prostitute to recognize *his* own subjectivity, but this requires that she acknowledge her own subjectivity as well, in the form of both of their bodily desires. The client might try to force the prostitute to unveil her selfhood by pretending to be concerned about her, trying to make her enjoy the encounter, or even injuring her to provoke a response. But the prostitute's job is to disassociate herself from her sexual activity, to appear as a body or a woman-thing without being a real self, which in reality she cannot do. Anderson and Estes conclude:

> When climax has been reached, neither can deny that he has been moved by her touch to pleasure and orgasm. His orgasm is a physical manifestation of a mutual presenting of subjectivity. . . . Despite their objectification of one another, the bodily nature of the encounter forces them to recognize their mutual humanity. This recognition is simultaneously a revelation of the harm they have done to one another and the harm they have done to themselves. In the prostitutional encounter, both the prostitute and the client attempt to use the other as a mere means to an end. Neither participant achieves his or her original objective, because the objectives are self-contradictory. . . . each walks away having given up more of themselves than was agreed to in the bargain.[49]

On Anderson's and Estes's view, the prostitute's subjectivity never goes away but is veiled or hidden in the act of prostitutional sex.[50] The prostitute is not actually objectified, though her client treats her *as if* she were an object. To treat her as a subject would be to respect her, which, in the sexual context, "requires the minimum criteria of mutual consent, concern, and desire to relate as individual subjects."[51]

However, even though Anderson and Estes have found a way to make Kant's view that persons never actually lose their subjectivity consistent with the idea that prostitutional sex seems to involve objectification, I am not convinced that prostitutional sex is unobjectionable for reasons relating to bodily autonomy and sexual identification. Even if prostitutional sex does not actually turn the prostitute into an object, by treating the prostitute *as if* she were an object, it still perpetuates the stereotype that women are sex objects, persons whose subjectivity does not matter or is denied, or whose autonomy is denied, or who are mere tools for another's purposes. Recall that these are exactly some of the ways Nussbaum defines (bad) objectification—none of them requires that the person actually *becomes* an object, just that the person is treated *as if* she were an object in one of a variety of senses. Any of these attempts to objectify the woman who engages in prostitutional sex can be seen, to use Hampton's terminology, as ways of diminishing the woman's value, which is to say that prostitutional sex gives the appearance of degradation, though it does not actually degrade the prostitute. Here I agree with Kant, Hampton, and Anderson and Estes that a person's value as a person cannot actually be degraded, though another can try to degrade it, that is to say, diminish it. But this is enough to perpetuate the stereotype that women actually are sex objects, since there is no outward difference between actually turning someone into an object and treating her as if she were an object.

5.3. Marino on Objectification: Choice Determines Wrongness

An alternative approach to explaining away the notion that the prostitute perpetuates the stereotype of women as sex objects hinges on admitting that the prostitute really is objectified in prostitutional sex, but showing that the objectification is not bad objectification after all. I have suggested that to be a sexual object is to be just a body or body part devoid of subjectivity as expressed in your own sexual desires. Patricia Marino defends the thesis that instrumentally using a person is morally benign when, and only when, it is in accordance with respect for autonomy.[52] While she agrees with Nussbaum that some kinds of objectification in sex are morally permissible, such as when the partners surrender to their passions in the heat of the moment, she disagrees with Nussbaum's view that the *context* of the partners' having a regard for each other's humanity that is typical in a healthy relationship mitigates the morally problematic instrumental nature of objectification. Instead, Marino argues that consent and respect for or nonviolation of autonomy make objectification in sex morally unproblematic.[53]

Marino believes that instrumental use in the *strong* sense where "A uses B as a genuine tool of A's purposes, really as a thing, when A fails to consider B's decisions, when A coerces B, or deceives B or simply forces B to do what A wants" is wrong because it clearly violates autonomy—it is the way we treat a person when we do not care about their ends, or take their general wishes and desires into account."[54] But Marino believes that the *weak* sense of instrumental use is morally unproblematic: it is morally benign for A to have sex with B and fail to take all of B's ends and desires into account while respecting B's autonomy and self-determination, and in the context of consent, whatever the relationship of the parties.[55] Marino explains that it is the *choices* of the partners in sex that matter to whether the partners are self-directing or autonomous and whether objectification is wrong. (And she acknowledges that one's choices might be constrained by patriarchy, in which case they count against autonomy.) It might be the case that the partners want and agree to ignore each other's desires and wishes. There is no moral rule, she insists, that pleasure in sex should be spread around equally; one partner may forego her own pleasure to focus on the other partner, either out of excitement or to make her partner happy. It is essential, though, that attention and respect be paid to the other in order to understand whether the partners participate in "a mood of ongoing consent."[56] Marino believes that this attention and respect is rather minimal, requiring only "a basic system of communication" (e.g., "checking" and asking when in doubt) and can occur between intimates and strangers alike.

Let's apply Marino's analysis to the prostitute. Suppose, as is typical, that the prostitute consents to have sex with her client, and the kind of sex she consents to have is one devoid of her own pleasure (or, at best, her own pleasure is a mere side effect of the encounter) but focuses only on the pleasure or desire satisfaction of her client. Is the prostitute self-directing or autonomous in this encounter because she *chooses* to forego her own pleasure (if this is what her client wants)? If prostitutional sex meets Marino's condition of weak instrumental use, then it does not involve morally wrong objectification. To repeat, for Marino, what matters for wrongful objectification are one's choices, not one's desires: one may forego the satisfaction of one's desires if one so chooses.

One problem—not with Marino's account, but with its application to prostitutional sex—is that the prostitute's choosing to suspend the satisfaction of her desires in favor of the satisfaction of her client's desires is at odds with there being a "mood of ongoing consent" in the sense that I think Marino wants. (Prostitutional sex might allow ongoing consent never to check the prostitute's desires, but I don't think this is what Marino has in mind.) There is only the initial consent, which is consent to surrender the satisfaction of the prostitute's desires if this is what the client wants, and he has no obligation to check—and I assume does not check in the ordinary case since his fantasy or desire is to have sex with a woman-thing who does not come with the baggage of subjectivity—to see whether the prostitute's consent to this kind of encounter is ongoing. Having an obligation to check, after all, is grounded in the fact that the entity checked upon has subjectivity and so is an appropriate recipient of the respect involved in checking. But when it comes to the client in prostitutional sex, at best he checks to see that the prostitute still consents not to have her desires matter, but he does not check to see whether her current desires are in line with what she consented to. So he can decide to become violent, or whatever, because he pays to treat her in ways satisfying just his desires, which is all she consents to. Thus, prostitutional sex does not involve weak instrumental use of the prostitute's body. The objectification involved is of the strong kind and thus is morally problematic after all.

A second problem is that I think desires matter much more to Marino's account than she admits, which I think is a good thing with respect to the right to bodily autonomy. Marino describes her view as one for which one's desires in sex can fall out of the picture since they are completely subject to choice, and only choice determines whether one is autonomous and ultimately whether objectification is morally wrong. But her stipulation that there must be "a mood of ongoing consent" brings desires right back into the picture. Where there is a true mood of ongoing consent to sex between intimates or even strangers, we hope and assume, in the spirit of Marino's argument, it means that one partner can pull out because she decides she does not want to have sex after all, or that the kind of sex the couple is having is not really what she wanted, and so on. Otherwise, what would be the point of ongoing consent? But this is just to say that the "mood of ongoing consent" reflects your desires and ensures that your choice is consonant with them. So if you choose to suspend the satisfaction of your desires but then change your mind along the way in the encounter because you realize that being treated a certain way mattered a lot more to you than you thought at first, then the "mood of ongoing consent" licenses you to change or end the encounter depending on your desires.

I think the view that desires, and not mere choice, matter to autonomy and the moral status of objectification is a good thing because desires are important for the right to bodily autonomy. I have defined the right to bodily autonomy as the right to determine what happens in and to your body. What makes a person self-directing in sex is, in part, that she has and can act on desires about the sexual aspects of her body. But this entails not surrendering the satisfaction of these desires. Here, Kant might help: he believes that the characteristic of humanity, as distinct from animality, is "the power to set an end . . . any end whatsoever."[57] Surely Kant meant to exclude the end of not setting any other end, as this would outright deny one's humanity. In consenting to suspend or even to veil the satisfaction of one's desires in sex, the prostitute gives up her very power to set her ends in sex, which is to give up her self-direction in sex, her bodily autonomy, and her humanity. She cannot autonomously consent to this. As Mill says, one cannot autonomously consent to give up one's autonomy, but the prostitute surrenders her own right to bodily autonomy in giving up the satisfaction of her sexual desires by consenting (only initially) to become an object for another. She foregoes the very basis of her ongoing autonomy and consent, which are her desires or her subjectivity.

Can the right to bodily autonomy ever be legitimately waived? It seems that Thomson suggests as much, for she says that no one has a right to use of your body unless you *give* him such a right.[58] But notice an important distinction, one that underscores the difference in good sex and prostitutional sex. Thomson says you can give a person a right *to use* your body, *not* a right *to determine what happens in and to* your body. In sex—even good sex—we can allow another person to use our body; doing so does not preclude your rationality or subjectivity because using a person's body is consonant with respecting their bodily desires. *You* are still determining the use of your body, through your desires about it. (Compare: the mother can let the fetus *use* her body, but she doesn't give the fetus the right to *determine* what happens in and to her body.) But to give someone a right *to determine* what happens in and to your body is to give him a right to determine what your bodily desires are and whether they are to be respected or ignored or violated. It is to give up your very subjectivity, or at least to act as if you lack subjectivity after the point of the initial consent. This is pure objectification, of a bad kind.

There are other cases in which we think we can legitimately waive our right to bodily autonomy. A heart surgery patient might be thought to waive this right by allowing the surgeon to do what is necessary if she encounters something unexpected during surgery rather than bring the patient back to consciousness in order to get his consent. Yet I do not think this is a proper waiver of the right to bodily autonomy, because the patient's initial consent is consent to the entire procedure, including certain unexpected happenings, with the goal being the patient's welfare. The goal in prostitution, in contrast, is exchange of money for sexual services, whether or not these promote the prostitute's welfare or desire satisfaction.

Another case which we might think of as involving a waiver of our right to bodily autonomy is that of a living will, when you sign over to another a right to make decisions about your body should your mental state deteriorate to the point that you no longer know your own bodily desires. Again, this is not properly understood to be a waiver of the right to bodily autonomy but a way of respecting it because you appoint someone you trust to be able to fulfill the desires you would have about your body when you can no longer be self-determining about them. In contrast, the prostitute is conscious of her desires and retains the ability qua person to be self-determining about them, and she does not entrust her client to respect them.

A third case is that of the boxer who initially consents to play a match for money knowing that he is likely to be beaten up. Again, I don't think this is a legitimate waiver of a right to bodily autonomy because the boxer doesn't consent to allowing his opponent to treat him any way the opponent wants, and he can perfect his sport so he doesn't take too many blows. He wants to, and is entitled to, defend his body against harm. He wants to beat up his opponent. Hence, his subjectivity is not veiled. His case is unlike that of the prostitute, whose sexual desires become irrelevant in the encounter.

In general, I think that our desires should inform our choices about the use of our bodies for the reason that Hobbes and Thomson give, namely, that having the right to bodily autonomy puts us in the moral game.

6. CONCLUSION

I have been defending the view that the right to bodily autonomy is necessary for a person's being able to identify herself sexually. I have claimed that in order to exercise fully the right to bodily autonomy, one needs to be free from external, internal, and social constraints. I granted the possibility that a woman could be free from constraints on her liberty and deformed desires and choose prostitution. That left the question of whether the prostitute had sexist stereotypes imposed on her, limiting the full exercise of her right to bodily autonomy. I began by saying that the prostitute might look like the paradigm case of someone who turns on their head sexist stereotypes about women's sexuality, namely, that it is dangerous and ought to be controlled by men. This would lead us to think that prostitutes control their sexual identity and exercise their right to bodily autonomy. I have argued that they do neither.

What, then, does this say about whether *women*, under patriarchy, control their sexual identity? Clearly women are constrained externally and internally. But one thing they can do to take them further down the road to full exercise of their right to bodily autonomy and to controlling their own sexual identity is to fight off sexist stereotypes that are imposed on them. They do not do this through prostitution, any more than the sinister characters of *Dangerous Liaisons* overthrew Victorian stereotypes about women by manipulatively seducing them to give in to their sexual temptations.[59]

I end with a positive suggestion, drawn from the character of Samantha on the HBO TV series, *Sex and the City*. Samantha has sex frequently (and mostly with men). She seems free and in control, without worry over being labeled "loose." She is often the one who pursues the man to whom she is sexually attracted. The sex she has is consensual, with each partner seeking their own pleasure. Her behavior flies in the face of sexist stereotypes and conservatism about sex. Samantha meets men on their own terms by thinking of sex without any attachment, just like the stereotypical male view of sex to which the prostitute's client conforms. But the difference between Samantha and the prostitute is that neither she nor her partners objectifies the other in a bad way because they are both attentive to satisfying their own and each other's desires. Because Samantha has sex often with men she has just met, she takes the risk that they will not respect her desires, but the show depicts her as having a radar that successfully picks out men who want an enjoyable sexual encounter all around, one that favors both parties' pleasure or desire satisfaction rather than one party's seeking to satisfy his conquest mentality.

I am not suggesting that women try to be like Samantha. Nor am I suggesting that real life enables women to be as safe sexually as is Samantha. Rather, I am suggesting that there are many ways to be, sexually speaking, that are expressions of women's exercising their right to bodily autonomy, including abstaining from sex. What they have in common is that they respect, not veil, ignore, or discount women's sexual desires. The right to bodily autonomy requires this.

Patriarchy undermines women's right to bodily autonomy. The right to bodily autonomy is a feminist concern in that it goes some way—perhaps a long way—toward ending women's oppression. Disrespecting it explains in large part the moral wrongness of denial of abortion rights, woman battering, rape, and sexual harassment, to mention a few. The prostitute, in surrendering her right to bodily autonomy to her client and perpetuating the stereotype of women as sex objects, risks lessening the grip of this right when it comes to these other issues. This does not bode well for ending women's oppression. For feminists, it is particularly salient that women have control over their bodies in ways that patriarchy does not allow.

ACKNOWLEDGMENTS

The paper is titled after the 1969 hit song by Rolling Stones, in a nod to Martha Nussbaum, who titles her paper on deformed desires, I presume, after the song, *American Women*, by The Guess Who. See Martha C. Nussbaum, "American Women," in *Sex and Social Justice*, ed. Martha C. Nussbaum (New York: Oxford University Press, 1999), pp. 130–153. *Honky Tonk Women* was inspired by Brazilian gauchos or taverns; a honky-tonk woman is a dancing girl in a western bar who may work as a prostitute. See http://en.wikipedia.org/wiki/Honky_Tonk_Women (Accessed 4/23/2009). For comments, I thank Scott Anderson, Ann Cahill, Alice MacLachan, Patricia Marino, Marina Oshana, Laurie Shrage, Helga Varden, and audiences at the Sexual Selves conference at the University of Illinois, Champaign/Urbana, and the University of Waterloo.

NOTES

1. I am concerned with sexist stereotypes imposed on women in their sexual relationships with men.
2. Dan Gardner, "Do Some Women Really Choose to be Prostitutes?," *The Ottawa Citizen* (Sunday, June 9, 2002), pp. 1–4. www.missingpeople.net/do_some_women_really_choose-june_9,_2002.htm (Accessed 4/1/2009).
3. Gardner, *Ibid.*, 3.
4. Martha C. Nussbaum, "'Whether from Reason or Prejudice': Taking Money for Bodily Services," in *Sex and Social Justice*, pp. 276–298.
5. Martha C. Nussbaum, "Taking Money for Bodily Services," in *Sex and Social Justice*, pp. 276–298, at 287.
6. See Nussbaum, "Judging Other Cultures: The Case of Genital Mutilation," in *Sex and Social Justice*, pp. 118–129.
7. Nussbaum, "Taking Money," p. 297.
8. Martha C. Nussbaum, "The Feminist Critique of Liberalism," in *Sex and Social Justice*, pp. 55–80, at 57.
9. The distinction can be found in Uma Narayan, "Minds of Their Own: Choices, Autonomy, Cultural Practices, and Other Women," in *A Mind of One's Own: Feminist Essays on Reason and Objectivity*, ed. Louise M. Antony and Charlotte E. Witt (Boulder, CO: Westview Press, 2nd edition, 2002), pp. 418–432. Not all constraints on liberty are bad—e.g., laws prohibiting sex with minors.
10. Nussbaum, "American Women," 149.
11. These can become internal constraints if internalized by the subject.

12. Cynthia Willett, *Irony in the Age of Empire: Comic Perspectives on Democracy & Freedom* (Bloomington and Indianapolis, IN: Indiana University Press, 2008).

13. See Susan Griffin, "Rape: The All-American Crime," in *Feminism and Philosophy*, ed. Mary Vetterling-Braggin, Frederick Elliston, and Jane English (Totowa, NJ: Littlefield, Adams and Co., 1981), pp. 313–332.

14. Catharine MacKinnon thinks that woman battering is a sexual issue, not just an issue of violence, because most of the cases take place in the bedroom. See "Sex and Violence: A Perspective," in *Feminism Unmodified: Discourses on Life and Law*, ed. Catharine MacKinnon (Cambridge, Mass.: Harvard University Press, 1987 and 1981), pp. 85–92, at 92.

15. MacKinnon, *Ibid.*, argues that pornography, sexual harassment, rape, and woman battering allow men to define who women are sexually.

16. Judith Jarvis Thomson, "A Defense of Abortion," *Philosophy & Public Affairs* 1 (1) (1971): 47–66, at 54.

17. Thomson, "Abortion," 53.

18. Thomson, "Abortion," 53.

19. Thomas Hobbes, *Leviathan* (New York: Collier Books, 1651 and 1962), 105.

20. Judith Jarvis Thomson, "Trespass and First Property," in *The Realm of Rights* (Cambridge, Mass.: Harvard University Press, 1990), p. 215.

21. Thomson, "Trespass," pp. 205–206.

22. Nussbaum also offers a possible grounding of the right to bodily autonomy. She defends the individualism of liberal feminism on the grounds that the individual is the basic unit for political thought. This means "that liberalism responds sharply to the basic fact that each person has a course from birth to death that is not precisely the same as that of any other person; that each person is one and not more than one, that each feels pain in his or her own body, that the food given to A does not arrive in the stomach of B. The separateness of persons is a basic fact of human life . . . " See "Liberalism," 62.

23. Scott A. Anderson, "Prostitution and Sexual Autonomy: Making Sense of the Prohibition of Prostitution," *Ethics* 112 (July 2002): 748–780, footnote #12 at 754. Many prostitutes are driven to prostitution because of sexual abuse, child abuse, drug and alcohol abuse, divorce, and racism, and many suffer from rape, slavery, poverty, posttraumatic stress disorder, and poor employment prospects either during or after prostitution.

24. Nussbaum, "Taking Money," 278 and 290.

25. Anne Barnhill discusses the phenomenon of women's "flaunting it" in "Modesty as a Feminist Sexual Virtue," in *Out from the Shadows: Analytical Feminist Contributions to Traditional Philosophy*, ed. Sharon L. Crasnow and Anita M. Superson (New York: Oxford University Press, 2012), pp. 115–137.

26. Sandra Lee Bartky, "On Psychological Oppression," in *Femininity and Domination: Studies in the Phenomenology of Oppression*, ed. Sandra Lee Bartky (New York: Routledge, 1990), pp. 22–32, at 36. Reprinted from *Philosophy and Women*, Wadsworth Publishing, 1979.

27. See my entry on "Feminist Moral Psychology," in the *Stanford Encyclopedia of Philosophy*, Section 2 on Deformed Desires. (http://plato.stanford.edu/contents.html)

28. Bartky, "On Psychological Oppression," 26. Rae Langton, "Autonomy-Denial in Objectification," in *Sexual Solipsism*, Rae Langton, p. 228.

29. Clelia Smyth Anderson and Yolanda Estes argue that while sexual relationships offer potential delight, they also are time consuming, inconvenient, and demanding in ways that the client prefers to avoid. See "The Myth of the Happy Hooker: Kantian Moral Reflections on a Phenomenology of Prostitution," in

Violence Against Women: Philosophical Perspectives, ed. Stanley G. French, Wanda Teays, and Laura M. Purdy (Ithaca, N.Y.: Cornell University Press), pp. 152–158, at 154.

30. Martha C. Nussbaum, "Objectification," in *Sex and Social Justice*, pp. 213–239, at 218.
31. Nussbaum, *Ibid.*, p. 228.
32. Nussbaum, *Ibid.* p. 229.
33. Nussbaum, *Ibid.*, p. 230.
34. Nussbaum, *Ibid.*, p. 230.
35. Alice MacLachan was one such objector.
36. Barbara Herman, "Could It Be Worth Thinking About Kant on Sex and Marriage?," in *A Mind of One's Own: Feminist Essays on Reason and Objectivity*, pp. 53–72, at 60.
37. Herman, "Kant on Sex and Marriage," 60, citing Kant, *Lectures on Ethics*, translated by Louis Infield (New York: Harper Torchbooks, 1963), 163.
38. Herman, *Ibid.*, 65, citing Kant, *Lectures on Ethics*.
39. Herman, *Ibid.*, 65–66, citing Kant, *Lectures on Ethics*, 167.
40. Herman, *Ibid.*, 66.
41. Of course, since Kant thinks he needs to invoke marriage to avoid the view that a person actually turns their partner into an object in sex, these passages might not be contradictory in the end.
42. The references to Kant are given by Thomas E. Hill, Jr., "Humanity as an End in Itself," *Ethics* 91 (1) (Oct. 1980): 84–99, at 86. They include: Immanuel Kant, *The Doctrine of Virtue*, trans. Mary Gregor (New York: Harper & Row, 1964), 85, 87, 88, 92, 113, 143, 122; or Immanuel Kant, *Metaphysical Elements of Virtue*, trans. James Ellington (Indianapolis: Bobbs-Merrill Co., 1964), 83, 85, 86, 89, 128, 137, 118.
43. Hill, *Ibid.*, 96, citing Kant, *Metaphysical Elements of Virtue*, 43.
44. Jean Hampton, "Defining Wrong and Defining Rape," in *A Most Detestable Crime: New Philosophical Essays on Rape*, ed. Keith Burgess-Jackson (New York: Oxford University Press, 1999), pp. 118–156. See especially the discussion on pp. 126–138.
45. Hampton, *Ibid.*, 135.
46. Anderson and Estes, "The Myth of the Happy Hooker."
47. Anderson and Estes, *Ibid.*, 154.
48. Anderson and Estes, *Ibid.*, 155.
49. Anderson and Estes, *Ibid.*, 158.
50. Ann Cahill suggested that the prostitute is neither objectified by her client nor objectifies herself but expresses desires that her client wants and, because of this, remains a subjectivity instead of becoming an object. But I think this doesn't leave the prostitute's subjectivity intact. Admittedly this makes her more of a subjectivity, an entity possessing desires, than a sex toy. But the desires she has are feigned, not truly hers, but belong to someone else. Kant might call them heteronomous desires. Even though for Kant, (reflective) desires are supposed to indicate the capacity for rationality, and thus, one's humanity or subjectivity, I doubt he meant for these heteronomous desires to mark a person's subjectivity.
51. Anderson and Estes, "Happy Hooker," 153.
52. Patricia Marino, "The Ethics of Sexual Objectification: Autonomy and Consent," *Inquiry* 51 (2008): 345–364, at 349. Although Marino is not concerned particularly with prostitutional sex, her argument bears directly on prostitution, since she takes up the question of whether objectification in sex is necessarily wrong.

53. Anderson and Estes believe that consent alone fails to safeguard an action from moral reproach: "If a person performs sexual acts for another without any interest in or desire for connection to that person, without any response to sexual needs of her own, or solely to accomplish some end extraneous to her sexual and emotional satisfaction, then her actions express no desire to interact sexually with her partner . . . Sex in such a context may be voluntary and consenting, but it demonstrates that the participants are using one another as mere means for some end." In Marino's terms, Anderson and Estes are saying that this is a wrongful form of objectification. See "Happy Hooker,"153.
54. Marino, "Objectification," 351.
55. Marino, "Objectification," 352.
56. Marino, "Objectification," 353.
57. Hill, "Humanity as an End in Itself," 86, citing Kant, *The Doctrine of Virtue*, 51, and the *Metaphysical Elements of Virtue*, 50.
58. Thomson, "Abortion," 53.
59. *Dangerous Liaisons* is a 1988 film based on the 18th-century French novel, *les Liaisons dangereuses*, by Pierre Choderolos de Laclos. At http://en.wikipedia.org/wiki/Dangerous_Liasons (Accessed 3/23/2014).

REFERENCES

Anderson, Clelia Smyth and Estes, Yolanda. "The Myth of the Happy Hooker: Kantian Moral Reflections on a Phenomenology of Prostitution." *Violence Against Women: Philosophical Perspectives*, ed. Stanley G. French, Wanda Teays, and Laura M. Purdy. Ithaca, N.Y.: Cornell University Press, 1998, 152–158.
Anderson, Scott A. "Prostitution and Sexual Autonomy: Making Sense of the Prohibition of Prostitution." *Ethics* 112 (July 2002): 748–780.
Barnhill, Anne. "Modesty as a Feminist Sexual Virtue." *Out from the Shadows: Analytical Feminist Contributions to Traditional Philosophy*, ed. Sharon L. Crasnow and Anita M. Superson. New York: Oxford University Press, 2012, 115–137.
Bartky, Sandra Lee. "On Psychological Oppression." *Femininity and Domination: Studies in the Phenomenology of Oppression*, ed. Sandra Lee Bartky. New York: Routledge, 1990, pp. 22–32.
Gardner, Dan. "Do Some Women Really Choose to be Prostitutes?" *The Ottawa Citizen* (9 June 2002), pp. 1–4. www.missingpeople.net/do_some_women_really_choose-june_9,_2002.htm (Accessed 1 April 2009).
Griffin, Susan. "Rape: The All-American Crime." *Feminism and Philosophy*, ed. Mary Vetterling-Braggin, Frederick Elliston, and Jane English. Totowa, NJ: Littlefield, Adams and Co., 1981, pp. 313–332.
Hampton, Jean. "Defining Wrong and Defining Rape." *A Most Detestable Crime: New Philosophical Essays on Rape*, ed. Keith Burgess-Jackson. New York: Oxford University Press, 1999, 118–156.
Herman, Barbara. "Could It Be Worth Thinking About Kant on Sex and Marriage?" *A Mind of One's Own: Feminist Essays on Reason and Objectivity*, ed. Louise Antony and Charlotte Witt. Boulder, CO: Westview Press, 1993, 53–72.
Hobbes, Thomas. *Leviathan*. New York: Collier Books, 1962.
MacKinnon, Catharine. *Feminism Unmodified: Discourses on Life and Law*. Cambridge, Mass.: Harvard University Press, 1987.
Marino, Patricia. "The Ethics of Sexual Objectification: Autonomy and Consent." *Inquiry* 51 (2008): 345–364.

Narayan, Uma. "Minds of Their Own: Choices, Autonomy, Cultural Practices, and Other Women." *A Mind of One's Own: Feminist Essays on Reason and Objectivity*, ed. Louise M. Antony and Charlotte E. Witt. Boulder, CO: Westview Press, 2nd edition, 2002, pp. 418–432.

Nussbaum, Martha C. *Sex and Social Justice*. Oxford: Oxford University Press, 2000.

Thomson, Judith Jarvis. "A Defense of Abortion." *Philosophy & Public Affairs* 1 (1) (1971): 47–66.

Thomson, Judith Jarvis. *The Realm of Rights*. Cambridge, Mass.: Harvard University Press, 1990.

Willett, Cynthia. *Irony in the Age of Empire: Comic Perspectives on Democracy & Freedom*. Bloomington and Indianapolis, IN: Indiana University Press, 2008.

11 Jewish Self-Hatred, Moral Criticism, and Autonomy

Marilyn Friedman

INTRODUCTION

Some people support Israeli policies toward Palestinians in the Occupied Territories, while other people criticize those policies. Some of the critics, both outside and inside Israel, are Jewish. Occasionally in these debates, one hears Jewish supporters of Israeli policies try to discredit the arguments of Jewish critics of Israeli policies by accusing the critics of being "self-hating Jews."[1]

This criticism turns up emphatically on the website Masada2000.[2] The Masada2000 website publishes a list of what its creators call "Self-Hating and/or Israel-Threatening Jews," in other words the "SHIT list."[3] This list names nearly 9,000 Jews worldwide who are supposed to be either Jewish self-haters or threats to Israel—or both. The website has stated about these self-haters that "They are the socialists, communists, anarchists and so-called 'human rights' junkies and 'peace and justice' activists. . . . Most of them know the Truth but hate their heritage to such a degree that nothing else matters to them except bashing Israel right out of existence." They "have a sick need to conspire with the enemies of Israel."[4] The Masada2000 list of self-hating Jews names Noam Chomsky and other scholars such as Martha Ackelsberg, Seyla Benhabib, Wendy Brown, Norman Finklestein, and Evelyn Fox Keller; celebrities such as Woody Allen and Richard Gere; political commentators such as Thomas Friedman and Ted Koppel; and the South African judge Richard Goldstone, who chaired the committee that wrote the UN report claiming that Israel's military operations against the Gaza strip in 2008–2009 were disproportionately excessive.[5]

Group-based self-hatred in general has been a widely studied phenomenon. It seems to occur especially among members of identity groups that have been systematically oppressed, scorned, and vilified. These groups are often immigrant or minority groups. Social scorn or vilification of an identity group can easily lead group members to hate their group-based identities.

However, there might be legitimate grounds for moral criticism of an identity group, even one that has been historically oppressed. Granted, moral criticism of an identity group is perilous and risks arousing unfounded prejudice. Yet even historically oppressed groups should be open to the possibility that they might be tempted into wrongdoing, perhaps by oppressive conditions.

Either being a member of a historically oppressed group or thinking that one's group engages in morally questionable practices—or both together—might well promote group-based self-hatred of a sort that undermines autonomy. Jewish self-hatred and accusations of it will serve as our example. The oppression of Jews took a massive and deadly form in the twentieth century. During the same time period, many Jews created the state of Israel, which is now the target of moral outrage for its treatment of Palestinians who dispute Israeli claims to land and sovereignty. Thus Jewish group-based identity at the present time is a vivid example to use for exploring whether group-based self-hatred undermines autonomy.

Jean-Paul Sartre's account of Jewish self-hatred as arising inevitably from anti-Semitism was an especially influential account in reaction to the Nazi era in Europe. I begin, in Part 1, with a summary of and partial disagreement with Sartre's account. In Part 2, I sketch some moments in the development of the concept of Jewish self-hatred over the twentieth century and draw out some general points about the phenomenon of group-based self-hatred.

In Part 3, I argue that a group member's criticism of her own identity group does not necessarily exemplify group-based self-hatred. Finally, in Part 4, I explore how mixed conditions in a historically oppressed group can offset the tendency of oppression and group-based self-hatred to undermine autonomy.

1. SARTRE ON ANTI-SEMITISM

I assume that, at the very least, personal autonomy in what someone does or how she lives her life involves her in some minimum of self-reflection in accord with her beliefs, desires, values, and commitments.[6] If she is to rely on her own beliefs and commitments, she must have some degree of confidence in them as the features of herself that define how she approaches her situations and her world. A self-conception derived from the identity group to which someone belongs is a kind of umbrella conception that can collect the ideas of these various aspects of self into a unified self-understanding.

If someone's identity group is the target of social oppression, then to the extent that group-based identity is central to self-identity,[7] this would seem to diminish the personal autonomy of group members for the following reasons. The oppression of a group is likely to be accompanied by negative stereotypes and other demeaning portraits of the group that circulate widely, "justify" the oppression, and reduce social esteem for the group. Such demeaning group conceptions would tend to infect the sense of self of each group member, perhaps leaving each one distrustful of what she believes and what she thinks she values. Her failures would follow from her inadequacies; her successes would be due to luck. Her own perspective, who she is, and what she has done, might seem to her to provide only a shaky foundation at best on which to base her critical reflections about how to act and how to live. Relationships with other members of her own group might not help her much because those others, after all, are disparaged persons as well.

A socially scorned group identity, especially when the scorn has lasted a long time and contributed to harsh victimization of the group, would seem to promote *self-hatred* among group members.

Jewish self-hatred is one such historical example. In *Anti-Semite and Jew* (1948), Sartre suggests that Jewish self-hatred in particular begins as a Jewish response to a context of anti-Semitism. For Sartre, a human being's authenticity is a matter of the person's "having a true and lucid consciousness of [her] situation, in assuming the responsibilities and risks that it involves, in accepting it in pride or humiliation, sometimes in horror and hate."[8]

In Sartre's view, authenticity for a Jew involves taking as given and definitive of who she is, the situation created and defined for her by anti-Semites.[9] Sartre claims that Jews do not have any community of "interests," "beliefs," homeland, or "history." He asserts that "The sole tie that binds them is the hostility and disdain of the societies that surround them."[10] Sartre claims that "society" is what makes someone a Jew, creates the "Jewish problem," and forces a Jew "to make his choices entirely within the perspective set by this problem." Sartre seems to be addressing only non-Jews when he writes, "It is our eyes that reflect to him the unacceptable image that he wishes to dissimulate. . . . It is we who constrain him to choose to be a Jew whether through flight from himself or through self-assertion; it is we who force him into the dilemma of Jewish authenticity or inauthenticity."[11]

Sartre writes further that "The authentic Jew . . . wills himself into history as a historic and damned creature; he ceases to run away from himself and to be ashamed of his own kind. . . . He knows that he is one who stands apart, untouchable, scorned, proscribed—and it is *as such* that he asserts his being. . . . [H]e accepts the obligation to live in a situation that is defined precisely by the fact that it is unlivable; he derives his pride from his humiliation."[12]

At the end of his essay, Sartre seems to change his position. Here he writes, "the authentic Jew *makes himself a Jew*, in the face of all and against all." The authentic Jew has *none* of the characteristics commonly attributed to Jews, Sartre claims. "[H]e is what he makes himself. . . . [H]e becomes again a man, a whole man. . . ."[13]

However, in Sartre's estimation, a Jew cannot make herself *whatever* she wants, for although a Jew can choose all sorts of character traits, she "cannot choose not to be a Jew."[14] For Sartre, Jewish authenticity must start with the "hostility" and "disdain" imposed on her by anti-Semites.[15] She can overcome this attitude and become a "whole man," but the path to that salvation starts with anti-Semitic regard. Self-hatred, on this view, is the authentic starting point for Jewish identity.

Many theorists now hold that personal identity and self-conception are grounded in interpersonal recognition.[16] Sartre, however, goes beyond this. He claims that the point of departure for Jewish self-conception is not just any interpersonal recognition but anti-Semitism in particular. However, Sartre's view prompts the thought that the self-conception of oppressed group members need not be based solely on the regard of outsiders.

Granted, the members of an oppressed group always have to be alert to the ways they are being regarded by people who might slander or slaughter them. However, the degree of exposure to hostile outsider conceptions can vary and might be minimal in some cases. As Philip Mendes writes in 2009, "it is hard to make an empirical case for Jewish self-hatred today given the absence of significant anti-Semitism in most Western societies."[17] Anti-Semitism has not disappeared, but we are a far cry from the Nazi era. Sartre was partly right that anti-Semitism *can* ground Jewish self-conception but partly wrong in that it need not do so. Social contexts involve multiple influences that can impart group identities combining both positive and negative aspects.[18] Even a historically oppressed group may find or create social contexts in which it is valued or esteemed. As a result, a group member may hate her group, cherish it, or feel any combination of these attitudes. Not all contexts for minority groups are as demoralizing and dehumanizing as the anti-Semitism that Sartre witnessed in the Europe of the Nazi era.

2. DEVELOPMENT OF THE CONCEPT OF JEWISH SELF-HATRED: A SKETCH

The concept of Jewish self-hatred pre-dates the birth of the state of Israel (1948) by at least half a century, having started to become prominent around the end of the nineteenth century in the early Zionist period. Before that time, Jews sometimes acted in ways we would now call self-hating, surely an understandable reaction to centuries of persecution, segregation, forced conversions to Christianity, and deadly violence.[19] But the explicit concept of Jewish self-hatred is historically relatively new.

The early Zionists scorned what they regarded as weakness and passivity in Jews. In the late 1800s, Theodor Herzl, the founder of modern Zionism,[20] argued that Jews needed a state of their own because when they tried to be good citizens in the many countries in which they lived, they never gained full acceptance and were often persecuted instead.[21] Herzl used the expression "anti-Semite[s] of Jewish background" to refer to Jews who betrayed other Jews under these oppressive conditions.[22]

From the start, the idea of a Jewish state was controversial among Jews. According to the historian W.M.L. Finlay, this was primarily because "there was already a long-established Arab population living in Palestine."[23]

Despite this resistance, Zionists urged other Jews to work for their own state in Palestine and to stop trying to assimilate into the non-Jewish countries of the Diaspora. According to Finlay, Zionists scorned weak and assimilated Jews as self-hating and encouraged Jews to "assert their Jewish identity, primarily through the nationalist project."[24]

During the first few decades of the twentieth century, the concept of group self-hatred, and Jewish self-hatred in particular, gradually became topics of scholarly research. In 1941, Kurt Lewin published his widely influential article, "Self-hatred among Jews,"[25] which introduced this concept to English-speaking audiences. His work was relevant to a variety of disadvantaged groups, not only Jews but also African Americans and various immigrant groups to the U.S., such as Greek, Italian, and Polish immigrants.[26]

Lewin thought that self-hating Jews had the aim of leaving the group altogether,[27] and he worked actively against this trend. He was concerned that any sort of dissent or group criticism weakened the group. Lewin thought that a "fundamental fact of group life" was that the fate of group members was interdependent.[28] He argued that a "positive" Jewish identity should be based on group "loyalty." Education for Jewish children and adults was needed to work against feelings of fear and inferiority that were primary in driving Jews to leave the group.[29] Jewish education, Lewin thought, should aim to make Jews feel a sense of belonging to a group "whose fate has a positive meaning." In Lewin's view, each individual had to "accept active responsibility and sacrifice for the group."[30]

In the 1940s and 1950s, Lewin's work on Jewish self-hatred contributed to an educational and cultural movement among American Jews for the development of a positive Jewish identity.[31] Jewish leaders in the U.S. promoted Jewish education and the development of Jewish community centers. Ironically, this movement increased the tensions among Jews. Historian Susan Glenn argues that a discourse on Jewish self-hatred "proliferated" in the 1940s and 1950s in the U.S., a period she is tempted to call "the age of [Jewish] self-hatred."[32] Glenn describes what developed as a "Jewish Cold War." It involved "a contentious public debate revolving around the question of Jewish group loyalty, Jewish group 'survival,' and Jewish nationalism" (100). In this debate, defenders of Jewishness regarded assimilation by Jews as an attempt to hide or escape from Jewishness. The failed assimilation of the German Jews, still so recent and so raw, was seen as a tragic example of what could happen to Jews who sought to abandon their Jewishness.[33]

In these battles, there was a group that provided a counterweight to the charge of Jewish self-hatred. This group consisted of what Susan Glenn calls a "small but highly visible cohort of self-described 'alienated' Jewish nonconformists, sometimes referred to as 'the New York Intellectuals.'" According to Glenn, they "openly expressed uncertainty about the meaning of their own Jewish identities, demanded individual rather than collective definitions of Jewishness, and advocated individual rather than group solutions to the various states of ambivalence and identity confusion that contemporaries called 'Jewish self-hatred'" (109). The New York Intellectuals included the art critic Clement Greenberg as well as Erich Fromm, David Riesman, and Hannah Arendt. Some of them challenged rigid definitions of Jewishness. The intensity of this debate is evident in the harsh terms in which it was framed. For example, one Jewish critic of the New York Intellectuals characterized them as "harbingers of Jewish 'moral suicide' and 'ethnic self-liquidation'" (109).[34]

Clement Greenberg typified the attitudes of the New York Intellectuals. He wrote that self-hatred was "almost universal" among Jews. However, he regarded the movement for positive Jewishness as just another example of chauvinism, like any nationalism.[35] Writing in 1950, Greenberg characterized the "nationalist Jew" as wanting the Jewish people to be more powerful. This Jew, he claimed, felt "humiliated by the ease with which the Nazis were able to kill most of our six millions."[36] Greenberg wrote that "The rise of a militant, aggressive Jewish nationalism is in large part an answer to this state of mind. . . . We have to show the world and ourselves that 'Jews can fight.'"[37]

Greenberg did not reject this struggle, but he argued that it had to be fought "inside ourselves." Jews had to convince themselves that "Auschwitz . . . was not a verdict upon our intrinsic worth as a people."[38] In direct contrast to Kurt Lewin, Greenberg called for Jews to shift the burden of dealing with anti-Semitism from the group to the individual level. Militant group resistance to anti-Semitism risked becoming "chauvinist and irresponsible" and fueling "rabid nationalism."[39] Greenberg claimed that "Jewishness . . . should be a personal rather than mass manifestation, and more a matter of individual self-reliance."[40] To him, this meant avoiding the "herd conformity out of which arise the ugliest manifestations of nationalism—as we saw in the German case."[41] Greenberg wanted to accept his Jewishness "implicitly" and use it to realize himself "as a human being in my own right."[42] He wrote, "I want to overcome my self-hatred in order to be more *myself*, not in order to be a 'good Jew.'"[43]

Tony Judt expressed a similarly individualistic attitude in some of his final writings before his death.[44] Recalling his time spent on an Israeli kibbutz, Judt wrote that there is "no general purpose answer" to the question of what it means to be Jewish.[45] He claimed that "it is always a matter of what it means to be Jewish for me—something quite distinct from what it means for my fellow Jews."[46] Judt thought there was something right about the American obsession with the Holocaust, but it was not easy to say what that was. He asked: "Are we really Jews for no better reason than that Hitler sought to exterminate our grandparents?"[47]

The individualistic emphasis by Greenberg and Judt has its appeal, but there are reasons to adopt it cautiously. The interpretation of any group-based identity has implications for others who are in the group. One Jew cannot alone forge the meaning of Jewishness as such. If I said that my way of being Jewish is to smoke peyote with my friends, this would be a comical way of saying I am not being Jewish at all. When an identity applies to a group of people, individual group members who are too inventive in deciding "what it means to me" to be a member of the group may find themselves disconnected from other group members. Individuality of self-definition is possible to a significant extent but it has complications. Group bonds may not survive over time with too much individuality.

At any rate, returning to the 1960s, we find Israel now existing as a modern state with a developing history. Holocaust survivors and other commentators are engaging in extensive retrospective reflections on the Nazi era. At that time, a landmark controversy emerges over Hannah Arendt's 1963 publication of *Eichmann in Jerusalem: A Report on the Banality of Evil.*[48] Arendt was widely denounced as a self-hating Jew. The accusation was based on at least three complaints about the book. First, the Nazi Adolf Eichmann, whose decisions sent many thousands of Jews to their deaths, was portrayed as an ordinary fellow who insisted he was just following orders. Second, Arendt criticized how Israel handled the Eichmann trial. Third, and perhaps most importantly, Arendt argued that Jewish leadership in Europe during the Nazi era had collapsed in the face of the Nazi onslaught and had even collaborated with the Nazis to some extent.

Arendt was suggesting that some perpetrators of evil might not be as bad as they seemed, while some victims of evil might be less innocent than they had seemed. This sort of analysis is bound to be shocking when the evils have been profound and the suffering of the victims has been extreme beyond imagining. Arendt thus presented several momentous "moral inversions," analyses that make surprising reversals of moral evaluation. Some victims become perpetrators, some perpetrators are exonerated, and right and wrong become indistinguishable or reversed at their deepest levels.

This historical sketch allows us to note a few of the common elements in debates over self-hatred. First, there are tensions between individually oriented and group-oriented ways of working out group identity. Second, there are radical moral disagreements over the nature of significant events and developments. For example, in the Jewish case, as noted, there were debates over Eichmann's role in the Holocaust, and there are debates today over Israeli treatment of Palestinians in the Occupied Territories. Third, there are concerns about the survival of the group. Does survival require uncritical group loyalty? When does group loyalty become what Clement Greenberg calls "rabid nationalism"? Fourth, threats to group survival may seem to arise both from the outside and from within the group.

3. SELF-HATRED AND OTHER BIASES

What sort of attitude is "group-based self-hatred"? Hatred is a severe attitude. It is not mere indifference or even mere dislike. Hatred can take the form of abhorrence, abomination, loathing, or repugnance, to name some of its manifestations.[49] In group-based self-hatred, someone regards her identity group as typically characterized in ways that she loathes or abhors. Also, she regards herself as tainted by those typical characteristics and abhors or loathes herself. Even if a person could come to hold this sort of attitude autonomously (and I do believe this is possible), what sort of autonomous attitude would that be? It could hardly be a desirable condition in which to live one's life. There is nothing to idealize in a condition of autonomously achieved, group-based self-hatred.

However, the attitudes that are characterized as self-hating might not actually be so. A Jewish person's criticisms, for example, of Israeli policies toward Palestinians in the Occupied Territories might not really manifest Jewish self-hatred. The state of Israel is not equivalent to the Jewish people globally. Anti-Zionism is not the same attitude as anti-Semitism, and Jews ought to be able to recognize the difference. Israel is a Jewish state, but Jews who live elsewhere might not feel that their own identity is bound up with the state of Israel. A Jew living outside Israel may feel as distant from Israel as she does from any other state in which she does not reside. Also, the Israeli government, like any government, has many policies. A Jew may reject some of those policies while accepting or being indifferent to others. Thus, Jewish critics of Israeli policies need not hate themselves, need not hate Jewishness, and need not feel hatred at all. A Jew's attitudes toward her own self, group, religion, and ethnicity are not necessarily predetermined by her attitude toward particular Israeli policies and seem to allow wide scope for individual choice and variation.

In debates over Israeli policies, it is very likely that the concept of Jewish self-hatred is used by Israel supporters to try to discredit Jewish critics of Israel without having to present any political arguments.[50] The charge of Jewish self-hatred suggests that Jewish criticism of Israeli policies is based not on genuine wrongness in the policies but instead on mere bias or prejudice and is therefore to be summarily discredited. The likeliest biases are anti-Zionism and anti-Semitism. The charge is that Jewish critics of Israel are Jewish self-haters, and these, in turn, are either anti-Zionist, anti-Semitic, or some combination of the two. However, neither of these biases is a necessary underpinning of Jewish criticism of Israeli policies.

Anti-Zionism covers a variety of beliefs depending on how one defines Zionism. The most common theme is a belief, roughly, that the current state of Israel should not exist. Philip Mendes makes a point of differentiating anti-Zionist Jewish critics of Israel from those Jewish critics who accept the existence of Israel and criticize only its policies.[51] Notice that simply to accuse someone of being anti-Zionist does not *refute* anti-Zionism. The label alone does not give reasons to think the position is wrong. Calling a particular person anti-Zionist might well be accurate, but the charge tells nothing about whether anti-Zionism is merely a bias or a reasonable position to hold.

What about the charge of Jewish anti-Semitism? This, too, is not necessarily involved in criticism of Israeli policies. As I already suggested, the Jewish state of Israel is not the same as the Jewish people globally. It is certainly possible to criticize the policies of the state of Israel without implying or feeling anything negative about Jewish people globally. Whether criticism of Israeli policies is justified calls for examination of the historical record. It also calls for a fair hearing of the different perspectives, Israeli and Palestinian at least, that are involved in the controversy.

Also, criticism of Israeli policies might manifest a sincere concern for the moral standing of Israel.[52] Caring about the moral standing of a group may well reflect overall concern for the group. Thus, criticizing Israeli policies on moral grounds, simply considered as moral criticism, need not manifest anti-Semitism. (More on this in Section 4.)

At the same time, it is certainly *possible* that criticisms of Israeli policies are biased by anti-Semitism. Some Jews—and, of course, some non-Jews—might be predisposed to finding fault with anything Jewish and might react to any evidence about the Middle East in a prejudicial manner. Israel supporters sometimes argue that criticism of Israel is selective, that Israel is singled out for criticism of policies that are no worse than the policies of some other states that are meanwhile being ignored.[53] Suppose this charge is accurate. Selective criticism of the Jewish state only, for wrongs that are also committed by other states, could easily manifest an anti-Semitic bias.

However, this argument has a problem of its own. The argument asserts that there are states in addition to Israel that do the same things that Israel does. This assertion concedes that there is something wrong with the policies of all these governments, including Israeli policies. Wrongdoing is not excused or justified merely because it is practiced somewhere else. Nor is it excused or justified merely because one's critics have ignored the other wrongdoers. So even if selective criticism of Israel sometimes manifests anti-Semitic prejudice on the part of the critic, pointing this out does not vindicate Israeli policies toward Palestinians.

4. OPPRESSION, CRITICISM, AND CHANGE

It should seem obvious that not all historically oppressed groups are alike. Forms of oppression vary and may be accompanied by a great diversity of conditions that aggravate—or mitigate—the conditions of oppression itself. The moral significance of oppression might vary in what any particular case of oppression calls upon its perpetrators and its victims to do. In this discussion, it is the moral impact on the victims that is particularly in question.

Members of a historically oppressed group might feel moral burdens arising from that oppression that seem to constrain their choices in an autonomy-reducing manner. For example, it might be morally problematic for the members of an identity group that has been historically oppressed to express public moral criticism of the group. Their moral criticism might injure their already oppressed group. Oppressive treatment of an identity group is typically laced with condemnation and defamation of the group that is being oppressed. Additional moral criticism of the group adds to the oppression of the group by reinforcing this condemnation and intensifying the societal conviction that the group deserves to be socially controlled. Members of the group who join in its public moral criticism risk increasing that oppressive treatment toward their own group. Even just thinking critically about their group might seem risky lest they express their criticisms inadvertently.

Criticism by group members would be even more damaging to an oppressed group than criticism by outsiders. Those who criticize their own group would acquire an aura of credibility by appearing to speak against their own self-interest.[54] Jewish criticism of Israeli policies seems to fall into this category. A Jew who criticizes Israeli policies is vulnerable to condemnation by other Jews for harming her "own people." In this way, the moral and social costs of self-group criticism could exert a painfully dampening effect on a person's autonomous reflections on her group.

The moral burden of not criticizing one's group can depend on how necessary the absence of criticism is to group survival. Israel supporters often argue that the existence of the state of Israel as a Jewish state is necessary to the survival of Jewish people globally. As noted, the early Zionists claimed that Jews living in the countries of the Diaspora were never accepted as full citizens and always remained in danger of persecution. In Nazi Germany, extreme persecution arose even after Jews thought they had assimilated.[55] Deportation out of Europe saved some Jews from the Nazi onslaught, but emigration was unavailable to most European Jews, partly because of immigration quotas elsewhere.[56] The existence of a Jewish state could have helped many more Nazi-era victims to survive. A Jewish state would have then provided—and will now provide—a refuge for Jews who are persecuted anywhere else in the world. It would constitute a homeland for Jews where, finally, Jews need not fear persecution. Thus, anything that threatens the existence of Israel would eliminate this refuge for Jews and might thereby constitute a threat to the future survival of the Jewish people.

The existence of Israel is by no means guaranteed. The state of Israel is surrounded by hostile Arab neighbors, some of whose leaders have called for Israel's annihilation.[57] The global Jewish community is relatively small: only 13.7 million people worldwide in 2012.[58] Historically, Jews have been persecuted and murdered because of preposterous falsehoods such as the "blood libel."[59] Thus many Jews conclude that Israel and Jews globally must be perpetually vigilant about self-protection. Any criticism of the state of Israel might contribute to international hostility toward Israel that would threaten Israel's existence and, derivatively, that of the Jewish people.

Does each person have a special moral responsibility to avoid under-mining the significant identity groups to which she belongs? This might be especially true when the group in question has endured a history of oppression. If the very survival of someone's historically oppressed identity group is threatened, an ethic of group loyalty calls for her to stand with her group and help defend it against the forces that threaten it. If she fails to help defend her group or, worse yet, adds to the threat against her group in any way, she *betrays* her group, according to an ethic of group loyalty.

Betrayal goes beyond merely inflicting harm on others.[60] The concept of betrayal presupposes a special relationship in which people expect mutual support from each other and trust each other to provide this support. Members of an oppressed group, especially, need each other in this way. After all, in extreme circumstances, they may have only each other to turn to for survival and protection. This responsibility implicates a person in the very survival of her group, a moral burden that could seem to diminish rather than augment the autonomy of her reflections about or from the standpoint of her group.

Granted, not everyone accepts an ethic of group loyalty. Clement Greenberg, as noted earlier, worried that group loyalty would descend into "rabid nationalism." Yet group loyalty does seem to be a widely accepted ethic worldwide.[61] To be sure, in practice there might be substantial variation in the commitments that people expect of the other members of their own groups for the sake of group loyalty and group survival. Some expectations might be excessive and unreasonable, as illustrated by the Masada2000 website noted earlier. Nevertheless, an ethic of group loyalty, however unreasonably demanding it might be, might partly explain—even if it does not justify—the view of a Jewish supporter of Israel who holds that a Jewish *critic* of Israel is anti-Semitic, self-hating, or a traitor to the Jewish people.

In this world, there are numerous historically oppressed groups, sometimes engaged in complex interrelationships with each other. Adding to the complexity is the fact that a historically oppressed group can become materially and economically more well off than it was previously. It can attain greater political and cultural influence than it had before. In rare cases, it can realize its ambition of creating a state that rules in its name or for its own interests, as is the case for the Jewish state of Israel.[62]

Improvements in the material, political, or cultural well-being of a historically oppressed group may remove that group from the category of the *currently* oppressed. This seems to be the situation of Jews today in the U.S.[63] It is also the situation of Jews in Israel.[64] Yet historically oppressed groups whose well-being improves might continue to think of themselves as oppressed. Group members might have difficulty realizing that they no longer occupy a currently oppressed status in a particular social context.

It is also important to note that a person's moral criticisms of her own group might be based on genuine moral wrongs in the behavior of her group members. A historically oppressed group is not necessarily insulated from wrongdoing. There may be certain tendencies and temptations to which historically oppressed groups are vulnerable that might lead them astray in their dealings with other groups. A group that focuses only on its own victimization, for example, might fail to grasp the oppressive nature of the treatment it is imposing on other groups, perhaps in the name of self-defense.

Granted, even if a group is no longer currently oppressed, it may remain vulnerable to a revival of oppressive treatment.[65] Jews often remind each other that Jews in Germany were the most assimilated of European Jews prior to the rise of Nazism.[66] A group's sense of being vulnerable to future oppression might have a sound historical basis and might therefore sustain a reasonable ongoing suspicion by group members that their current security is fragile. The continuing vulnerability of a historically oppressed group to future victimization makes a legitimate claim for group self-defense, and this, in turn, suggests a claim on the loyalty of members of the group. Thus, Jews today face a complicated social context in which genuine historical oppression has bequeathed a legacy of painful memories along with anxiety about the future. That is the context in which some Jews criticize Israeli policies toward Palestinians while some other Jews criticize the critics.

The autonomy of a person's reflections on her oppressed group's identity and practices can be influenced by her awareness of the moral significance of that identity and those practices. One objection raised by some critics of Israel is that Israel exploits, for political purposes, a portrait of itself as a "victim" of the Holocaust.[67] Victim status makes relevant a highly significant sort of moral narrative. A group that is persecuted, attacked, or oppressed may deserve an important kind of moral leeway. An oppressed group may be justified in doing things in self-defense that would otherwise be morally wrong. This moral asymmetry is incorporated, for example, in the rules of Just War Theory, according to which an attacked state is entitled to use a degree of military power in self-defense that would be impermissible for a state not under attack.[68] Legitimate self-defense licenses a range of responses to others that might be morally unacceptable if they were "first strikes." Supporters of the Palestinians often regard Palestinian terrorism against Israel as morally excusable self-defense. Both the supporters and the critics of Israel seem to accept the idea that the use of force in self-defense is excused to a degree that would be considered illegitimate if it were the *initiation* of violence. (The supporters and critics disagree over which side is using force legitimately.)

Wendy Brown explores the way an oppressed group can become invested in its victimization as an identity. In her view, this is problematic because the group thereby perpetuates its own impotence in the form of Nietzschean *ressentiment*.[69] While impotence is a condition that can indeed arise in this way, Brown misses a more serious possibility. A historically oppressed group can invoke a narrative of genuine historical oppression at the same time that it acts quite potently and aggressively, perhaps toward other oppressed groups. The legitimation provided by a victimization narrative can serve to "justify" the group's aggression as self-defense. Thus a potentially more serious problem than impotence, in the case of victim narratives, is a highly potent harm inflicted aggressively on other oppressed groups that are treated disproportionately as threats.

In a related way, Garrath Williams observes that Israelis use a narrative of historical, Holocaust victimization to justify their aggressive treatment of the Palestinians.[70] Williams thinks the problem is that contemporary (Jewish) Israeli claims to have been victims of the Holocaust are false. Williams has a significant point to make about victimization (more on that in what follows), but his criticism of Jewish-Israeli victim claims seems wrong. There are probably today (2014) some direct victims of the Holocaust living in Israel and certainly bereaved descendants.

As well, Williams has an unduly narrow conception of an identity group. Identity groups are not limited only to those members who are alive today. Identity groups also include all the ancestors who were members of the group. The historical narrative of an identity group includes significant events experienced by those ancestors. Group members alive today may well feel personally the significance and impact of historical, group-based tragedies that affected their ancestors. Just as contemporary African-American blacks may still feel the legacy of slavery and contemporary Native Americans may still feel the legacy of the European conquest of their lands, so, too, the tragedy of the Holocaust might still be personally wrenching to Jews alive today. A Jew who is alive today might not be indifferent about the fact that she was not supposed to have existed, according to the Final Solution.

Thus Williams is wrong to charge that Israelis alive today are claiming falsely to have been victims of the Holocaust. At the same time, Williams does draw attention to a real problem. The problem has to do with the degrees of connectedness that members of a historically oppressed group might bear to the tragedies that historically oppressed their group. If Israeli Jews are warranted in appealing to their victim status, especially when trying to justify the treatment of other peoples such as Palestinians, that victim status should be authentic, deep, relevant, and morally overriding. One problem arises when group members treat the claim to group loyalty as overriding all moral responsibilities to avoid harming persons outside the group.

It seems that for victimization to be morally overriding—that is, to justify strong measures of self-defense—it should still be current and not yet offset by positive well-being. However, despite the ongoing risk of a resurgence of the oppression of Jews, the condition of Jews in the world today, both inside and outside Israel, seems to be one of relative well-being. The formation of the state of Israel has provided a degree of sovereignty and security to Jews that was historically unknown to them for two thousand years. (It is a tragedy calling for amelioration that this political autonomy of Israeli Jews has come at the cost of oppression to the Palestinians who suffered during and from that process.) The very existence of the state of Israel creates a sea change, a momentous reversal in the historical moral narrative of the oppression of the Jewish people. This change in political status for Israeli Jews decisively alters the moral equations surrounding the position of Jews in the world. It is not irrelevant that, despite the long tragic history of the Jews, there is now a Jewish state complete with a modern army to defend it. Jewish self-identity includes a long history of some of the worst forms of oppression ever known. Yet Jews now face a complex global situation. Israel may be threatened, but it is equally capable, if not more so, of threatening others in return.[71] Also, Jews in the U.S. and elsewhere enjoy relative socio-economic well-being.[72] These crucial changes of material and political status make all the difference.

Debates among Jews about Israeli policies seem to be part of an ongoing struggle among Jews to survive as a people and to reshape Jewish identity in response to a changing world. "Moral inversions" can turn up anywhere. "Victims" might be perpetrators, and "right" could be wrong. Any historically oppressed group may acquire new power and use it to oppress other groups in turn. Oppressed groups may attain a secure status that requires a different moral outlook than one of untarnished victimization.

Because the historical oppression of Jews has been, at times, so enormous and deadly, its reemergence should never be discounted. Jews must continue to be numbered among historically oppressed groups. However, the possibility that oppression may once again erupt against a historically oppressed group is not the same as facing currently active oppression. The key point is that social complexity and change over time may reduce or eliminate the situation of *current* oppression experienced by a historically oppressed group.

Historically oppressed groups that are currently doing comparatively well also need to be alert to the possibility that they are becoming *oppressor* groups, as some have charged against Israel.[73] New options and means for self-defense can be used for ill against other groups. Means for the military self-defense of Israel, for example, are at the same time means by which Israelis can set up checkpoints in the Occupied Territories that control and stifle the movements of Palestinians who live there. Those same Israeli military forces can also protect the growing number of Israelis who move into the Occupied Territories as settlers.[74]

Group loyalty, even among historically oppressed groups, is not an absolute moral requirement overriding all others. A contrary idea is that one should not support one's own group in wrongdoing. Group wrongdoing could consist of unjust or oppressive treatment toward other groups. Even a historically oppressed identity group might now be wielding power unjustly over another, still-oppressed group. The extreme form of group loyalty is something like "My country (or identity group): right or wrong." Fortunately, the ethics of group loyalty allows for intermediate positions. A less extreme form is "defend my country when it is right; *change* it when it is wrong (and *then* defend it)." Promoting improvement in the moral character of one's group is also a form of group loyalty. It might indeed be one of the noblest forms of group loyalty and, thus, not a betrayal at all.

Jews can now entertain the luxury of being able to make a plausible case that their moral criticisms of Israeli policies could be the expression of group loyalty. Thoughtless charges of self-hatred and anti-Semitism against Jewish critics of Israel should be dismissed as the logical irrelevancies that they are. The socio-political complexities that make this critical stance morally available to Jews today offset the tendencies of historical oppression to undermine the personal autonomy of Jews.

These complexities illustrate the obvious point that not all oppressed groups are alike. Even for historically oppressed groups, there may be liberating and empowering conditions that open up rather than foreclose possibilities for the personal autonomy of group members. One moral burden that comes with such conditions is to use the empowerment wisely and not toward the oppression of other groups.

ACKNOWLEDGMENTS

An earlier version of this chapter, under the title "Authenticity and Jewish Self-Hatred," was presented at the Workshop on Autonomy, Authenticity, and Culture; Royal Flemish Academy of Belgium for Science and the Arts; Brussels, Belgium, 2–3 December 2010. Also, I am grateful to Marina Oshana for helpful comments on the penultimate draft.

NOTES

1. It should be noted that there are Jewish defenders of Israel who deliberately refrain from accusing all Jewish critics of Israel of being self-hating Jews. See, for example, Dershowitz 2003 and Mendes 2009.
2. This website is named after Masada, a famous fortress in Jewish history that symbolizes a kind of Jewish heroism. In the first century C.E., a Jewish sect called the Zealots, which occupied the fortress, was attacked by the Roman armies. The Zealots' situation was hopeless, but they chose not to surrender to the Romans, who would have enslaved them. Instead of slavery or defeat, they chose to die together by their own hands.

   The website is said to be maintained by people from the United States, Israel, Switzerland, and Brazil with an extreme pro-Israel, anti-Palestinian orientation. See Wikipedia, "Masada2000," 2013.
3. www.masada2000.org/shit-list.html, accessed on 13 Aug. 2010.
4. www.masada2000.org/shit-list.html, pp. 2–3, accessed 3 Sept. 2010.
5. Goldstone later moderated his report after he was targeted for serious intimidation that involved his family. Wikipedia, "United Nations Fact Finding Mission on the Gaza Conflict."
6. This is not meant to be a complete account of personal autonomy.
7. The discussion in this section is influenced by my reflections on Oshana 2005.
8. Sartre 1948, 90.
9. This claim about authenticity may seem implausible, and I will later disagree with it.
10. Sartre 1948, 90–91.

11. Sartre 1948, 134–135.
12. Sartre 1948, 136–137.
13. Sartre 1948, 137.
14. Sartre 1948, 89. Sartre also claims that "To be a Jew is . . . to be responsible in and through one's own person for the destiny and the very nature of the Jewish people" (Sartre 1948, 89). There is a bit of hyperbole here. These responsibilities are surely shared with several million others, and each individual Jew's contribution is likely to be miniscule.
15. Sartre 1948, 91.
16. Much of the recent writing on this theme was prompted by Taylor 1994.
17. Mendes 2009.
18. See, for example, Weir 2013.
19. Cf. Gilman 1986.
20. The book's title is usually translated as *The Jewish State* (Herzl 1997), first published in 1896. A more recent translation is *The Jews' State* (1997). The translator, Henk Overberg, argues that this translation comports better with the original German, *Der Judenstaat*, and coheres better with Herzl's idea that the state would be for Jews as a people but would not have a particularly Jewish character; pp. 3–6.
21. Herzl 1997, 129–132.
22. Herzl 1997, 134.
23. Finlay 2005, 212.
24. Finlay 2005, 211.
25. Lewin 1948.
26. Finlay 2005, 101–102.
27. Levin 1948, 137–138.
28. Levin 1948, 135.
29. Levin 1948, 140.
30. Levin 1948, 141.
31. Glenn 2006, 106.
32. Glenn 2006, 97–98.
33. Glenn 2006, 101–102.
34. The critic was Ludwig Lewisohn; Glenn is here quoting Ralph Melnick, *Life and Work of Ludwig Lewisohn*, Vol. 2 (Wayne State University Press, 1998), p. 378.
35. Greenberg 1993, 47–50.
36. Greenberg 1993, 51.
37. Greenberg 1993, 51–52.
38. Greenberg 1993, 53.
39. Greenberg 1993, 53.
40. Greenberg 1993, 53.
41. Greenberg 1993, 54.
42. Greenberg 1993, 56.
43. Greenberg 1993, 56; italics mine.
44. Judt 2010.
45. Judt 2010, 21.
46. Judt 2010, 21.
47. Judt 2010, p. 22.
48. Arendt 1963.
49. Kipfer 1992, p. 424.
50. See Mendes 2009.
51. Mendes 2009.
52. See Lerner 2003.
53. Writing in 2003, Dershowitz gives the examples of Libya, Sudan, Iraq, Cuba, and North Korea; p. ix.

54. See Dershowitz, *op. cit.*, p. 221.
55. See, for example, Lerner 2003, pp. 51–55.
56. Arab residents in Palestine did sometimes react violently against Jewish Zionist settlers in the 1920s and 1930s and did refuse entry to a large number of Jewish migrants seeking to leave Europe before and during the Holocaust. However, it is arguable that their reason for doing so was self-defense; they sought to block the national Zionist ambitions of Jewish settlers, ambitions that were becoming known during those times. See, for example, Lerner 2003, pp. 45–57.
57. See, for example, Fathi 2005. However, there is also evidence of mixed attitudes toward Israel on the part of the citizens of Arab states; see Khashan 2000.
58. Jewish Virtual Library 2012.
59. See Anti-Defamation League 2013.
60. See, for example, Scheindlin 2012.
61. See, for example, Druckman 1994.
62. Of course, a group can become worse off in all these ways than it was before; this discussion focuses only on Jewish people in the twentieth and twenty-first centuries.
63. See, for example, the PEW Forum on Religion & Public Life, "Income Level by Religious Tradition," 2008. In that study, Jews were one of the highest-earning income groups among religions in the U.S. See also Mazur 2007.
64. See Wikipedia, "Standard of Living in Israel," 2013. Approximately 20% of Israelis live below the poverty line, but these are largely either Arab Israelis or Haredi Jews, who comprise a type of Orthodox Judaism that isolates itself from the mainstream economy.
65. This is illustrated by some of the recent incidents recounted in the otherwise optimistic report by Mendes-Flohr 2010, 186–187.
66. See, for example, Elon 2002.
67. See Finkelstein 2000/2003, pp. 48–52.
68. See, for example, Orend 2005, p. 5.
69. Brown 1995, pp. 70–76.
70. Williams 2008.
71. Israel has a modern army, one that has in some cases inflicted casualties on its enemies in the ratio of 100 to 1 (as in the 2008–2009 conflict with Hamas in the Gaza strip). Wikipedia, "Gaza War."
72. See, for example, Mazur 2007, accessed online 2 March 2014.
73. See Wikipedia, "Criticism of the Israeli Government."
74. See, for example, Human Rights Watch 2012. This report also documents rights violations by Palestinian armed groups. See also United Nations News Center 2013.

REFERENCES

Anti-Defamation League. "Glossary of Key Terms and Events in Israel's History: Hezbollah." http://archive.adl.org/israel/advocacy/glossary/hezbollah.asp; accessed 4 July 2013.

Arendt, Hannah. *Eichmann in Jerusalem: A Report on the Banality of Evil*. New York: Penguin, 1963.

Brown, Wendy. *States of Injury: Power and Freedom in Late Modernity*. Princeton, NJ: Princeton University Press, 1995.

Dershowitz, Alan. *The Case for Israel*. Hoboken, NJ: John Wiley & Sons, 2003.

Druckman, Daniel. "Nationalism, Patriotism, and Group Loyalty: A Social Psychological Perspective." *Mershon International Studies Review*, Vol. 38, No. 1 (April 1994), pp. 43–68.

Elon, Amos. *The Pity of It All: A History of the Jews in Germany, 1743–1933.* New York: Henry Holt & Co., 2002.

Fathi, Nazila. "Wipe Israel 'Off the Map' Iranian Says." *New York Times*, 27 October 2005, www.nytimes.com/2005/10/26/world/africa/26iht-iran.html?_r=0; accessed 4 July 2013.

Finkelstein, Norman. *The Holocaust Industry: Reflections on the Exploitation of Jewish Suffering.* 2nd ed. London: Verso, 2000/2003.

Finlay, W.M.L. "Pathologizing Dissent: Identity Politics, Zionism, and the 'Self-Hating Jew.'" *British Journal of Social Psychology*, Vol. 44 (2005), pp. 201–222.

Gilman, Sander L. *Jewish Self-Hatred: Anti-Semitism and the Hidden Language of the Jews.* Baltimore: Johns Hopkins University Press, 1986.

Glenn, Susan A. "The Vogue of Jewish Self-Hatred in Post-World War II America," *Jewish Social Studies: History, Culture, Society*, n.s., 12, no. 3 (Spring/Summer 2006), pp. 95–136.

Greenberg, Clement. "Self-Hatred and Jewish Chauvinism: Some Reflections on 'Positive Jewishness.'" *Commentary* 10 (Nov. 1950). Reprinted in *Clement Greenberg: The Collected Essays and Criticism, Volume 3: Affirmations and Refusals, 1950–1956*, Ed. John O'Brian (Chicago: University of Chicago Press, 1993), pp. 45–58. Page references are to the reprinted version.

Herzl, Theodor. *The Jews' State: A Critical English Translation.* Henk Overberg, trans. Northvale, NJ: Jason Aronson Inc., 1997 (first pub. 1896).

Human Rights Watch. "World Report 2012: Israel/Occupied Palestinian Territories." www.hrw.org/print/world-report-2012/world-report-2012-israeloccupied-palestinian-territories, accessed 4 July 2013.

Jewish Virtual Library. "Judaism: Jewish Population of the World (1882–2012)." www.jewishvirtuallibrary.org/jsource/Judaism/'jewpop.html, accessed 16 July 2013.

Judt, Tony. "On Being Austere and Being Jewish." *New York Review of Books*, Vol. LVII, No. 8 (May 13, 2010), pp. 20–22.

Khashan, Hilal. "Arab Attitudes toward Israel and Peace." Washington Institute for Near East Policy, 2000. www.washingtoninstitute.org/policy-analysis/view/arab-attitudes- toward-Israel-and-peace; accessed 4 July 2013.

Kipfer, Barbara, ed. *Roget's 21st Century Thesaurus.* New York: Dell, 1992.

Lerner, Michael. *Healing Israel/Palestine.* Berkeley, CA: Tikkun Books, 2003.

Lewin, Kurt. "Self-Hatred Among Jews." *Contemporary Jewish Record*, Vol. 4, no. 3 (June 1941), pp. 219–232. Reprinted in Kurt Lewin, *Resolving Social Conflicts*. New York: Harper & Row, 1948.

Masada2000 SHIT-list. www.masada2000.org/shit-list.html. Accessed 15 November 2010.

Mazur, Allan. "A Statistical Portrait of American Jews into the 21st Century." On-line http://faculty.maxwell.syr.edu/amazur/Jews.pdf, 2007; accessed 2 March 2014.

Mendes, Philip. "The Strange Phenomenon of Jewish Anti-Zionism: Self-Hating Jews or Protectors of Universalistic Principles?", *Australian Journal of Jewish Studies*, Vol. 23 (2009), pp. 96–132.

Mendes-Flohr, Paul. "Anti-Semitism and the Jewish American Political Experience." In *Perspectives on Race, Ethnicity, and Religion: Identity Politics in America*, eds. Valerie Martinez-Ebers and Manochehr Dorraj. New York: Oxford University Press, 2010, pp. 174–187.

Orend, Brian. "War." *Stanford Encyclopedia of Philosophy.* 2005. http://plato.stanford.edu/entries/war/, accessed 5 July 2013.

Oshana, Marina. "Autonomy and Self-Identity." In *Autonomy and the Challenges to Liberalism: New Essays*, eds. John Christman and Joel Anderson. Cambridge: Cambridge University Press, 2005, pp. 77–97.

PEW Forum on Religion & Public Life. "Income Distribution of Religious Tradi-
tions." 2008. http://religions.pewforum.org/comparisons; accessed 5 July 2013.
Sartre, Jean-Paul. *Anti-Semite and Jew.* George J. Becker, trans. New York: Schocken
Books, 1948.
Scheindlin, Dahlia. "Dear Liberal American Jews: Please Don't Betray Israel." +972,
pub. 14 February 2012; http://972mag.com/dear-liberal-american-jews-please-
dont-betray- israel/35396/, accessed 4 July 2013.
Taylor, Charles, et al. *Multiculturalism: Examining the Politics of Recognition.*
Princeton, NJ: Princeton University Press, 1994.
United Nations News Centre. "Independent UN Inquiry Urges Halt to Israeli Settle-
ments in Occupied Palestinian Territory." 31 January 2013. www.un.org/apps/
news/story.asp?NewsID=44045.
Weir, Allison. *Identities and Freedom: Feminist Theory Between Power and Connec-
tion.* Oxford: Oxford University Press, 2013.
Wikipedia. "Criticism of the Israeli Government." http://en.wikipedia.org/wiki/
Criticism_of_the_Israeli_government, accessed 12 July 2013.
Wikipedia. "Gaza War." http://en.wikipedia.org/wiki/Gaza_War, accessed 11 July
2013.
Wikipedia. "Masada2000." http://en.wikipedia.org/wiki/Masada2000, accessed 5
July 2013.
Wikipedia. "Standard of Living in Israel." http://en.wikipedia.org/wiki/Standard_
of_living_in_Israel, accessed 5 July 2013.
Wikipedia. "United Nations Fact Finding Mission on the Gaza Conflict." http://
en.wikipedia.org/wiki/United_Nations_Fact_Finding_Mission_on_the_Gaza_
Confl ict, accessed 6 July 2013.
Williams, Garrath. "Dangerous Victims: On Some Political Dangers of Vicarious
Claims to Victimhood." *Distinktion*, No. 17 (2008), pp. 77–95.

Contributors

Paul H. Benson is Dean of the College of Arts and Sciences and Professor of Philosophy at the University of Dayton, U.S.

Ann E. Cudd is Vice Provost and Dean of Undergraduate Studies and University Distinguished Professor of Philosophy at the University of Kansas, U.S.

Marilyn Friedman is W. Alton Jones Chair of Philosophy at Vanderbilt University, U.S.

Suzy Killmister is Assistant Professor of Philosophy, with a joint appointment in the Human Rights Institute at the University of Connecticut, U.S.

Catriona Mackenzie is Professor of Philosophy and Director of the Macquarie University Research Centre for Agency, Values and Ethics in Australia. She is currently Associate Dean (Research) in the Faculty of Arts.

Marina A. L. Oshana is Professor of Philosophy at the University of California, Davis, U.S.

Beate Roessler is Professor of Philosophy at the University of Amsterdam, The Netherlands.

Natalie Stoljar is Associate Professor of Philosophy at McGill University, Canada.

Anita M. Superson is Professor of Philosophy at the University of Kentucky, U.S.

Jennifer Warriner is Adjunct Instructor in Philosophy at Simon Fraser University, Canada.

Andrea C. Westlund is Associate Professor of Philosophy at the University of Wisconsin–Milwaukee, U.S. She holds a joint appointment in Women's Studies.

Index